"Finding Work without Losing He ...
package any compassionate organization ...
rated employees. This book is a valuable ...
from one job to another."

David E. Maguire
President, Janotta, Bray & Associates, 1989-1994

"Finding Work without Losing Heart *displays a welcome sensitivity to*
the problems faced in rebounding from job loss. It is a hopeful book that will
stimulate both renewal and recovery for all job seekers."

Mary Frestel
Outplacement Consultant

"More than just useful advice and helpful role models, this book offers
a deep inspiration to get up, go out, and implement a critical transition in
one's life."

William F. Baker
President, Thirteen • WNET

"This book is a must read for executives in transition, as it offers truly
insightful and inspiring personal witnesses of executives who have experi-
enced an extended job loss. It richly details the anchors that help them sur-
vive and in many cases thrive during the difficult ordeal of unemployment."

Kevin Dolan
Manchester, A career consulting firm

"This is a terrific, wonderfully useful book full of helpful advice; an
awful lot of people are going to benefit from its tips, strategies, and general
all-around wisdom about life."

Trevor Armbrister
Senior Editor, The *Reader's Digest*

"Knowing all the best ways to support a spouse in mid-career job loss
can make all the difference in a family's survival of the crisis. Here at last is
a comprehensive book that gives concrete tools to help spouses move forward
with integrity—to meaningful employment and a fuller appreciation of life
as a whole."

Peggy Treadwell, LICSW, Family Psychotherapist
Director, St. Columbia's Pastoral Care Center, Washington, D.C.

FINDING WORK
-*without*-
LOSING HEART

BOUNCING BACK FROM MID-CAREER JOB LOSS

WILLIAM J. BYRON, S.J.

Adams Publishing
Holbrook, Massachusetts

Published by Adams Media Corporation
260 Center Street, Holbrook, MA 02343

ISBN: 1-55850-481-8

Printed in the United States of America.

J I H G F E D C B A

Library of Congress Cataloging-in-Publication Data
Byron, William (William J.)
Finding work without losing heart : bouncing back from mid-career job loss / William J. Byron.
    p.   cm.
Includes bibliographical references and index.
ISBN 1-55850-481-8
    1. Job hunting. 2. Mid-career. 3. Middle aged persons—Employment. I. Title.
    HF5382.7.B97 1995
    650.14—dc20
                             94-46695
                                 CIP

This book is available at quantity discounts for bulk purchases.
For information, call 1-800-872-5627.

For

Harold J. Byron, M.D.

… my psychiatrist brother
and childhood sparring partner,
who specializes in putting people back on
their feet to deal peacefully and productively
with the challenges of life.

TABLE OF CONTENTS

FOREWORD

Manager's Journal

The Hawaiian Room

By John Rocchi

They joked a lot about it in the executive dining room, and at least once during every annual officers' banquet someone with a few drinks under his belt would imitate a guitar playing "Aloha" and get a big laugh, but I don't think any of them seriously believed that they would ever end up in the Hawaiian Room. I certainly didn't.

Things had gone reasonably well for me over the years: steady salary increases, good performance reviews and a number of promotions which led to a comfortable spot in a job I enjoyed.

But then last year, the company re-organized some of its divisions, and my job was abolished. The personnel department assured me that I would be successfully placed elsewhere within the company. To spare me embarrassment, it was suggested I remain at my desk and continue what was left of my normal activities. But I soon learned that others in the company weren't exactly clamoring for the services of a middle-aged man with a large family and a specialized background.

After three months of fruitless search, the personnel officer advised me that all avenues of inquiry had been exhausted. He handed me the company telephone directory and suggested I scan through it and try to find anyone who, through friendship or past associations, might offer me a job. I stared at the book for a moment or two, thinking of the wife and the kids and the mortgage, laying it back on his desk without anger but advising him that I would prefer to move on to the Outplacement Center, the infamous Hawaiian Room. We were both relieved.

From The *Wall Street Journal*, Dec. 29, 1980

As I thought about it on my way home, it really didn't seem all that bad. I had been an officer in the company, and so I would be extended many benefits and privileges not offered to the regular staff: a phone, a desk, assistance in the preparation and printing of résumés, employment counselors if requested and, most important of all, full salary for up to a year while I was looking for a job. Any depression I had felt seemed to be gone now, because I wanted to leave as much as the company wanted me to go.

Also, and of the utmost importance in seeking a job, was that, in theory anyway, the whole procedure was to be treated with complete confidentiality. Outside inquirers were to be told that I had merely been transferred to another department—which explained the new phone number, and even placed me in a better bargaining position in my overtures to prospective employers. After only two days in the Hawaiian Room, however, I began to get calls from headhunters, employment agencies and even outside business associates who were calling to offer their condolences.

The Outplacement Center turned out to be a suite of separate offices off to the left of a long corridor. From time to time, during my first few days there, the whole group (there were usually from eight to 10 occupants) would get together for light and airy conversations, with no references to the real subject. Though I didn't know everybody, every effort was made at first to make the newcomer feel at home and among friends.

Gradually, the conversations became more serious on a one-to-one basis, with each recounting why he was there. Many had legitimate grievances, it seemed to me: bosses who were tyrants, scapegoats for the negligence of others, perhaps just at the wrong place at the wrong time. But there were, of course, obvious cases of drunks, chronic complainers and inept and totally unqualified executives, who probably deserved to be let go.

After a while, life fell into a regular pattern. Everyone was busy looking for work; some more, some less. Some men had told their families, some were delaying the bad news. And some, perhaps, would die with their secret, or what they hoped was a secret. Some men were continuously close to tears while others pretended a false bravado. Some sat in stunned silence; others were loudly adamant, retelling the story of the fate that had befallen them. For some, it was a blow from which they would never recover, while others just got up, went out and found a job and never looked back.

The most seriously affected seemed to be those who had been with the company all of their lives. Others who had been unbearable snobs, strutting arrogant peacocks during their careers, were also vulnerable, unable or unwilling to face their misfortune. And some of the saddest cases were those whose wives had left them because they were no longer members of the elite.

The worst days seemed to be toward the end of the week, especially on rainy or overcast days when some had elected to remain home. It was an eerie feeling, sitting alone with the silence broken only by the soft padding of the secretary passing by the door, the muffled sounds of the vice president jogging in place in the next office to relieve the tensions, or the quiet sobbing behind the closed door of the office at the end of the corridor. The atmosphere was closely akin to the solitary confinement scenes dramatized in "Papillon."

Not many ever again lunched in the executive dining room, most preferring to eat their lunch in a quiet corner of the regular employee cafeteria, sometimes almost shunned by their former associates who passed them in the halls with averted eyes, fearful of being "tainted" by any association which would impede their forward progress with the company.

There were days for rejoicing when a fellow inmate would land a good job, but these times were not that frequent, with many people still there close to a year and still looking. Eventually, they would be dropped from the payroll and never be heard from again. My time came too and, though I didn't have a job yet, my days in the Hawaiian Room were concluded.

Aloha.

The author, who is using a pseudonym, was formerly an officer with a major New York company.

HOW TO READ THIS BOOK

Although this is quite obviously a book, you should think of it as a compass. It is written for managers and professionals who, in mid-career, are separated from their jobs. Adrift, sidelined, streeted, beached, on the bricks—whatever the image you use to describe your situation, you are out of work. You are "looking." This is a book for you and those who most want to help you look for and find a job—your spouse, closest friends, counselor, pastor, neighbor. You will come to see most of those who want to help as points on your compass. But the needle on that compass also points to you, to the new corporate culture, and, if you are a believer, to your God.

With this compass in hand, you will be invited first to take a reading of yourself. That's the business of Chapter 1. But before you do, read the Foreword. It is not intended to cheer you up, just to fix your attention on someone else's experience of the problem as you take your bearings for a job campaign.

You have a self to serve; that's the message of Chapter 1. You have to let yourself get comfortable with that idea. You also have to resist the impulse to omit thinking deeply about yourself so that you can be off prematurely on an uncharted course in hot pursuit of some undefined "next job."

Chances are, you are married. Your spouse is in this job search with you. Chapter 2 is reading for two; don't move on without talking about the contents of this chapter with your partner.

You will come out of Chapter 2 much better prepared to deal with discouragement, the theme of Chapter 3. You will also have learned that men and women respond to job loss differently; the difference should be respected as you face up to the management of your personal discouragement.

When you see "The Literary Mirror" at the top of Chapter 4, be prepared to pause to see yourself in the snippets of literature quoted there. Be prepared as well to return to the reading habit (or cultivate it for the first time), not for diversion during the job search, but to discover some of that hidden substance in the soul of the searcher—you.

You have probably already begun networking. If not, Chapter 5 will convince you of its importance. In either case, you should read this chapter for both motivation and method in weaving a network of contacts that will lead to your next job.

"The Relevance of Religion" may not have occurred to you in connection with the business immediately at hand. But there it is—one full chapter to open up an important question to be dealt with entirely on your own terms. Skip Chapter 6 if religious faith is irrelevant to you. The chapter is there simply because religion is part of the reality of most job searches; it provides an important point on the compass for many job seekers.

Chapter 7 should be read with an eye to what you will find yourself talking about in interviews directed toward your reinsertion into the new corporate culture and your reconnection with a new corporate contract. If you expect to find nothing but the furniture rearranged when you return to the world of work, allow time to read this chapter twice.

The self-assessment prompted by your reading of Chapter 1 can trickle down now to your personal notebook of maxims and "Guiding Principles." You will find in Chapter 8 an array of principles—answers from within—that worked for others, guiding and even propelling them back to meaningful employment. Without clearly articulated principles of your own, you will not be ready to begin the final chapter, "Your Job-Search Strategy," which requires that you have at hand a blank sheet of paper so that you can begin to write your personal strategic plan.

Drills and diagrams are not "required elements" (to lift an expression from judges of figure skating competition) as you go through these chapters. Just read the book, one page after another—with time out, when you are ready to take it, for conversations with yourself, with your spouse and/or your closest friends, and with your Creator, if faith draws you in that direction. You will want to converse and consult with others along the way; the needle on your compass will point them out for you. And you should mark up these pages with underlining and marginal comments to provide yourself with a set of notes for ready review at any time. You will surely want to order your thoughts and refresh your memory from time to time in order to produce your own best answers to the question of your own employment future.

Acknowledgments

A grant from the Lilly Endowment, Inc., supported this project during the 1992–93 academic year. I am most grateful to the endowment and to program directors Jeanne Knoerle and Fred L. Hofheinz for their encouragement, advice, and backing.

The 150 participants in this study, virtually all of them strangers to me when I began, were remarkably open in disclosing their unique transition experiences. (I often remarked that each of them is the world's leading expert on his or her own experience of job loss.) Without their generous cooperation—painful for some, therapeutic for others—this book would not be in your hands.

My initial anxiety about finding willing participants was eased considerably by offers of help from executive search professionals Gerry Roche and Ron Walker, and from outplacement specialists Dave Maguire, Tom Holman, and Rose Begnal. John Fontana introduced me to the Crossroads group in Chicago, Torrey Foster to Job Seekers in Cleveland Heights, and Dick Hanscom to the Career Initiatives Center in Cleveland. John Tydings opened the door to potential participants in the Washington business community. Kevin Dolan contributed many good ideas that are acknowledged in the text; he also provided excellent leads to many persons in the New York metropolitan area who proved to be willing subjects for this study. John Leahy and Marylin Dyer sharpened my focus at the outset; Gene Croisant and Tom McHugh helped me to pretest the questionnaire and offered helpful suggestions for the final revision. And Charlie Hennessy came to my rescue when I found myself, as this project began, sitting in front of a brand new personal computer that was really a desktop 747. I knew how to type but not how to fly; Charlie was a patient tutor.

The paradigm underlying the chapter on spousal support began to take shape in my mind thirty-five years ago in conversations with my late Jesuit cousin, Fr. Jack Scanlan, who both taught and practiced marriage counseling. Two psychiatrist friends, Ellen McDaniel and Ned Cassem, provided me with reassurance, as this study began, that the theory outlined in Chapter 2 does indeed hold up in practice. Virgil Nemoianu pointed me in the direction of most of the literary figures presented in Chapter 4.

Helpful comments on the first draft of the manuscript came from Trevor Armbrister, Mary Frestel, Bill Johnson, Jack Limpert, Anne and Roger Stroh, Marty Walsh, and Peggy Treadwell. Also generous in their willingness to read the manuscript were several of those mentioned above: Torrey Foster, Dick Hanscom, Dave Maguire, and Gerry Roche. My agent Michael Snell knew that Bob Adams, Inc., was the right publisher for this book; my editor there, Dick Staron, was more than helpful in bringing this project into print.

To these, and to many others who provided insights and assistance along the way, my abiding thanks.

WJB

INTRODUCTION

If you skipped the Foreword, take a moment to note that it originally appeared in 1980, long before the recession that had a lot to do with the transfer of presidential power from George Bush to Bill Clinton. The Foreword is a depressing essay written by a senior executive who lost his job in the late 1970s.

He was ousted—"displaced" instead of effectively "outplaced"—a victim of what later came to be known as downsizing in the American economy. His severance occurred a full decade before the days when just about everyone knew someone who had been "streeted" in mid-career. And, as the reader accustomed to tracking gender references in written accounts will have noticed, his companions in the "Hawaiian Room" were all male.

In truth, involuntary separation happens all the time. In good economic times and bad, high- and mid-level managers are at risk of losing their jobs. It happens more to males than to females only because there are more males than females at the middle to upper levels of managerial responsibility. The experience of involuntary separation among executives in corporate America is predominantly, but by no means exclusively, a male phenomenon.

I began noticing the problem—as a problem for the disconnected, mid-career, male executive—around 1975. I was forty-eight, a priest with a doctorate in economics, a university president, and a corporate board member. Old friends from college days—all within a year or two of my own age, all beneficiaries of the take-off economy that swept the class of 1950 into jobs that soon became positions of influence and power in the American economy—started renewing their contact with me by making quiet inquiries. Confidentiality was important. Networking was essential. A new job was the objective. After twenty-five years or so of uninterrupted employment, they found themselves in the embarrassing and often frightening position of looking for work.

This is a book for them and for those men and women who now face, or want to prepare for, the midlife search for a meaningful job. I write for experienced managers who find themselves looking for employment. This is a book for men and women (now, in the 1990s, there are indeed many women in this situation) who, voluntarily or involuntarily, have left positions of managerial responsibility and are trying to reconnect with meaningful employment. I think I understand where they're hurting and why. This book is intended to assist dislocated managers in getting themselves back on track.

Reading over their shoulders, I hope, will be those who want to help—spouses, friends, pastors, counselors.

I write also for those who have made it through the transition into new positions and now want to fold that experience into an interpretive envelope to be filed away for further reflection. It is an experience they surely will never forget, but they may not yet understand it.

Also in view throughout the project that produced this book were students preparing to step onto the corporate ladder and young managers on their way up. Both should realize that job loss is a possibility at any time and that career rebounds, like fortune, have a way of favoring the well prepared.

After more than twenty years in academic administration—a college deanship and two university presidencies—I decided to spend a transitional year, before returning to the classroom, by studying the phenomenon of executive separation. I used the survey instrument appended to this book, but I realized from the outset that this would be a study, not a survey that could produce statistical comparisons and data that would explain the universal experience of managers who move in mid-career, voluntarily or involuntarily, from one job to another.

This population cannot be randomly sampled. There is no directory or registration list from which every seventh name can be culled. Those who left voluntarily fear being tarred with the same brush that touches those who were fired. Typically, they politely decline invitations to be interviewed. Some ousted executives are still hiding, or just unwilling to talk, or still smarting from the pain of the layoff. It is not surprising that many, from both the "pushed" and "jumped" categories, do not want to relive the experience, even in an analytical, academic context. Nor is it surprising that others are more than willing to talk. They find the discussion therapeutic. They welcome the opportunity to reflect on their experience, articulate the guiding principles that worked for them in the reconnection process, and communicate, through this writer for the benefit of others, bits of wisdom they acquired along the way.

Fortunately, by virtue of a networking process not unlike those used by successful job seekers, I found a sufficient number of willing subjects to make this book possible.

What I offer in these pages is the result of experience, my own and that of two sets of persons: the twenty or so I have helped personally over the years, and the 150 executives, male (90 percent) and female (10 percent), from middle managers to chief executive officers, geographically and industrially diverse, who participated in this study. Since the relevance of religion in their lives is one of the themes I highlight, it should be noted that religious identification of the participants is approximately (and I say "approximately" because some were vague and imprecise in this regard) 40 percent Protestant, 45 percent Catholic, 8 percent Jewish, and the rest identified with no organized religious denomination. Participation involved completion of the questionnaire and, in many cases, a face-to-face or telephone interview.

Participants in this study are the world's leading experts on their individual, intensely personal experiences. I have caught a lot of that for inclusion in this book. I managed to assemble a representative, but by no means perfect sample. That, however, did not deter me, nor does it detract from the utility of my findings for the intended readers—those who are immediately affected and those who could be affected by job loss, and persons who want to help them.

My own experience as a CEO, a board member in the for-profit and not-for-profit sectors, and a priest-counselor has influenced my approach and provided the vantage point from which I examined this relatively uncharted area of personal and organizational reality. A useful metaphor in explaining the purpose this book is intended to serve is that of a compass. A compass differs from a road map; the needle on a compass provides direction, not detailed and precise information on how to reach specific destinations.

Without overloading this metaphor excessively, it can be noted that portions of this book correspond to major points on a personalized compass in the hand of a job seeker: the relationship to self, spouse, God, the corporation. And the 360 degrees on the face of the compass suggest the countless networking contacts needed to find the right job. And, pushing the metaphor one final notch, if the compass can be imagined to have a glass cover capable of reflecting an image, the reader can hold up Chapter 4, "The Literary Mirror," as a looking glass to see him- or herself in literary portrayals of persons dealing with discouragement—persons set adrift, not necessarily by separation from a job, but by some form of broken connection that results in personal dislocations.

If the Surgeon General were to preview this book, he or she would probably approve it as beneficial for the mental health of any dislocated manager. But a warning might be attached not to permit the early sections to depress you; the second half of this book will have you on your feet and ready to roll.

Job seekers can expect to be spending more time alone than they would like. Not only do you spend more time with yourself during the search for reemployment, you have to devote time, perhaps for the first time, to self-assessment, self-renewal, and cultivating (or combating the forces that tend to negate) self-respect and self-esteem. Chapter 1 reminds you that you have "A Self to Serve," and that knowing that self—its strengths, weaknesses, talents, and genuine occupational interests—is prerequisite to a successful job campaign.

Repeatedly, persons I interviewed stressed the importance of having an understanding spouse before, during, and after severance. Those without a spouse acknowledged the value of having a close friend for encouragement and support. A paradigm for understanding the way this personal reinforcement can counter the stress of unemployment is offered in Chapter 2, "Spousal Support."

"Dealing with Discouragement" is the focus of Chapter 3. Discouragement cannot be avoided, but it can be managed during what often proves to be a painfully long search for the next position. Personal accounts of the way job seekers have dealt with their own discouragement are outlined here for the consideration of others who have to map their own strategies for managing discouragement.

Chapter 4 holds up "The Literary Mirror" so that you can see yourself in the character delineations fine writers give to persons in situations like yours. It can be both clarifying and encouraging to find what you are thinking, or see what you are feeling, in the images and words crafted by good writers and embodied in the characters they present in the pages of fiction and drama, or the intensity of meaning that good poetry can convey. This chapter is not a course in literature, just an excursion along literary lines to stimulate the imagination and, perhaps, feed the soul of managerial men and women in transition.

"Networking," the subject of Chapter 5, is indispensable to anyone looking for light at the end of the transition tunnel. Those who have been through it before you will tell you to "Network, network, network!" This chapter offers ideas, gleaned from the experience of others, on weaving networks that function as lifelines and safety nets throughout the search, or, to try still another metaphor, hiking trails that can take you to your next job.

"The Relevance of Religion" is the title of Chapter 6. For many, religion is part of the reality and thus has a place in a book focused not on religion, but on management concerns. For others the issue is not "religion," which they perceive to be an irrelevant, institutionalized stained-glass distraction far removed from the urgent business of finding work. They prefer to talk about spirituality—a clarifying, integrating, reflective experience involving oneself and a higher power. Some that I met during the course of this study had neither religion nor spirituality to draw upon for assistance in their search for employment. Most in the sample, however, drew strength from their religious faith and regarded themselves as open to help from organized religion, however that help might be made available.

Going into this study, it was not my expectation to find severance to be a window through which an observer could see structural change and a culture shift within the American corporation. What I found, looking through that window, is contained in Chapter 7, "The New Corporate Contract." Company loyalty has disappeared in some quarters and is waning in virtually all parts of corporate America. The "womb to tomb," quasi-tenure-track security managers enjoyed in the giant corporations and financial institutions of decades past is gone; smaller companies and nimble managers represent the wave of the future. The old corporate battleships are yielding to new, more maneuverable corporate cruisers, with corresponding adjustments in crew.

Managers and companies are now quite literally coming to terms in an environment of new corporate contracts that are explicitly contingent, less relational and much more transactional in nature. Your relationship with the organization employing you is more like an over-the-counter transaction than an identification that will last a working lifetime.

Chapter 8 outlines "Guiding Principles"—the originating impulses of action, the directional guidelines participants in this study used for their own benefit. They are articulated here for the benefit of others. It is important for job seekers to clarify for themselves and adopt for their own guidance principles capable of keeping themselves and their search on track during the job campaign.

Chapter 9 sketches a strategy for the manager in transition. This is about as close as this book comes to the "how-to" genre. Suggested strategies are based on the advice participants in the study wanted to pass along to others who find themselves in the same boat. The books these participants read are noted here— many of them practical manuals on how to find a job; some of them reflective works that reinforced their spirits or changed their outlooks during their job campaigns.

As I mentioned earlier, this book is intended to function more as a compass than as a road map. If it helps the reader get his or her bearings in the pursuit of employment, my primary goal in writing will have been met. If, in addition, this book helps those who want to help the job seeker and assists those who have been through it all themselves to understand better their own experience, so much the better from my point of view. If, finally, these pages encourage anyone to "be there" for another person in any way at any time during the lonely experience of trying to reconnect with meaningful employment, I will be happy to have had a hand in reducing the pain of an almost always painful process.

Gerard R. Roche, chairman of the executive search firm Heidrick & Struggles, was described in 1994 by *Business Week* as "headhunting's high priest." Executive recruiters focus on people who are in place—at work, content, and successful—not the typical person you will meet in the pages of this book. Headhunters try to interest managers in moving to new, and usually better, positions of higher-level executive responsibility. Their clients are organizations looking for executives, not executives looking for work. It interested me, therefore, to hear an admiring competitor speak of Gerry Roche as "legendary," and immediately add, "He built his business by making time for folks who are out of work."

It will please me enormously if anyone who reads this book will, as a result, decide to make some time for persons looking for work.

Chapter 1

A SELF TO SERVE

*We set up all kinds of monsters in our heads. They
don't exist outside, just in our heads.*

—James J. O'Connell

"Losing a job after giving yourself so totally to one organization is
like getting cancer," said a veteran of twenty years as director of
personnel in a large publishing company. With no notice, he was
on the street, "truly frightened that I would never find another
suitable job," he told me. "You know perfectly well on one level
that it can happen and you try to prepare yourself, but the reality
is so totally stunning that it's like walking into a steel beam in the
dark." It took him eight months to find comparable employment in
another industry in the same metropolitan area. He credits "a mar-
velous outplacement counselor" with "saving" him. That person
"put the old starch back in me and restored my faith in myself.
Alternating between stroking my ego and kicking my butt, he
instilled in me the belief that I would find another job and a good
one, and he was right."

"My story is not 'Gloom-and-doom, pity me.' It is 'Work hard,
do good, keep the faith, and you'll prosper.'" This is a forty-six-year-
old manager speaking, one-time head of the international corporate finance department of a major New York bank. He received
three days' notice and a six-figure lump-sum severance payment,
and then took eighteen months to look for work. The time was
spent in self-renewal, getting himself ready for a new career.
"What, sell life insurance?" he claims to have asked himself:
"You've got to be kidding!" No, he says, he wasn't kidding himself
or anyone else when, after serious reflection and extensive networking, he came to the conclusion that there was a future for him
in "serious, high-tech financial services," the new environment in

which he now enjoys both satisfaction and financial success selling insurance products of one of the industry's leading companies.

You have a self to serve during the transition from one job to another. You are your sole client, your chief concern. Throughout the transition, you are the center of a process of personal self-assessment and self-renewal; you must be or become the object of your own self-esteem and self-respect. You are the one who has to guard against self-pity and loss of self-confidence. You are the agent of change. If you are to find new employment, you have to take the initiative. The process is fundamentally self-serving, and there is absolutely nothing to apologize for in acknowledging that it is. Ultimately, the job search is a test of character. And character, as both history and literature attest, is proved in action.

There will probably be a humorous side to the self-service dimension of life that necessarily opens up for you as you move into transition. You will, in all probability, be scheduling yourself, purchasing for yourself, getting things repaired on your own, placing and taking your own calls, handling your own mail—in and out. If you were "above that sort of thing" earlier on, or simply prevented, in the interest of efficiency, from taking care of the practical details you would otherwise have enjoyed attending to, you will find yourself bumping into reality checks that remind you of your membership in the human race and your citizenship in the real world. For instance, an ousted company president who flew, he told me, "on the Concorde to Europe once a month, and in a company plane virtually at will anywhere in the country" expressed the slightly exaggerated realization that upon his separation, not just from his job but from his chauffeur-driven car as well, "I didn't even know how to get to the airport." But to the airport he had to go as his job campaign began. "So I drove myself out there and saw a 'parking' sign, left the car there, and returned eight days later. How was I supposed to know it was short-term parking? It cost me 192 bucks!"

As a fifty-five-year-old vice president for marketing discovered for himself while in transition, "I am my own salvation; the end result will vary with my imagination and effort." He also convinced himself "that I will feel good when I act." In the process of looking for work, he came to believe "that I am certainly good enough to be my own boss," and, accordingly, set himself up in a business of his own.

You have to recognize that you are both the product and the sales force in your personal job campaign. You are the "corpus" to be moved from here to there; you are the "corporation" that does the moving. Getting to know the product is, not surprisingly, an indispensable first step toward making this important sale—the reconnection of yourself with meaningful employment.

"Make at least one networking telephone call every day of your working life," says the banker who found a new career in insurance. That's a reasonable call quota while you are fully occupied with gainful employment, but many more calls than that must be made every day by anyone who is, as they say in show business, "between engagements."

The self you serve during what you can expect to be long months, possibly years, of transition will be better served if you pause at the outset to analyze why you hesitate to make those calls. Fear of rejection is the basic reason, according to one outplacement specialist. "I will dial the phone, hand it to them, and then walk out" (of the office where he counsels clients), explained Dr. James J. O'Connell, a psychologist who is senior vice president of Drake Beam Morin, Inc., a major outplacement firm. "We set up all kinds of monsters in our heads," he said. "They don't exist outside, just in our heads." Clients say to him, "I'll do it, but." He tells them, "Get rid of the but and just do it."

"I was so ashamed," said a senior manager in a major advertising firm, who was fired without notice in 1991 from her $250,000-a-year job as executive vice president and director of operations. In those "terribly tough" first days of separation, she said, "I wanted to pull the covers up over my head each morning and not get out of bed; I was so ashamed." Shame, the experts say, can be triggered by betrayal. It also follows upon the revelation of something you prefer to keep hidden. This lady felt betrayed when she lost her job, and she certainly didn't want the world to know that she had been fired. Shame imparts a feeling of inadequacy and unworthiness tied together by a sense of helplessness.

A fifty-year-old foundation executive told me that "an element of shame" was attached to his summary ouster. "I appreciate a little more the humiliation of the rape victim. The whole damn world tells you how terribly you were treated, but something is different in all your normal relationships. You may be good, loyal, smart, effective, even exceptional—but you have no power; you have lost a war that was never declared."

Shame can make it hard to pick up the phone. So can pride. Neither condition is necessarily a vice or a virtue. Each comes naturally; each has to be contained. The advertising executive certainly had nothing to be ashamed of, but shame, compounded by anger, was the emotion with which she had to deal. The banker experienced neither guilt nor shame, just anger, and he directed the anger positively ("Don't harbor grudges. I was a marine—we didn't quit on ourselves or our families").

Timidity is a vice that is often confused with humility, but true humility is courage. Timidity makes it hard to pick up the phone. Humility will keep you at the phone and on the trail of meaningful reemployment through a courageous, persistent, personal job campaign. Severance, whether voluntary or involuntary, puts time on your hands. It is up to you to use that time productively for self-renewal.

Voluntary separation can leave a person unexpectedly off balance. Involuntary separation inevitably shakes a person's self-confidence. Some are initially stunned, immobilized physically and intellectually. "He had to be told several times. It didn't quite compute with him what had taken place," said a General Motors insider, describing a senior executive's reaction to news of his demotion as part of the outside directors' coup that restructured management within GM in 1992. Even when it does compute, especially when the computation results in a person being zeroed out, personal withdrawal into time-frozen immobility is not a promising strategy for successful reemployment.

"Stunned" was the word used by a fifty-five-year-old software CEO who was fired just a couple of months after his board gave him an 11 percent raise and a commendation for excellent year-end results in the face of a worldwide recession. With the help of racquetball and long bike rides, he got himself in gear for the job campaign.

Doing versus Being

There is in this country what I like to call the great American heresy: What you do is what you are. Therefore, when you find yourself "doing nothing," you conclude that you are nothing. One man I met in the course of this study put it this way: "If you are what you do, when you don't, you aren't."

Your employment has been terminated, yes, but you falsely and foolishly conclude that you've been terminated. You forget that you are a human being; you think and act as if all you've ever been is a human doing. That conclusion requires reexamination right at the beginning of a new job search.

When I made this doing-versus-being distinction in a conversation with a major banking executive who had lost his job as a result of a merger, he recalled advice heard thirty years earlier in a college classroom. The professor said, "You should want to do, rather than simply be; but you shouldn't want a certain position in life just to have the position. Take a position in order to do something good." The banker went on to recall that it was in a big freshman history lecture hall that he had heard that advice, along with about 280 classmates (all male). He also recalled the professor saying, "Gentlemen, we want you to be individuals and nonconformists. But we don't want you to nonconform in matters of attire and grooming; we want you to conform in that way because those things are incidental and unrelated to the fundamental aspects of your humanity. Where we want you to nonconform is in how you address problems, how you think, and how you stretch your mind." Acknowledging that he fell short of that ideal, the banker said, "I never forgot what he thought we ought to do, and I think about that a lot now as I'm working my way through this transition with no end in view."

It is wise, of course, to tell just about everyone willing to listen that you are out of work and looking for a new opportunity. Those close to you, who fit into the category of what some would call colleagues or associates, but whom I would label, simply to make the present point, "functional friends," should be asked to tell you what, in their view, are the ten things you do best. You will probably be surprised to see listed some skills or strengths you had not noticed or had underestimated in yourself; they could, if cultivated, qualify you for productive activity in fields not within your immediate job-seeking range-finder. By the way, be prepared to find that you have fewer functional friends than you thought you had. A former bank chairman explained to me, "When you are riding the top of the wave, you have many friends and lots of acquaintances. When you crash, you discover who your friends are and who your acquaintances were."

More important, as you begin the reflective, self-renewal stage of your job search, will be responses you receive (only if you ask!) from another set of friends, those who know you and value you for who you are, as opposed to what you do. Ask them to list your ten top qualities as a human being. Both lists—positive descriptions of your being and your doing—provide you with an agenda first for reflection and then for appropriate action.

If you are disappointed not to find qualities that you assumed would be listed, or if you note the absence of qualities that should be there, make your own "to do" list, identifying workable objectives within reasonable limits for the assimilation of qualities that should be part of the self you serve. Again, within reason and respecting the limits, only you can provide your self with these enhancements to your personal being. If you think you need help from an adviser, counselor, or even therapist, ask for it. You are your own project now; getting another job is the goal, but not the entire goal. You can't afford to forget that you are, now and always, a unique human being, not an interchangeable and suddenly dispensable human doing.

Most of the job seekers who will speak to you in these pages were jolted into a self-assessment by involuntary separation; they were fired from their jobs. Most, but not all. Barry Sullivan, chairman of the First Chicago Corporation, was thrown into a self-reflective mode by a hurricane. It struck his beach-home community on New York's Long Island in August 1991 while he was vacationing there. He had left Chase Manhattan for the First National Bank of Chicago eleven years before. Secure in his job, he fully intended to remain in the chairmanship at least a while longer, because he had four years to go until retirement. Five days without electricity, due to hurricane damage, meant long hours for walking hand in hand on the beach with his wife. Processing memories of years past, assessing the present, and wondering what their future memories might be, they "kind of said, that's it." So he returned to Chicago and told the board, "Let's get on with succession."

What he really wanted to do was get into community service. He didn't have to worry about personal finances. So when his former mentor at Chase, David Rockefeller, had lunch with him on his first day back in New York and made a suggestion, Barry Sullivan, at age sixty-one, was ready for a challenge. Sullivan was thinking community service, not public service. But Rockefeller was persuasive; he had breakfasted that very morning with the mayor of New York City, and the mayor needed help. Mr. Sullivan became Deputy Mayor for Finance and Development in the City of New York, a job that gave him "the sweep of the most complicated city in the world," he told me with obvious enthusiasm eight months into his new public-sector responsibilities. He loved his new job. It enabled him to make both a contribution and a difference. He didn't miss the bank. And it all began with long, reflective, self-assessing walks on the beach.

Whether you are on the job or out of work, you can't afford, as I mentioned earlier, to forget that you are a unique human being, not an interchangeable and dispensable human doing. Of course, if you are out of work, you want to do something productive and satisfying again. But first assess yourself as a human being as you examine your opportunities to do something in the workplace. Incidentally, the example of Barry Sullivan's move into executive-level government service might serve to remind you to widen your view of future possibilities to include public service or something else you've never done before.

The self you serve is, at the opening of the job campaign, not likely to be very demanding. Typically, it will be a wounded self in need of help, not a sidelined self voluntarily withdrawn from the fray. Quite probably, fear and fatigue are there to aggravate the blow to self-confidence, to magnify the wounded pride. In this condition, it is hard for the ousted executive to rebound. A health-care CEO, fired from his $200,000-a-year responsibility by an unhappy board, told me he turned immediately to "the old triangle: daily Mass, pumping iron, and working the phones." Why so fast? Why no time off before the search? "If you don't connect reasonably fast, you get that black band around your arm, and then you diminish." He said, "you diminish," although he meant to say that your chances of reconnecting diminish.

"In between jobs, quiet desperation is the operative mood initially," an automotive industry executive told me. "There is a denial akin to the feelings surrounding the death of a loved one, except you feel that you have died a little, and a lot. The realization of the enormity of the occurrence has a numbing effect that translates into taking no overt action that could result in rejection." As an ousted president of a large manufacturing company described the initial feeling, "I came home that night feeling like someone had torn my insides out." A bank chairman described his reaction to involuntary separation: "It's like a terminal illness. Someone you meet on the street asks, 'How are you?' You're not going to say, 'I'm dying,' but that's exactly how you feel."

Many find it difficult to pick up the phone right away because they believe that they, not their jobs, have been terminated. Not only is the wound personal, if their actions are to be believed, it would appear to be fatal. "It's as though you have been killed, but you still walk the earth," said an executive vice president exiled from a health-care corporation. But he came back to life with the realization that, "Since nothing worse can happen to you, it is easy to speak and write plainly and without reservation." So he wrote for an entire week, the first week after severance. It got him through what he calls the "shock trauma period."

"How you handle this shock period may be important," he told me. "It will help you rise above the situation or display whatever character flaws you may have. For me, it was a good time, that week." What did he write? "Personal handwritten notes to board members, both business and personal letters and communications to the new CEO [who had let him go, but who had, upon arrival, given him the assurance, 'I hope you'll retire here'], light-hearted printed messages to the department heads; all of it very much appreciated, well received. Everyone who mattered learned about this situation from me. That, I think, was part of the need to restore some dignity and control to a professional and personal life."

This obviously sensitive and reflective person acknowledged that he and his wife wanted to avoid people, but did not. "We took the offensive and dealt with friends head on. We managed to keep a cheerful and positive outlook and projected it without exception. Every single critical comment from friends and associates about 'the stupid bastard who let you go' was turned around immediately. We had stock statements: 'He's really a decent guy; he just needs to work with his own people, people who balance off his own strengths and weaknesses; he wants to build his own team.'"

You serve yourself poorly if you fail to distinguish between yourself and your job, and, after the separation, act as if you've been terminated (a "mercy killing" was the way a Westinghouse vice president described his separation after twenty-nine years with the company), instead of acknowledging candidly to yourself and others that your employment, and just your employment, was terminated. You also serve yourself poorly if you expect the sting to wear off fast. "The hurt will only disappear (wrong word—only lose a lot of its power) over time," a corporation president, fired at age forty-five, explained in writing to me following successful legal action to gain severance compensation. Hurt feelings are no justification for inactivity.

"The 'mourning' ends as it began, with the realization—not so profound—that life goes on and that you need to be a vital part of it. At that time, a 'new' you emerges and the process of rejuvenation begins." For this former auto executive, the process took him, at age fifty-five, into the oil business.

Just about everyone will tell you they hate to ask anyone for money, even for charitable gifts to very good causes. They just can't bring themselves to ask for money. What they are saying, in most cases, is that they cannot bring themselves to risk personal rejection. They take a negative reply as a direct rejection of themselves, not a turndown of their request. Similarly, the displaced or dislocated executive will shy away from the phone for fear of rejection.

The self you (and only you) can serve is indeed quite ill-served by procrastination, by deferral of the calls, by substitution of written (although the written will also be necessary) communications for direct voice-to-voice or face-to-face contacts. Your wounded self will suggest the need to "smell the roses" for a while, the need to rest and recuperate. And that may indeed be not only necessary but wise before the serious search gets underway. Your responsible self, your "steering" self, so to speak, can permit you some downtime, but you should accept it as a slow-paced preamble to the demanding regimen of the upcoming job campaign. This reflection from a forty-year-old female health-care executive who went through a tough separation is good advice for anyone in similar circumstances: "Don't be too hard on yourself or set too many demands; expect to be tired and depressed and not feel like doing much. Remember that this—like anything—will be resolved one way or another, sooner or later." For her it was resolved, and happily, but only after an eight-month search.

The account of "The Loneliness of the Layoff Survivor" in The New York Times (Jan. 3, 1993) is instructive. For those who survive the cut, writes reporter Glenn Rifkin, there is "fear and uncertainty, heightened by the constant threat that more layoffs will be coming, perhaps with less lucrative severance packages." To compound the problem, "those who remain must take on increased workloads, often adding 20 hours or more to their workweeks." Peter DiToro went through that tension at Prime Computer, only to face an eventual cut himself. Here is how the newspaper story recounts his experience:

> 'They cut a group of 55 down to 15 in one morning,' he said. 'They just called us into a room in groups of eight or nine and

handed us the severance package. My manager was tough, and people were afraid to work for her, but that morning she cried.'

"While the others went out for a tearful group lunch, Mr. DiToro got on the phone. 'I had three interviews lined up by the time they got back from lunch,' he said. Forty-eight hours later, he had a job.

This is not typical. But it is, quite obviously, possible. The moral of the story (and the reason for including it here) is simply this: Pick up the phone.

Bruce Springsteen sings about being on the "downbound train." The self you serve, knowing perhaps what it's like to have been sidetracked, if not railroaded, may need some immediate rest and relaxation. But withdrawal into self—into self-imposed isolation to dwell on the past—means running the risk of missing the rebound train. In some cases, and yours may well be one of them (it's your call), a short vacation could be just the right thing immediately after severance. A corporate vice president in California, who lost his job at age fifty and had a severance arrangement giving him full salary for six months and half salary for the following six, offers this advice: "Get lots of exercise and start looking for a job right away, although if you can afford it, take a trip with your spouse—two weeks—and don't talk about it [job loss or job prospects] on the trip."

A high-level transportation executive chose, at age forty-five, to leave his job with the top firm in his sector of the industry because of personality differences with the chairman. Although his transition was brief and his job search successful, he has this advice to offer, drawn from reflection on his career up to that point:

In my personal life, I experienced mixed emotions over the stupidity of my workaholic habits, my literal marriage to a company, my perfectionism, and the question of what life might be if I had worked only five days weekly and under fifty hours a week. But I still had not learned. I did not stay out (of the field) long enough to reflect, ponder, and smell the roses. Instead, I decided to do better in terms of business achievement. In retrospect, I probably was misguided in my focus, albeit I was doing the only thing that I could do to reach my goals for my family. I should have taken six months off, made a retreat, and just unwound with my family. I did not. I was self-driven to go even faster. Before charging forward to conquer new worlds, I would suggest to anyone that staying out a little longer to make more considered decisions would be beneficial.

Two years later, at age forty-seven, he was again in transition, again voluntarily. His higher-paying, higher-responsibility job in the same industry was just not the right fit. He quickly found a job with a comparable level of responsibility and higher pay, still in the same industry, only to exit voluntarily three years later to take a CEO position in transportation marketing that he has now held for fifteen years.

When asked to translate his own experience into advice for someone who anticipates loss of executive employment soon, he replied:

Begin discreet inquiries concerning possibilities elsewhere; think through objectively your strengths, weaknesses, and potential value to another employer; reassess your career path. If you are in a stagnant or recessive industry, consider changing to another, and, time permitting, do what's necessary to make yourself marketable in the anticipated new industry through attending seminars, reading extensively, studying, taking crash courses, and developing new contacts.

That is a good, but only partial outline of what you have to do to be genuinely helpful to the self you serve.

Stages of Reaction

In a restaurant in a Chicago suburb, an ousted soft-drink company president, age fifty-two, listed for me, two years after the fact, the "life cycle" of his personal job-loss experience. He moved, he said, from disbelief, to anger, to self-doubt, to emotional paralysis, to forgiveness (of himself "for being human"), to a final stage he labels simply "getting on with it." Books that helped him get off the ground in his job campaign had titles indicative of his need: *Man's Search for Meaning, The Road Less Traveled, Wounded Healer*. (In Chapter 9, you will find listed some of the books and authors that participants in this study credit, from personal experience, with the power to assist in various stages of the job campaign.)

The need to forgive oneself for being human is worth noting. If that need is present and unrecognized or unattended, the job search will not go well. You'll be walking with a "limp" that others will surely notice. Refusal to forgive oneself or others is self-maiming. Most job seekers realize that if they are ever to get on with their lives, they need to forgive others in the former workplace who may have "done them in" or "taken them out." Most who leave unwillingly have, for understandable reasons, great difficulty in forgiving anyone who had anything to do with the separation. But they usually recognize the need to work at it, avoid talking about it—in the sense of bad-mouthing former superiors or associates— and thus reduce, if not altogether eliminate, the limp. But they may not recognize the need to forgive themselves. The soft-drink executive explained to me that he had been a successful athlete in high school and college days. He knew then what it was to lose, of course, but in those days he almost always knew as well that the loss was not his fault. He pointed out that in business no CEO can always play well. Every manager is human, and all humans make mistakes. If you are not prepared to forgive yourself while still acknowledging ownership of your personal failures, you have a problem that needs attention very early in the job campaign.

The Career Initiatives Center (CIC), a low-budget, modestly quartered, nonprofit, charitably financed organization in Cleveland, provides displaced managers and professionals with "career transition services," including an eight-session "Self-Marketing Class." The first sheet put into the hands of new arrivals is headed "Coping with Job Loss." It enumerates the "stages of job-loss crisis," as outlined by Robert B. Garber in *The*

Psychology of Termination and Outplacement: (1) shock or relief, (2) denial/disbelief, (3) self-isolation, (4) anger, (5) bargaining , (6) guilt and remorse, (7) panic—the degree depends on the severance situation, (8) depression, (9) understanding of and resignation to the situation, (10) acceptance of reality, (11) building a positive outlook, and (12) opportunity, growth, and new direction. Just reading this list should be enough to convince you that you are not unique in your reaction, wherever you happen to be at the moment in the range of stages and emotions associated with the job-loss crisis.

Successive handouts to clients of CIC sketch, in effect, the remaining topics to be covered in the Self-Marketing Class: (1) self-assessment, (2) correspondence, (3) résumés, (4) networking, (5) reference books, (6) telemarketing, (7) job interviewing, (8) factors to consider before accepting a job offer, and (9) (happy day!) salary negotiation.

Coping with job loss means recovering from the shock of employment termination. Self-assessment means the hard work of figuring out who you are, what you want to do, what you do best, what you hope to be or become, and where you fit best in the world of work. This is the service you must render to yourself. Others can help, but only you can write the ticket, even if it's going to be punched by someone else.

It is important that this be done in a focused way, not necessarily with pinpoint precision, but with sufficiently clear direction to set the course for your job search. Returning for a moment to the compass analogy (and I would hope that this book will be something of a compass in your hands), listen to one of my respondents, speaking of his personal job campaign: "A point in every direction is the same as no point at all; focus on a goal-oriented job search."

All the topics listed above will be touched upon later in this book. The next three chapters—dealing with spousal support, management of discouragement, and your own reflection in the literary mirror—together with a subsequent chapter on the relevance of religion, are offered to provide you with an interpretative framework. They will be useful for purposes of self-understanding in the early stages of your job campaign; or, if you have success-fully negotiated your transition, they can help you locate the self that may have been hard to find when you were down, but will be with you always—how-, who-, and wherever you are, and whatev-er you do.

In a poem titled "The Time It Takes to See," Samuel Hazo explains:

> *Years*
> *afterward we find the words*
> *for what we had no words for*
> *then, which means the past*
> *is simply what we make (re-make)*
> *of it, which means we're always*
> *in arrears.*

And then he observes:

> *We sort our memories*
> *like players who arrange the cards*
> *they're dealt into a kind of order.*

You play the hand you've been dealt, you tell yourself, but don't forget to sort out what it all means and arrange your cards "into a kind of order."

One of the participants in my study, who now runs her own executive search firm, came to see that her involuntary separation from another search firm was, in fact, "initiated by a realization of a values conflict that I had been unwilling to admit." She wanted out, but didn't know why. After her release, she realized that the values conflict had occasioned both her discontent and her termi-nation. She therefore focused on identifying and understanding her deepest-held values during the downtime created by her sepa-ration. This gave her, she says, not only insight but "more psychic energy, because I wasn't so disappointed or angry with myself as I previously had been." When a thirty-nine-year-old construction executive in my study found himself "on the bricks," he came to realize "what a great relief it has been to leave a job that constant-ly pushed me to compromise my values. Now, through study, self-

assessment, exercise, and just trying to organize my life, I'm redis-
covering important values and some neglected areas of my life."

In a certain sense, your values are yourself. You are what you
value. And it takes honest reflection to identify your deepest values. It is important to spend time in that quest at the very outset
of your job search. And it may be helpful to recall that a value is a
quality attached to a person, idea, or thing, so that it is prized and
cherished. It therefore has worth. Association with or possession
of that which you value is worth your while, your time, your
thought, your money. In the principles that organize your life, you
can find the values that define you and that disclose your ultimate
concerns. Simple logic suggests the wisdom of knowing your values (and thus yourself) before you set out to select the job that will
be a major part of the context within which you and your values
will be spending a lot of time together. If the job context does not
provide a very high antecedent probability of congruence between
your values and your work, let the opportunity pass. "Don't let
yourself be picked by a job," advise outplacement experts William
J. Morin and James C. Cabrera in *Parting Company* (Harcourt
Brace Jovanovich, 1991), an excellent book to be read before or
during the transition. "Discover what's important to you and then
find a job that fills those requirements."

It takes both courage and a capacity for risk taking to do what
a forty-seven-year-old manager of R&D for a major brewing company did in the interest of "keeping an even keel" while riding the
initial "cycles of depression and confidence." "I had a job offer
within one week of severance," he told me; "I rejected it and then
went ten months before finding employment." After the fact, he
could say it was worth the wait. As the months of idleness added
up, he wasn't so sure.

One senior executive, who had perhaps the most attractive
"golden parachute" I saw in the course of my interviews, told me
that his anger, his sense of pride, and his determination "to show
them they were wrong" in letting him go put him on a rebound
route that brought him very close to taking the wrong job. An older,
wiser friend cautioned, "You don't want to do that job, you just
want to get that job." Through the clearer vision of a trusted friend,

the ousted executive saw the opportunity in sharper focus and decided to pass it up. He never regretted the decision.

Similar advice comes out of the separation experience of a fifty-five-year-old chairman and CEO of a large bank. His advice to others who find themselves out on the street: "Stop—slow down—don't jump too soon into a position that you think you want. Wait. Patience is very important." He had experienced pressure from an unexpected quarter—his eleven-year-old daughter. He and his wife had a "split-level family," two young adult sons and the eleven-year-old daughter. It was his custom to drop her off at school on his way to the office. When he stopped working in January, he continued to do this—dressed, however, in casual clothes and returning home after the drop-off, instead of continuing on downtown. He and the family were economically secure as the result of a generous financial severance package. He planned to work again, but was in no great hurry. In the car on the way to school, the child would ask questions like, "Where are you going today?" "Don't you have any work to do today?" This, he said, "began to bug me, although I realized she was totally unaware that her questions were putting pressure on me." On the last day of school, before getting out of the car, she turned to her father and said, "When I go back to school in September, you'll have a job, won't you?" This did it; he decided to take an available job. He was back at work when September rolled around, but not sure he had waited long enough for the right opportunity to present itself. And he later discovered that schoolyard teasing—"Your dad lost his job; your dad got fired!"—was behind the innocent questions. Other children had heard their parents, some of them bank directors, discussing the dismissal in dinner-table talk at home.

I mentioned patience to an executive whose involuntary departure from the presidency of a major corporation became the subject matter of a *Business Week* cover story. He was angry, was anxious to relocate fast, and wanted to run something big and complex—perhaps a university, he confided to me. I explained that academic management is quite different from business, and that persuasion and patience have to be part of the academic CEO's tool kit. "Patience," he acknowledged, "is not my strong suit." But he pressed me to nominate him for two vacant university presidencies and would have grabbed either, had the offer been made. And that, of course, would have been a mistake both for him and for the institution.

The job he lost—chief operating officer—was one he didn't really want, he told me. He took it because his son had complained, "Dad, we move so often, and this one is right down the street." When he was a rising young star on an executive search firm's preferred list for high-visibility Number Two jobs, he had not yet learned what he readily passes along by way of advice to persons on similar launching pads today: "Don't go, if you can't get the top job." He eventually got the top job—twice—in high-technology firms and lives with a certain resentment against executive recruiters: "As soon as you're off their top list, wham! They disappear. They drop you because you're 'shopworn.'"

Not in his case, but in another like it, the recruiter told me, "He never learned. We placed him again and he made all the same mistakes all over again."

What Sets You Apart?

The self you serve can be hurt by hasty rebounds made in anger without reflective self-assessment and personal strategic planning. Strategic planning begins with strategic thinking, and good strategic thinking for an executive in transition begins with the question, What sets me apart? What (or where) is my comparative advantage? First, however, you have to know who you are. When you were working, you probably resisted self-examination; most people do. Perhaps you resisted it resolutely, concentrating on your work to avoid confronting yourself. You may not yet realize that you've been doing that. Or, perhaps, introspection is not uncomfortable for you; you've done it, and you like it. But lately you just haven't had the time. Well, if you left your most recent job involuntarily and do not now clearly understand what went wrong, and, in particular, if you are not absolutely sure that the fault is not within yourself, you may well fail in your next job simply because you bypassed this crucial stage of self-assessment. This happens easily and all too often, especially as layoffs are routinely explained in terms of "the economy," "restructuring," "downsizing," "foreign competition," and other variables unrelated to one's personality, knowledge, attitude, and skills. Your problem could be right there between your ears, and you don't know it.

Whatever your record of reflection and self-awareness, you have to begin anew (or perhaps for the first time) to get to know yourself. That will take time—quiet time, intervals of solitude. It is important to remind yourself that solitude is not loneliness. Solitude is a chosen form of isolation; it is good for you. It provides you with the necessary dimensions of space and time to figure things out, to work things through. Loneliness is never good; it is a kind of living death. You will need friends—visible, tangible, audible human support—to help you fend off loneliness as you try to get to know yourself, plan a strategy to market yourself, and then stick to your plan, without losing heart, as you work through the implementation stage (which may prove to be long and painful) of a well-planned strategy.

Of this, however, you can be sure: If you know yourself, have a plan, and stay the course that your plan lays out, you will reconnect; your job campaign will succeed.

In response to my inquiry about "bits of wisdom" picked up along the way that might be helpful to others in transition, a financial services manager in California put it briefly and simply: "Getting a new position is my responsibility, and working to that end calls for dedication, innovative thought, and persistence. Personal networking is extremely important. I'm preparing a larger nest egg in case it happens again. Finally, I'd advise others: don't be bitter or vengeful." That just about sums it up as a package of advice you can present to the self you serve, assuming, of course, that you know that self well—in depth and along all the fault lines.

"Never lose your sense of humor or sense of purpose; keep on going," advises a fifty-year-old broadcast communications executive, who, in the face of unemployment, described himself as "an emotionally stable person" who "knew exactly what I had to do." In response to a question about how his time was spent between jobs, he replied, "The job search is a full-time job, with overtime.

Even during times of recreation and leisure activity, one still needs to remind oneself that the search is an ongoing one, and that opportunities need to be seized at the moment. The great football coach Vince Lombardi used to say, 'Luck happens when preparation meets opportunity.'"

As I indicated, I'll list for you later on the books that others found to be helpful in focusing their respective job searches. Among those recommended readings will be *What Color is Your Parachute?* by Richard Bolles. His words, responding to the "what do I have to do now?" question and addressed repeatedly in different parts of his book to job seekers of all types, never change: "Know your skills. Know what you want to do. Talk to people who have done it. Find out how they did it. Do the homework, on yourself and the companies, thoroughly. Seek out the person who actually has the power to hire; use contacts to get in to see him or her. Show them how you can help them with their problems." That's preparation. Luck inevitably follows.

Jannotta, Bray & Associates, a well-known outplacement firm, provides its clients with a "Job Search Skills Workbook." On the outside cover, a user finds these words: "A Message from Your Future Employer: 'I'm not here to give you a job. I'm here to solve problems. Show me how you can help me, and I'll be interested.'" Once that cover is opened, a process of self-assessment and opportunities research begins that prepares the job seeker to present him- or herself to a future employer as an attractive solution to the potential employer's present problem.

It can be helpful to job seekers who tend immediately to look for a solution beyond the borders of self, and who hope upon outwardly focused hope that someone somewhere will present them with a job, to see if there is a lesson to be learned from this story that the writer Isaac Asimov was fond of telling. A young would-be composer approached Mozart and sought advice on how to compose a symphony. Mozart responded that a symphony was a complex and demanding musical form and that it would be better to start with something simpler. The young man protested, "But Herr Mozart, you wrote symphonies when you were younger than I am now." And Mozart replied, "I never asked how." I've heard the same story, by the way, attributed to Beethoven. No matter where and with whom the story originated, the point is one that should be assimilated by the self you are there to serve.

You will and should ask a lot of people a lot of questions about how to prepare and proceed with your job search. But the self you serve will be quite badly served if you expect others to do it for you, or if you presume that you are capable of handling all the complexities all at once. Get the help you need for the task of measuring up to your responsibility of finding yourself another job. If you asked David Maguire, president of the outplacement firm Jannotta, Bray & Associates, how to proceed, he would tell you to ponder the difference between activity and passivity. You are being passive if you simply float your resume and let "them" know you are available. Maguire would press you to get out there, face to face, with potential employers and stimulate demand for what you have to offer. However, he would have you first be prepared to say with confidence, "This is what I'm good at; this is what I really enjoy." And finally, he would encourage you to be able to say, at least to yourself, "And this is the pay I'd be comfortable with." His point is that although you may have good reason to accept lower pay in a new position than you had in your last, "You don't want to be embarrassed, even though you are keeping that information to yourself."

I want to leave you here, at chapter's end, with one of the worst stories I heard in the course of this study, not to make you feel good by learning of someone much worse off than you, but to make the point that the self you serve can indeed be an isolated self that simply has to rebound from within—in this case the needed job vanished at the moment this executive was most needed by the ones he loved.

A top manager I talked to, a CEO who reported only to the chairman, received high praise and the largest salary hike he had ever received only three weeks before the following exchange took place. Just as he was leaving home one morning, the CEO received bad medical news from his wife—she had been diagnosed the day before as having breast cancer. He had an important meeting that morning with the chairman and top staff; distressed as he was, he had to go to work. The chairman, noticing that some-thing was wrong, inquired about the problem written into the fur-rows on this troubled husband's brow. "I got some bad news this morning; Pat has cancer." Incredibly, the chairman's response was, "Well, maybe you ought to get all your bad news on the same day; you're fired."

Through networking and a series of consulting engagements on the way to permanent employment, he recovered from that set-back; so did his wife recover from hers. Concern for his wife helped him keep his concern for himself in perspective. He gave his attention exclusively to her for three months, and then began looking for his next job. I met them both two years later. "She and I were best of friends when we got married," he said. "We're bet-ter friends today." His employment contract called for a severance of 100 percent of salary for nine months; it was cut to 90 percent for six. "I decided not to sue and just made up my mind not to look back. A good friend suggested, 'It's time to be repotted'; I took his advice and got moving. I'm happier now than I've ever been." The self-service route worked very well for him. It can work just as well for you.

Chapter 2

SPOUSAL SUPPORT

Leave the advice-giving to others outside the relationship; it may be perceived as criticism. View the crisis as an opportunity to be vulnerable with your spouse and thus strengthen the relationship.

—Unemployed Construction Executive

Most readers will come to this chapter with an understandable, but undetected bias. Some will presume that the issue of spousal support throughout a period of unemployment is exclusively one of emotional affirmation from wife to husband, from female to male, even though females also lose jobs and, like their male counterparts, need unquestioning support from a spouse or close friend. Many presume the typical case—married male job seekers—to be the norm, forgetting the many female victims of corporate downsizing and the many divorced persons, male or female, who are out of work and in need of help, not to mention the never-married career men and women who lose jobs and can lose heart just as readily as anyone else.

An often unexamined presupposition, in these days of widespread agreement that men and women are equal, is the mistaken idea that men and women are identical. They are not, of course, and there are emotional and psychological differences that require attention on the part of job seekers and those closest to them who want to be supportive through a stressful and often extended transition period.

The Paradigm

I begin with the construction of a paradigm—a theory, or frame of reference, intended to sharpen the reader's focus on this important issue. It is based on my own personal observation, pastoral experience, and extensive reading over more than three decades. I have found that in addition to the obvious physical complementarity between the sexes, there is a little-noticed and seldom-reflected-upon psychological complementarity.

Both men and women at all stages of their lives experience varying degrees of discouragement and loneliness, emotions easily activated by job loss. The male, however, is more bothered by and sensitive to discouragement, while the female tends to be more often beset with loneliness than with a feeling of failure. This is not to say that women do not feel discouraged at times, or that men do not experience loneliness. They clearly do. I have observed, however, that men tend to be more achievement-oriented and women more relational in their approach to work and life. Again, this is not to say that women have no drive to achieve and men are uninterested in forging relationships.

What I am getting at is this: There appears to be a male propensity toward discouragement and a female propensity toward loneliness. Men's and women's psychological vulnerabilities differ because their psychological propensities differ. Failure to achieve can activate discouragement; a failed relationship can trigger loneliness. Whether these propensities are genetically rooted and unalterable is not a question I intend to pursue. I simply remark that, generally speaking, different tendencies are there. And it is my experience that an awareness of the difference can enable spouses or friends to draw closer to one another by permitting their psychological complementarity to come into play. It works this way.

The male needs encouragement in the face of an abiding (it has been there all along, not just in a moment of career crisis!) sense of inadequacy and self-doubt, and a propensity toward discouragement. The female needs the presence of another, along with the conversation, consideration, and attention that the other person can bring. This provides her with emotional security—a sense of being connected—in the face of a propensity toward loneliness.

If each is attentive to the deeper psychological need of the other, each will enhance the likelihood of having his or her own psychological need met. The wife who gives encouragement, praise, and personal reassurance to her discouraged spouse makes herself a significantly more attractive target for the attentive presence she needs and wants. (This is remarkably consistent with a principle of religious faith—"it is in giving that we receive"—that many of us admire but most of us neglect.) In stressful circumstances, like those surrounding unexpected job loss, criticism and resentment from a wife will repel the husband, deepen his sense of failure, and create a chasm rather than a union between the spouses. Similarly, if the wife is the victim of job loss, insensitivity on the part of the husband will only aggravate the relational failure, the feeling of disconnectedness, and the concomitant loneliness.

In *Toward a New Psychology of Women* (Beacon Press, 1976), Jean Baker Miller writes that a woman's sense of self is "organized around being able to make and then maintain affiliations and relationships" (p. 83). Woman feels the need to connect; *affiliative* is a word that helps to describe her natural tendencies and related vulnerabilities, Obviously, it helps the relationship if the male partner is sensitive to this, particularly when a woman's employment relationship or corporate affiliation is abruptly and involuntarily severed.

When I raise the question of discouragement, I should point out that I am not talking about clinical depression. It is a well-known fact that more women than men present themselves for therapy because they are depressed. This is not due simply to the culturally conditioned male reluctance to discuss personal problems with others. The American Psychological Association's Task Force on Women and Depression reported in 1990 that twice as many women as men are depressed in contemporary America. Factors that put women at greater risk include physical and sexual abuse, poverty, discrimination, low wages, unhappy marriages, and a tendency to focus on depressed feelings rather than take steps to overcome them. It is a gross oversimplification to suggest that the two-to-one ratio, female to male, in the statistics of clinical depression is explainable in terms of a woman's relative ease in talking about her feelings of depression. Women do, however, tend to speak more freely about depression.

Professor Maggie Scarf, a member of the APA Task Force and author of *Unfinished Business: Pressure Points in the Lives of*

Women (Doubleday, 1980), writes of "the female's inherently inter-
personal, interdependent, affiliative nature—her affectionateness
and orientation toward other people—that underlies her far
greater vulnerability" (p. 527). These qualities, it should be noted,
equip her to be particularly helpful to her spouse when he is down;
they also help to explain the unique character of her pain when the
unemployment axe falls on her.

I have no special competence to discuss depression. My interest throughout this study is in the more common problem of discouragement, and how dislocated job seekers deal with it. Chapter
3, "Dealing with Discouragement," will have more to say on that
theme; the present chapter considers discouragement as one of
the many variables to be managed when unemployment puts
stress on the spousal relationship.

A full-page advertisement placed by the UJA (United Jewish
Appeal) Federation in *The New York Times* on April 15, 1992, pic-
tured a woman staring out through the words of this printed (and
timely) message: "My husband got laid off from work eight months
ago. Some days are so terrible. He breaks down and tells me he's
afraid he'll never find a job. He's afraid I'll stop loving him. And I
tell him that's ridiculous. And then I go into the bedroom and cry
because I'm not so sure anymore." At the bottom of the page,
potential donors to the UJA Federation are told that they can
"make it possible for thousands of people to find training, jobs, and
most important, dignity."

Dignity is a central issue. Each partner to the relationship
should, in the context of job loss, consider him- or herself to be the
protector of the other's dignity. And human dignity, you must
always remind yourself, is rooted in who you are, not what you do.
Recall the great American secular heresy: What you do is what you
are. And the unfortunate corollary to this proposition, the one that
causes so much grief, is the tendency on the part of those who find
themselves "doing nothing" to conclude all too readily that they are
nothing. No one needs to be driven deeper into that hole by an
insensitive spouse. Pity the husband of the financial executive
who explained to *The Wall Street Journal* (Jan. 28, 1993) that she

and others who shared her success "weren't raised as women to think we were going to be married to losers."

One of my respondents, a forty-year-old vice president of a construction company, who was still unemployed when I met him, has a direct suggestion for spouses: "Leave the advice-giving to others outside the immediate relationship; it may be perceived as criticism." He also acknowledged that the crisis can be viewed "as an opportunity to be vulnerable with your spouse and thus strengthen the relationship." I have seen many cases where that is exactly what happened. A woman of forty-eight, who lost a position of executive responsibility after six years with a large insurance company, has this advice for couples in anticipation of either partner experiencing involuntary employment separation:

> Talk to each other candidly. Explore all the possibilities for the future together, being sure to specify—on the table and in writing—the upsides and downsides of all options. Take some downtime together. Make financial plans and stay realistic. And start doing this before the severance comes; it will be helpful to the marriage even if job loss never occurs.

On this point, a married woman who has counseled hundreds of executives in transition remarked to me that if the marriage is strong, it strengthens under this stress; if it is already weak, it can be destroyed. Therefore, simply to be in this situation amounts to a test of the marriage.

A fifty-four-year-old president of a publishing company had a relatively brief (three months) transition and found that

> It can be a binding experience for the spouses, if shared with complete and thorough integrity. We discussed the situation most candidly, and I was surprised to learn that my wife was very concerned about the amount of pressure that I was under at the time. She was fearful of heart problems, stroke, and ulcers; she was also very concerned that my alcohol consumption was on the increase.

He saw this not as unwelcome interference or uninvited criticism. Instead, it translated into genuine, caring concern that reinforced his fragile ego. Another participant in the study, far less fortunate in marriage than this man, understated his own situation with the comment that "a rocky relationship will probably not get better when unemployment hits." His own marriage came apart because "unemployment is humiliating; it reduces comfort levels, collapses day-to-day defenses, and lifts the masks in a marriage. If a relationship is not something that spouses continuously reaffirm as Number One, you can't count on it to hold up under the weight of job loss." He admitted that his seventy-hour workweeks destroyed his marriage. His wife had nothing to say when he came home jobless; it was another woman who said, "I hurt for you," words that he repeated with warm appreciation years later.

One of the women in my study, a human resources manager, divorced, and out of work at fifty-one, explained her special circumstances. Her children are grown; she lives alone.

> *I think my experience is quite different from that of the married men who make up the majority of my support groups. Their wives work. They have income and benefits (health coverage) this way. They have someone to discuss options with. I think it is even harder doing this completely alone—your friends are not so involved, although they listen, up to a point.*

Another woman in my study, divorced for fifteen years, agrees entirely: "This is much harder for divorced people who live alone."

You are completely alone when friends no longer listen, and when, despite the existence of support groups, there is no one with whom you can review the options. The remarks about the difficulty of going it alone prompted me to recall the comment I heard years ago, "When Adam was lonely, God didn't create for him ten friends, just one wife." The need for human understanding and support is always there on both sides, male and female, of the spousal relationship. If that relationship is working well, the need will be met and a confident, eventually successful job campaign will be waged.

At an earlier stage in a successful career that took an unexpected detour into unemployment, one of my interviewees had written a book. A copy, inscribed to his wife, was available for my inspection when I visited their home to talk about the issues that constitute the themes of this study. That inscription, written decades earlier, defined the spousal relationship that supported this fortunate husband through two subsequent transitions: "To my beloved Mary, who has helped me far more than she has ever known, or I have even admitted to myself." He needed encouragement; she never failed to provide it.

Another man I interviewed received criticism from his wife and encouragement from his daughter, a nine-year-old who came up with just the right word at just the right time. He had broken down at the dinner table one night saying he "had failed as a father-provider." His daughter smiled that one aside and said simply, "You'll be able to spend more time with us." His child "sensed the agony I was going through." His wife was "ambivalent between wanting to help me and feeling I had betrayed her" by losing not only his job, but the medical insurance that went with it and upon which she was heavily dependent. His problem pales in comparison with the situation encountered by the founder and general manager of a communications company in the Midwest. He lost his stock in the company to his former wife as part of a divorce settlement, and then she fired him!

Mention above of the sympathetic daughter prompts me to report that a woman who lost her job in publishing said that her adolescent daughter was "supportive but annoyed that I was now at home and more aware of her activities!"

I asked everyone I interviewed to describe the spousal response to the news of job loss. In most cases, anxiety was there, but so was understanding. Rarely was there overt criticism, although in some few cases insensitivity released words or actions that were read as criticism. For example, an innocent inquiry about whether or not they were going to send the kids to summer camp in a few months was taken as criticism of his inability to provide, rather than an indication of her concern for planning ahead.

The paradigm I outlined earlier invites elaboration. Men tend to sell themselves short. They often regard themselves as failures waiting to be discovered. This applies to males at all stages and in all circumstances of life. Those men who are rising toward or holding positions on the many managerial mountaintops in contemporary society disguise, even from themselves, their inner fears that they are doing it all with smoke and mirrors, so to speak, and that sooner or later, probably sooner, they will be "found out," "put down," even "let go." Then what? That's the scary question.

This undisclosed anxiety, experienced by women as well as men in the heady atmosphere of higher-level management, stems from an honest assessment by managers of their own limits measured against the complexity of their tasks. They have insecurities based on the realization that they are not using a specific skill that is readily marketable elsewhere. Rather, they are generalists. They manage complex organizations where just about anything can go wrong. When reversals come, they are at risk of finding themselves ousted. Defensive strategies against this unhappy personal outcome range from stacking the board with loyalists to dictatorial dominance over subordinates. But ousters do occur, as readers of the business press discover every day. Once out, the manager has to find another complex organization to run, settle for something less, or depend on a previously negotiated financial-severance package to cushion the fall and meet future financial needs. Rarely, if ever, will a generous financial-severance arrangement repair the damage to the manager's bruised ego. Virtually all displaced executives or sidelined managers want to run something again, even if there is no financial necessity for them to do so. They want to prove themselves. They want to achieve.

This is generally true of men, young or old, in all walks of life. Men and women differ in this regard—certainly in degree, if not in kind. And husbands and wives have to understand this. Even when it is clearly a "no-fault" job loss related to legitimate restructuring, in the quiet of their hearts men tend to question their basic competency.

For a perspective on women and achievement, consider the view of Betty M. Vetter, executive director of the Scientific Manpower Commission, who spoke at Williams College in 1980, at a meeting designed to encourage more young women to follow research careers in science. She explained that men and women are not alike in their approach to scientific achievement. "A woman scientist," she said, "at the end of her life, looks back and exclaims, 'Look how far I've come.' But a man looks back and says, 'Look how many went ahead of me.'"

Robert I. Gannon, S.J., the famous orator who was president of Fordham University in the 1930s and 1940s, had an engaging expression for this phenomenon. He had sympathy but no praise for "mere trailing men." The phrase, applied to Irish-American Catholic males, derives from more primitive times when the tribe's hunters and gatherers returned exhausted from their labors. In reflecting on Gannon's speeches (and the mindset behind them), Peter McDonough speaks of "the gruff masculinity of 'trailing men' whose regrets and memories of struggle were intermittently more riveting than their success." Gannon's essential message for Irish-American Catholic couples was plain enough and powerful. McDonough sums it up in these words:

> *Men could be chivalrous even if weak and not fully successful. The family was sacred.... Mothers and daughters were the carriers of the ideal of simultaneous sweetness and strength.... Benevolence meant compassion for the defeated and solidarity in grief, the sentimentality of tribal bravery and stoicism, not generic altruism. Failure was forgiven in the home as sins were forgiven by the church.... The all-embracing sempiternal hierarchy was the church itself that sanctified women as acolytes of endurance and that comforted and did not threaten men* (Men Astutely Trained, *Free Press, 1992, p. 331*).

There is no Irish-Catholic monopoly on this dynamic. As I meet American men of all religious backgrounds, clinging to jobs that represent a broad range of rungs on the occupational ladder, I think of Carl Sandburg's poetic insight:

> *Those who order what they please*
> *when they choose to have it—*
> *can they understand the many down under*
> *who come home to their wives and children at night*
> *and night after night as yet too brave and unbroken*
> *to say 'I ache all over'?*

These are the trailing men of modern times. They are showing up on the managerial mountaintop these days, as well as in positions "down under." They are also losing their jobs. "The American workforce is being downsized and atomized," reported *Time* magazine on March 29, 1993:

> *Millions of Americans are being evicted from the working worlds that have sustained them, the jobs that gave them not only wages and health care and pensions but also a context, a sense of self-worth, a kind of identity. Work was the tribe. There were Sears men and GM workers and Anheuser-Busch people. There still are, of course. But their world is different.*

And those who are no longer there, at work and in the tribe, are hurting. If married, they need support from an uncritical, affirmative, understanding spouse. If single, they need affirmation from a close friend. Do women need similar support? Of course. And as women in managerial work accommodate themselves to unisex managerial roles, the need will become more obvious. But even then, the approach and emphasis will differ, and I will be addressing that point later in this chapter.

In a curious twist, the "trailing men" label has, in recent times, been applied not to worn-out males returning from the hunt, but to men the *Wall Street Journal* referred to as "Husbands in Limbo." The cascading headline on April 13, 1993, continues: "As More Men Become 'Trailing Spouses,' Firms Help Them Cope." "Many," the headline goes on to say, "Are Unable to Find Job When Wife Is Relocated: Some Pay Psychic Toll." "Who's the Boss as Home?" asks the final line over a page-one story about "the trailing husband problem ... or 'accompanying partners,' as they are also called." The story quotes an official of a Family and Work research institute as saying, "As companies get serious about moving up women, they've got to get serious about the trailing-husband issue." You will not have to tax your imagination to understand the headline hint that this rather recent phenomenon exacts a "psychic toll." The story puts it bluntly:

> *Many American men feel torn between traditional social values and some demands of modern life, but few are torn more*

brutally than those who are following their wives as the
women ascend the managerial ladder.... Many men suffer for
months over the double whammy of sex-role conflicts and
extended unemployment.

A *Business Week* cover story (Sept. 12, 1988) called middle managers the "silent majority" of American business.

Seldom heard. Rarely seen by the brass. And hardly ever pro-
tected when the going gets rough. No golden parachutes....
Ask a middle manager about life on the frontlines of the cor-
poration these days, and you're likely to hear a bitter story.
The ranks have been so decimated by the corporate trend to
'downsize' that some middle managers feel as if they are an
endangered species.

No less an observer than Peter Drucker is quoted in the story: "Middle managers have become insecure, and they feel unbelievably hurt. They feel like slaves on an auction block." I'll be exploring the implications of this in Chapter 7, "The New Corporate Contract." The point of mentioning it here is to observe that most (by no means all, but most) of these unsettled middle managers are male, many are disillusioned, and all of them would be better off if they were talking about it with their spouses. For that ongoing conversation to be productive, spouses have to understand their reciprocal relationships within the paradigm presented here.

One of America's best-known executive search consultants told me of an ousted CEO who said to him, "I just wish I were female, so I could cry; but I can't let them know how much it hurts." He hadn't read Robert Bly's *Iron John* (Addison-Wesley, 1990) or Sam Keen's *Fire in the Belly* (Bantam Books, 1991). These are books about men and their struggle for identity. In the 1950s, writes Bly, "man was supposed to like football, be aggressive, stick up for the United States, never cry, and always provide." But along came the 1960s, and "another sort of man appeared.... As men began to examine women's history and women's sensibility, some men began to notice what was called their *feminine* side and pay attention to it" (p. 2).

I recall hearing William Sloane Coffin, then chaplain at Yale, remark on a Sunday morning television program in the late 1960s that "the woman most in need of liberation in America is the woman inside of every man." There is a woman inside every man and a man inside every woman. (There is also, inside of every older person, a younger person wondering what happened!) The influence of the feminine in the man and the masculine in the woman is noticeable now, where previously there had not been a trace of one in the culturally conditioned preserve of the other. But there are differences that remain and require respect. The sensitive spouse will want to be ready to deal with those differences.

Many men could make these words their own: "After all the hard years, you start getting a little attention. You feel like a champion. You think you are something. But your wife knows you're not. She knows you're a jerk. She saw it all. She was there." This comment by actor Brian Dennehy in Life magazine was borrowed by Chuck Conconi for his *Washington Post* "Personalities" column (July 24, 1990) because, said Conconi, "It could have come from any major player in Washington as well." Perhaps it could. But the important question is, How will that knowledge of the other's vulnerability be used—as a weapon, or as a reminder that the male always needs reinforcing encouragement? Men, too, have both a wand and a weapon in their hands. They can give attention or withhold it. Given, attention becomes reassuring balm; withheld, it freezes into calculated disregard.

The Turn at Fifty

The problem of personal dislocation can, of course, be influenced by chronology as well as psychology. The famous milestone birthday referred to as the big Five-O ushers in a new era of doubt and disappointment for many males. Psychologist Daniel Levinson thinks "there may be more taboo about looking at your life during the fifties than any other decade." Why? "For many there is a silent despair, a pressing fear of becoming irrelevant in work or marriage, with no real alternative in sight. And for others, who are able to make vital choices during their 50's, there is a hard time of personal struggle early in the decade" (*The New York Times*, Feb. 7, 1989). Dr. Levinson's book, *The Seasons of a Man's Life* (Knopf, 1978), explores those struggles and acknowledges that although not universal, they are common through the decade of the fifties in a normal male lifetime.

In Connecticut, male job seekers, typically veterans of the insurance industry, sometimes speak of the "50-50 Club." If you make more than $50,000 and are over fifty years of age, you are a likely candidate for membership in this no-dues, no-meetings, no-headquarters organization. Once there, you have a lot of time to think about the issues the Levinson analysis raises.

Given the delayed entry of females into the labor market and the lag in their rise to positions of executive influence, men and women in their fifties can have opposite attitudes toward their careers. Sociologist David Karp, quoted in the same *New York Times* article just cited, says, "The men are developing an exit mentality, calculating how many years are left at work. But the women of the same age are thinking about making their mark." If one such woman is married to one such man, they have some serious talking to do without delay.

Further complexity is introduced from a source that is not simply psychological or chronological, but occupational. There are occupations that generate their own dark clouds over the workplace. Consider "professorial melancholia," a label devised by psychologist David F. Machell, who teaches justice and law administration at Western Connecticut State University. He explained to *The Chronicle of Higher Education* (Nov. 1, 1989) that he sees something inherent in the professor's job and in the academic environment that has created a "crisis of low self-esteem." Faculty members tend to be perfectionists. They like recognition, but don't get it. They know their pay is less than the compensation most other professionals receive. The fact that faculty jobs are relatively unstructured can contribute to the problem. But the point to note, says Professor Machell, is this: "Professorial melancholia is a disease of intense perfectionism. The criticism, the anger, the nothing-is-ever-good-enough aspect is really at the center of this disease."

It has been said that most of Thoreau's "men" live their "lives of quiet desperation" on university faculties. Faculty wives surely have better things to do than reminding their spouses that they come up short on relative shares of professional income. Faculty husbands should know that their professionally achieving spouses are underappreciated and late starters, for the most part, on the lower rungs of an already low faculty pay scale.

I want to attend more directly now to the female side of the spousal-support relationship I've been constructing in this chapter. One of the books that millions of spouses have found helpful is Georgetown linguistic professor Deborah Tannen's *You Just Don't Understand: Women and Men in Conversation* (Ballantine Books, 1991). The psychological underpinning for the linguistic enlightenment this book provides is instructive for spouses burdened with one or the other's job loss. The typical male, writes Professor Tannen (pp. 24–25), engages the world

> *as an individual in a hierarchical social order in which he was either one-up or one-down. In this world, conversations are negotiations in which people try to achieve and maintain the upper hand if they can, and protect themselves from others' attempts to put them down and push them around. Life, then, is a contest, a struggle to preserve independence and avoid failure.*

The typical female, on the other hand, approaches the world "as an individual in a network of connections." For women, as Dr. Tannen explains it,

> *conversations are negotiations for closeness in which people try to seek and give confirmation and support, and to reach consensus. They try to protect themselves from others' attempts to push them away. Life, then, is a community, a struggle to preserve intimacy and avoid isolation. Though there are hierarchies in this world too, they are hierarchies more of friendship than of power and accomplishment.*

And Deborah Tannen makes the further point that serves to remind all of us that sexual equality does not mean identity between the sexes. Men and women differ in their experience of loneliness and failure, even though men and women both experience loneliness and failure.

Women are also concerned with achieving status and avoiding failure, but these are not the goals they are focused on all the time, and they tend to pursue them in the guise of connection. And men are also concerned with achieving involvement and avoiding isolation, but they are not focused on these goals, and they tend to pursue them in the guise of opposition.

One appreciative reader of Tannen's book told me what a bargain it was—it saved him thousands in marriage counseling fees! I would certainly recommend that it become a shared-reading project for any couple at the very beginning of the job campaign. Even before the job-loss trauma strikes, many American couples who have been married for two decades or more are lonely together in marriage. One woman put it this way for me: "We are going our separate ways together." Noncommunication is not the root of the problem; nonunderstanding is. Inability to communicate leaves the deeper feelings, and questions, unexpressed. This results in a loneliness that is real in both partners, but more acute on the distaff side.

Job loss is typically regarded, by both women and men, as a failure of one kind or another. I was struck by the findings of Carole Hyatt and Linda Gottlieb regarding the different male and female reactions to failure. In *When Smart People Fail* (Penguin Books, 1988), these authors devote a chapter to "The Male/Female Difference." Here is a set of points culled from their fourth chapter (pp. 85–97) that can serve to highlight the differences and alert spouses to be on guard against misreading the way the other reacts to job loss.

- Many women who fail consider quitting work; almost none of the men who fail regard this as an option.
- Men returning to work after failure emphasize their "feminine" side; women returning to work after failure emphasize their "masculine" side.
- Most women have an easier time coping with career failure than most men.

- ◆ Success and failure are moral judgments to women and game calls to men.
- ◆ Sex-based differences regarding success and failure are less pronounced in younger people than in older people.

The subtitle of this helpful book is "Rebuilding Yourself for Success." If that rebuilding process is to go well for you after job loss, not only do you have to assume personal responsibility for your recovery and reentry into meaningful employment, but you should be as clear as you can in disclosing to your spouse or close friend "where it hurts." Consider yourself blessed if, in response, you receive support targeted on your need and sensitive to your vulnerability.

Writing in the *Personnel Journal* (August 1991), Stanlee Phelps and Marguerite Mason discuss "When Women Lose Their Jobs." And to ensure that readers will not miss the message, the layout editor highlighted the following words and placed them immediately beneath the title of the article: "If there's one thing to remember when outplacing employees, it's that men and women are different." How so? In order to learn the different approaches men and women take to outplacement—the professionally assisted process of transition from one job (lost) to another (not yet found) where the former employer pays for, but does not provide, the assistance—the writers interviewed and observed sixty-four executives (eighteen of whom were women) in a southern California office of a national outplacement firm. They found that women often take longer than men to move through the transition, that women approach outplacement in a way that perplexes the men in their personal lives, and that older women "may opt out of the corporate track altogether, excited by the prospect of blazing more rewarding trails as entrepreneurs or consultants." What is it about the female approach that perplexes the males around them?

Phelps and Mason note that having satisfying relationships in all areas of life, including the workplace, is tied in closely to a woman's fundamental identity. "Therefore, a job loss throws her into an examination of her relationships, her career choice, and the balance between the various facets of her life." Women, the authors explain, *are accustomed to working globally—integrating work, partner, kids, household, school and community. A change in one of these areas, such as a job loss, affects all the other areas. On a normal day, women may experience identity confusion because their lives are very complex. A job loss exerts even more pressure on the balance among these many responsibilities.*

Since work is only one of many female roles, the loss of work has less direct impact on female identity. This is not to say it doesn't hurt, only to note that the hurt is normally not part of an identity crisis.

One man I met during the course of this study, unfazed by the risk of being accused of stereotypical incorrectness on both sides of the gender divide, called women "nesters" and men "hunters." He proceeded to make the following point: "Although women now leave the nest to participate in the hunt, the tendency toward the nest is still there; so is the heart-on-the-hunt in the case of the typical male." In the interest of balance, I should note that an outplacement specialist (more on outplacement in Chapter 5) had men in mind when he told me that his New York City office had several nesters. The outplacement space and support services paid for by their former employer enabled some "to set up housekeeping here. This place becomes a club. One guy was here for five years."

The male identity—unquestioned and culturally reinforced—is typically focused on achievement, on doing, on success. If you lose your job, you set out directly and immediately to hunt for another. Men depend on spouses or close friends for encouragement and suppport during the job search. Not only do they want no criticism, they are not inclined toward critical review of themselves and their options. They have a need to perform; they are driven toward the goal of a job, maybe not any job at all, but some job without delay.

For women, say Phelps and Mason, losing a job "opens up emotional fallout, sense of loss, grieving." They "join with other women for creative problem solving, support." They are able to "integrate job search with personal growth, friends, family, and community." Women see the loss of a job "as an opportunity to take stock, shift gears"; they put the "focus on 'what's my life all about?'" and they see "job loss as a personal rejection." This view is affirmed by one of the female participants in my study; she told me, "Women are more resilient than men in dealing with job loss." She characterizes what she has observed in her own reaction to separation and that of other women as "constructive anger" and "recognition of a new opportunity." "I'm not saying that it is easier for women," she explained, "just that they deal with it better."

Men, by comparison, "downplay or deny the emotional side of losing a job." They proceed alone. Although support groups are available, "support groups for executive men are rare," say these writers, although I think this point applies only at the most senior levels. Those a notch or two down the scale—vice presidents and directors—have no difficulty finding support groups and are less reluctant to join them.

Unlike women, men tend to "compartmentalize the job search from other aspects of life," and they see the loss of a job "as a misfortune that needs to be fixed right away." They tend immediately to focus on the question "What's my job all about?" while sidestepping the antecedent question "Who am I and what's my life all about?"

Quoting other studies that show that about 95 percent of senior male executives are married and that close to 90 percent of their wives do not hold paying jobs, Phelps and Mason suggest that the traditional marriage can be both a plus and a minus for the job-searching male executive:

> *The wife may have been a support system for him during his days of career development and success, but now that he's unemployed, she may exert considerable pressure on him to get out there and get a job. At the same time, she may be unwilling or unable to get a job herself.*

The dynamics are different when a woman loses a high-level job.

> *For a woman to have attained a senior position, she had to have made her job her top priority. Men tend not to want to be a spouse in this situation, so many executive women are either divorced or never married.... Typically, these women didn't enjoy a spousal support system during their career*

development, nor are they subject to 'get a job' pressure from
a nonworking spouse.

Both men and women expressed to me the opinion that women at these higher altitudes of executive responsibility are tougher than their male counterparts.

Respect the Differences

The point to be repeated in these pages, and both understood and acted upon by the spouse of a person looking for work, is that men and women are different in their reactions to job loss and in their approach to the job search. The search will go a whole lot better if the person trying to be supportive is also sensitive to and respectful of the differences. Moreover, the nonworking spouse "has to understand that emotions run the gamut," said an ousted national director of real estate services for a major accounting firm. "Even in a person whose confidence has not been affected," he told me, "emotions cannot be 'up' all the time." He admitted to hiding his feelings from his wife on occasion simply because he didn't want to spread the gloom to her. He felt that his wife "didn't *really* want to know my true feelings; they would have made her afraid." His advice to others in transition: "Keep a stiff upper lip and a smile on your face when dealing with the family."

Robert Bly, in commenting on our tendency to partially trust rather than completely trust even those closest to us, tells readers of *Iron John*, "It is said that in marriage, the man and woman give each other 'his or her nethermost beast' to hold. Each holds the leash for the 'nethermost beast' of the other. It's a wonderful phrase" (pp. 76–77). The phrase is all the more wonderful for those who remember that *nethermost* means "lowest," the area all the way down at the deepest depth—not just the inner world, but the personal netherworld, as mysterious as that region may be. Marriage partners have to know the nature of the beast whose leash they are handing to or holding for the other.

Opposites may well attract (there will always be arguments about that), but values certainly bond. Shared values, deeply held, will hold partners together through periods of job anxiety. The senior male executive who remembers Tommy Dorsey's music with Frank Sinatra and the Pied Pipers singing "There Are Such Things," might admit to a need deep in his own nether world for "Someone to whisper/ 'Darling, you're my guiding star/ It's not what you own/ But just what you are.'"

Probably the most affirmative, supportive spouse I met in the course of this study is the wife of an automotive executive.

> *He was so strong through the whole experience that I wonder if we withheld some of the support we should have given him. He never complained or felt sorry for himself—and wouldn't let the children or me do so either. We were full of self-pity over the loss of our on-demand transportation (no new cars in the driveway), but Tom taught us the positive side of that too—taking cars in for service and making a few repairs ourselves, something we had never done before!*

Her closing comments offer a clue to the type of person she is:

> *Our family unity was never threatened, and through the whole painful experience Tom continued to do what he does best— be a perfect husband and father. He thinks young, looks young, acts young, and everyone thinks he is. Makes it very hard for a wife who is the same age as her birth certificate!*

I asked many men and women who had moved through or were still in the job search to articulate advice they would offer to married couples in anticipation of one of the partners encountering the dislocation associated with job loss. Here are some examples of what I received. From a very creative sales executive who moved into television production and back to sales:

- ◆ Don't postpone fun time together.
- ◆ Work separately on your "Life Priority" lists and then compare them to pinpoint the incompatibles and the unrealistic expectations. Work out your mutual goals and face up to the tradeoffs you will have to make.

◆ Holding is a form of communication that can be more effective than speaking, especially if you don't know what to say or if what you would like to say would be hurtful. Twenty minutes of holding a day (per pair) is good for parents, children, and spouses.

A corporate tax manager acknowledged that spousal and family love was strong. However, anger directed at him, not at the boss who fired him, came from inside the family. It was, he said, "frequent but short-lived, but it hurt." It took this form: "Why you? What did you do wrong? What aren't you telling me? You saved them so much money; you must have done something wrong." He didn't do anything wrong. In fact, he did something heroic, but his spouse wasn't pleased. He had been asked by his superior to name two people in his department who should be let go if cuts were mandated. He responded by pointing to the large contribution the department was making and that it was not overstaffed. He could not run a department with fewer people and still do the job. If cuts were mandated, he told those higher up, "it would be better to let me go." One month later they did. This forty-three-year old manager, now practicing the same specialty in another industry at twice his former salary, has this advice for spouses:

◆ Honestly assess to what extent either one of you contributed to the job loss and deal with that failure or innocence early on. Reaffirm your love for each other, "for better or worse."
◆ Once the issue of guilt is faced squarely, learn from it, but drop it and focus on building each other up and achieving your objective of reestablishing your source of income.
◆ A supportive spouse is very important, as rejection is a frequent occurrence if you are sending out enough resumes.
◆ Also, quickly establish a new budget with timetables for action.

As downsizing found its way into his Pittsburgh law firm, a fifty-four-year old attorney lost his partnership and had to search for corporate legal work. He reports that his wife was neither understanding nor personally supportive; she was critical and anxious. His advice takes a practical tone:

> *Deal honestly with your children and spouse. Tell them how it is and don't sugarcoat the realities. Explain what must be done on expenditures. (Cut!) And explain the job-search strategies and techniques to the nonsearching spouse. In short, plan for the worst.*

The most unfocused, discouraged person in my sample was a fifty-five-year-old male, who showed all the physical signs of a worn-out life and described his present position in one telling word: "adrift." He had lost a job as director of communications two years earlier and had not yet been successful in his efforts to reconnect. His wife worked as he searched, but he wasn't looking very hard. He needed her both emotionally and economically, "to ballast him," as a character in Ford Maddox Ford's *Parade's End* says, referring to another fellow's need for "a good woman's backing."

He comes as close as anyone I encountered in this study to fitting the description of a discouraged man novelist Jon Hassler provides in *North of Hope* (Ballantine Books, 1990):

> *"What are you feeding with all those calories?" [asks a therapist].*
> *"My big leak," was Frank's reply. "I've sprung a very big leak, and my spirit is draining away."*

The former director of communications, now "adrift," says he has spent a lot of time thinking about his problems in dealing with other people. "I still don't know what motivates others." His advice to any other couple anticipating job loss: "Reduce debts, avoid financial commitments, and recognize that it can happen any time for any reason. Don't rely on an employer's goodwill, understanding, or words of reassurance." Now there is a man in need of spousal support. That support, as you will see in the next example, could come in the form of a not-so-gentle push.

In a role-reversal marriage, the breadwinning wife of an unemployed trade association president reported it was "a difficult balancing act" to locate herself somewhere "between encouragement and pushing/prodding." She explained,

I was the one who had to keep encouraging my husband and telling him that he had various skills and qualities that would make him a good candidate for a particular job. There were times when he needed a good push. It was particularly difficult as he became increasingly discouraged, especially each time after being turned down for a job for which he was very well qualified. Occasionally I even went through the want ads and circled jobs for him. I'm sure there were some jobs he applied for just to get me off his back. Yet we rarely fought or argued during this time. We both knew we were in this together.

She had some additional insights on how to deal with waning support over time from those outside the family.

At first, all of your friends and family are very supportive and encouraging. As time goes on and you haven't found a job, they start to give advice. Much of this is unwelcome, because you have tried all of it yourself. Pretty soon you find yourself avoiding people because you don't want them to ask if you have found anything. When you have been in a prominent and powerful position, you have certain recognition that puts you on a par with people in similar positions. After a while, there is nothing to say, so you avoid these people. Then you develop a cover story that you are in business for yourself. Never mind that you aren't, but at least it gives you some dignity in the eyes of others.

She realized, however, that contact with close, nonjudgmental friends had to be maintained. In making that point, she highlights a growing problem in America, the difficulty that friends and relatives of the unemployed have in figuring out how to be of help.

Friends and relatives often wish there were something they could do to help. Everyone knows what to do for the family with a serious illness or death, yet no one knows how to deal with someone who has lost a job. It is a very fine line, because the unemployed are suffering from low self-esteem and do not want charity. However, some nice things friends have done for us include having us over for dinner, giving us tickets that they couldn't use for the theater or sporting events, and offering to let us use their beach house. These things were all done in the spirit of friendship; never were we made to feel that our friends were doing it because they felt sorry for us. The most important thing is to keep in contact, since the unemployed person is disconnected from the normal daily living of the working world and all the interactions that go with it.

One man in this study lost a vice presidential position in the automobile industry at age forty-two, and was "still looking" for the right position four years later. He was doing some consulting, and his wife returned to work. "I resent having to go to a job every day," she told me. "I don't find it satisfying. I loved being home taking care of my family. I would prefer having gone to work because I wanted to and because it was the thing to do at this stage of my life—not because I had to." I asked them both to write down for me an assessment of her reaction to the severance. He gave me one word: "fright." She wrote, "The following describes my immediate and present reactions to his job loss and the resulting challenge to our life together: fear, anger, devastation, anger, helplessness, anxiety, anger, disappointment, anger, isolation, despair, an overwhelming doubt in the existence of a personal God, anger." She added that she is "grateful for a strong family that has so far survived" and indicated that "some facets of our life together have actually improved." He was now closer to the children, more involved in church and school, "things he never had time for before."

Family psychotherapist Peggy Treadwell remarked to me, "How the spouse handles the situation has everything to do with the survival of the entire family" during the unemployment crisis. She makes the added point that typically there will be a still-employed spouse who should be encouraged to take care of him- or herself. The provision of necessary support must not become an all-consuming thing. She thinks the spousal-support relationship has to be viewed from a "family systems" perspective. Unemployment should not be narrowly perceived as the problem, and certainly the person who is out of work must not be seen as the problem. In fact, the spouse who has not been laid off should seize the opportunity to "get so clear about him- or herself and the future of their family that he or she can emerge as an enabling leader in the family, and as a nonthreatening challenger (a desirable form of support) to the other." This is tricky terrain, best negotiated, I would think, with the guidance of a skilled professional.

Use the situation, says Peggy Treadwell, as "an occasion to see how the *family* is functioning." If she were invited in and asked to help, she would be inclined to focus on the spouse (not necessarily the jobless one) who is "motivated to change." And she would work to facilitate that change on the assumption that the other spouse cannot then not change. In Peggy Treadwell's view, if the wife is still employed, she "needs to separate herself sufficiently so that she can do some clear thinking about what is important to her." This is not to be selfish; it is simply to be appropriately supportive. If you're going to "be there" for another person, you should first locate and assemble the self that hopes to help.

The best-known executive in my sample, a name immediately recognizable to even casual readers of business news, described his mood after job loss in these words: "I felt very lonely—rejected; my wife tried hard to keep up my spirits. Suddenly you have a lot of time on your hands." He was tempted, he told me, to lose confidence in himself. He credits the calm reassurance and affirmation from his wife as essential in enabling him to maintain stability.

Reflecting on her own experience after separation from the job of vice president for operations in a health-care corporation, a married woman had this advice for the spouse of the person being let go: "Recognize the anguish and self-doubt your spouse is experiencing and cut him or her some slack! Be supportive and try to understand that this is a time when you will have to give more than receive."

Another observer told me that one of the psychological issues underlying stresses in the spousal relationship during a job transition is what he calls "male grandiosity." Men tend to forget that "when the dream dies, it dies for *both* husband and wife, and indeed, the wife may have sacrificed more for it."

A former president and chief operating officer of a bank said, as many others also noted, that it is important for the spouse to understand the search process. The search "will involve rejection; the spouse must recognize this, understand it, and compensate for it." He added: "She has to resist the urge to provide a list of 'things to do around the house in all your free time.'" He wished, he said, that his wife had been able to "forget what might have been job-wise, and look with confidence toward the future." He subsequently found an executive vice presidency in a commercial bank.

During an eighteen-month migration from a divisional presidency in one of the nation's best-known advertising agencies to a "more fulfilling" but lesser executive responsibility in the same industry, a fifty-year-old executive learned this about the spousal relationship: "The same mutual support that served so well during the good times, serves even better after job loss. We were forward-looking and maintained positive attitudes. We were up-front with people about being out of work. We knew it would be counterproductive to deny the loss of employment."

Another executive, who had been through the transition twice, would want both spouses to realize that "this is a planning opportunity that few people take full advantage of." His advice:

- ◆ Communicate with each other early and often.
- ◆ Have a dose of reality, early!
- ◆ Consider these factors in setting your next job goal: future life goals; the job content (of both jobs, if the spouse works or wants to work); relocation—yes or no; the quality of the life you want to lead.

Keep Communicating

Repeatedly, unemployed managers mentioned the importance of communication between the spouses during the transition. "Communicate, communicate, communicate!" was the terse response several gave to my inquiry about any words of wisdom they would have for other couples in anticipation of job loss. Interestingly enough, it was a vice president for external communications who spoke to me, after his separation, of the importance of *mutual* support and understanding. He put it this way: "Be mutual; *both* people are going through the transition. One cannot let the external threat the transition brings harm the love that the relationship is based on."

Communication—before, during, and in those happy days after the experience—would be virtually unanimous advice for other spouses from marriage partners who had weathered the employment-separation storm. Some warned that the employed spouse can be "unintentionally insensitive" and that "specific job-seeking strategies should not be discussed unless *both* spouses find it useful." Many used navigational metaphors to convey the importance of mutual support in negotiating the choppy waters of a job search. A stressed job seeker, aware of his own impatience, underscored his dependence on his wife to keep a calm atmosphere at home. One person recalled an image from childhood to point to the need to manage emotional ups and downs together: "You must try to flatten the roller coaster."

Some offered very practical advice:

- Keep each other fully informed and involved in your finances.
- Live well within your means and don't take too seriously your "right" to the luxuries a high income buys.
- Reduce expenditures. Know the difference between discretionary and nondiscretionary expenditures.
- Pay off or restructure high-interest debts.
- Make sacrifices to meet the requirements of a reduced budget.
- Inform the kids of sacrifices all will have to make.
- List goals—in writing: long-term, mid-term, short-term.
- Choose someone other than your spouse to be a backup confidant. Find both a corporate and a spiritual mentor.
- The sooner both spouses talk to relatives and friends about the situation and ask for help, the quicker they will have many supportive allies to help them through the process.
- Do free things for entertainment; watch out for increased consumption of alcohol.
- Fight your desire to withdraw.
- Assume nothing about where your spouse wants to live and what he or she wants to do. Push for her (or his) answer.

- Recognize that it is every bit as hard, or even harder, on your spouse, who ordinarily cannot do much to solve the problem.
- Don't keep anything from your spouse, even if it means full disclosure of your own insecurity and doubt.
- Avoid unstated differences in expectations during a predictably trying time when mutual support is essential.
- No surprises.
- Respect the need for privacy felt by the spouse whose job was lost.
- Prepare yourself for the fact that during the transition it is going to be tough being together so much of the time.
- Realize that too many people stay in the denial or anger stage far longer than they should. It's old news; move forward!
- Don't place a "hiding-it" burden on the rest of the family; agree on what will be said about it up front and just say this whenever appropriate.
- Love each other and say so often.

Many of my respondents stressed, in this context of advice to spouses, the importance of accumulating savings in advance of the separation event, even if that event was considered unlikely to happen. Some spoke of this in terms of reserves, and one person specified the need to build up psychological as well as financial reserves in advance. A sales manager, out of work at age fifty-three, was quite specific on the financial issue: "You must have at *least* six to twelve months of salary set aside in a savings account, over and above what you may have been able to invest toward retirement. Finding a new position may take two weeks; it could easily take as long as two years."

Communication between spouses is the necessary infrastructure for both kinds of reserve endowments—psychological and financial—to support the spousal relationship during the stress of transition from a job lost to a job not yet found. Many of the managers I met in the course of this study referred to their spouses as "my best friend." That friendship strengthened the support system that sustained those partners through the ambiguities and uncertainties of the job search. Without that support, they invariably say, they would not have been able to make it.

Chapter 3

DEALING WITH DISCOURAGEMENT

He that lives in hope dances without music.
—George Herbert

In Chapter 1, I invited you to consider why you might hesitate or procrastinate when it comes to picking up the phone and initiating the contacts that are the building blocks of a successful job campaign. Fear of rejection is one of the reasons. So is immobilizing discouragement. This chapter deals with discouragement, or, to put it more accurately, this chapter offers you insight and assistance in dealing with your own discouragement—your flatness, dryness, diminution of hope.

"Until you've sat at home, as I did, waiting hours, then days, even weeks, for the phone call that never comes, you'll never know how important it is for me to return a call," said a senior vice president for human resources, who invited me into his corner office to discuss his personal experiences (three times) of job loss. I had thanked him for being so prompt in getting back to me when I telephoned for an appointment. He said that during his job search, he decided to make the baggage of discouragement a positive force, pushing him toward the phone and out the door for an endless series of interviews. Now back at work, he used the memory of the pain of waiting for unanswered calls as a stimulus to leave no call unreturned for long. "When you're looking for work and someone doesn't return your call," he told me, "you go lower than a whale's belly."

"You don't *have* to have the patience of Job," said an international banker, "but—phew!—people don't get back to you. And when you're waiting, every day is like a week, every week is like a month, every month is like a year."

You've seen how important spousal support is in dealing with discouragement. Empathy, not sympathy; positive reinforcement, not solution giving—that's what is needed from spouse or close friend during the job search. A subsequent chapter will look at the relevance of religion, a help for many in dealing with discouragement. Faith and friends are usually sufficient to pull a person through discouragement. An indispensable dimension of that faith, however, is faith in self—quiet confidence (the word means "with faith"), not arrogant self-sufficiency.

Of course you're discouraged. You wouldn't be human if you didn't feel down when you're out of work. Besides, chances are you've lived long enough to be able to relate to George Kennan's remark that if someone "lives more than half a century, his familiar world, the world of his youth, fails him like a horse dying under its rider." Good image, but don't forget that the rider can get up and start moving again. You are a human being with options, far better options than the one a not-so-helpful career consultant had in mind when he thought about the opportunities out there and told an aging inquirer, "If you are fifty-six and blown away, you might as well open up a candy store." You have a choice. You can convince yourself that you're looking into an empty future, or you can believe instead that an opportunity awaits you just around a future corner and that you will turn that corner soon.

The intensity of your personal discouragement while unemployed will vary from person to person, and normally it will be in direct proportion to the duration of the quest for work. As his job search moved into its second year, a fifty-two-year-old sales executive in San Francisco said to me, "I'm running out of ideas and contacts, I'm running out of money, I'm running out of life."

Several levels of discouragement may be activated simultaneously; for some, it may settle in at the level of the unconscious. When that happens, professional help may be required, as a displaced sales executive discovered with the realization that his job loss had triggered a host of unresolved feelings of grief related to his wife's death eighteen months earlier. He dealt with discouragement by learning how to deal with grief.

Some job seekers find themselves for the first time asking someone else for help. They find this distasteful. Unaccustomed as they are to asking for help, they are even less prepared for the refusal and rejection those requests will draw. Not flat-out rejections; those will be rare. But letters have a way of being set aside, résumés get lost, promised calls become promises broken, and the "anything I can do to help" messages become forced or muted, not followed up by prompt delivery. This leaves the job seeker even more alone and much discouraged. After the fact, some can joke about it. One man told me he kept careful count of the response ratio to the resumes he mailed out. It was three to forty—only three responses "of any nature, even 'go to hell.' You got to the point where 'go to hell' was nice to hear; I mean, you got a response. The guy knew you were alive. It was wonderful! You got a rejection letter. It made your day!"

With considerably less glee, an ousted computer executive, age forty-six, acknowledged that

> there were very few people I felt comfortable talking to or asking for help when I was separated from the company. I had always been independent and successful; that was my image, and I felt I had to protect that image. People I helped along the way—finding jobs, advancing their careers—didn't seem to have time to pick up the phone and call. This was probably my biggest disappointment in the entire experience.

Below these surface-level disappointments, these flesh-wound experiences of discouragement, lies a substratum of discouragement in many that calls out for the durability of hope, a call that does not ordinarily get an immediate and effective response. Hope is needed to provide the courage to endure, to overcome the all-too-human tendency to personalize what Yeats saw as part of the human condition: "Under every dancer is a dead man in his grave." I was astounded when one young man I was attempting to help some years ago referred to himself as "a walking graveyard." No one would have suspected that this handsome, well-dressed young professional was carrying with him that kind of baggage of low self-esteem. He should have been building up some personal reserves of hope to draw upon when he was in his fifties. As Thornton Wilder saw so clearly, "We strengthen our souls, when young, on hope; the strength we acquire enables us ... to endure despair."

I think the German poet Hebbel saw something that is at work within most of us and expressed it well in these lines: "The one I am sadly salutes/ the one I could have been." A displaced health-care executive, after first thanking me "for putting me in touch with my feelings by giving me the opportunity to complete the questionnaire," echoed Hebbel in articulating this advice for others: "Don't engage in recriminations, backbiting, or 'if-only' exercises; don't look back."

The circumstances of age, sex, occupation, and other personal "environmental" impacts on the displaced executive's psyche make this a complicated issue. The "sad salute," usually directed to opportunities missed, is made by different people in different ways and goes out in different directions. Although its meaning is unique to the discouraged person, the experience is shared almost universally among members of the human community by virtue of their being human. Even back in the eighteenth century, poet Edward Young framed the question in a poem called "Born Originals." If indeed we are all "born Originals," he asks, "how comes it to pass that we die Copies?"

To be is to be disappointed eventually, to have somehow fallen short. But, "That which we are, we are," wrote Tennyson in "Ulysses," and we simply have to accept this and get on with life:

> *Tho' much is taken, much abides, and tho'*
> *We are not now that strength which in old days*
> *Moved earth and heaven, that which we are, we are.*

Those who experience job loss need immediate and repeated assurance that they have not been laid off from life, despite the downward-pointing psychological signals their personal sad salutes might be sending to them. Some draw comfort from Mark Twain's observation [cited by Joseph E. Persico in *Edward R. Murrow: An American Original* (McGraw-Hill, 1988), p. 496]: "It is not likely that any complete life has ever been lived which was not a failure in the secret judgment of the person who lived it." Sayings like that may be useful for after-the-fact reflection, but they offer little consolation to someone still in the job-search tunnel with no sight of the light at the other end. One woman in my sample reported that at the end of a long interview with a job counselor, when she had been out of work for four months, she said, "Let me ask you a question. Am I ever going to get a job? And he just sat and he said, 'Well, I don't really know.'" She held her composure there, but shortly afterward, when she sat down to join a friend in a restaurant, she burst into tears.

Ousted from his company presidency, a telecommunications executive went, as he put it, "into a funk" when he clicked on the E-mail feature he had been accustomed to using on his home computer and discovered that he was "not valid"!

Back in the 1960s, when college students were supposed to be unreflective activists, Jim Beek, a student at Loyola College in Baltimore, wrote a poem for the Winter 1968 issue of *Ignis*, the campus literary quarterly, that can speak to the heart of the problem the person searching for work brings to this book. It was titled "Catharsis" and opened with the line, "I awoke in the silent fist of the night gagging on loneliness." Then, several lines later, Jim Beek writes:

And I opened my books for something to ease the cramp
But they only grumbled at me for awaking them at an odd hour.
And the fear that my existence wasn't doing anyone any good
Was under my fifth rib.

So the poet prays "to a god who would have nothing to do with a stained glass window," and gets this reply:

Son—
This is the pain that lets you know you're alive.
Much of you is grown, and the rest is trying hard to catch up.
You have raked many words from books, and now you must
  put some back ...

If you put up your guard and go through life with a sand-
    bagged soul,
You may fend off a blow, but you'll also stop a kiss.

The fear that your existence isn't "doing anyone any good" adds a lot of heavy freight to your discouragement. If, as the psychologists remind us, depression is inverted anger—i.e., anger turned in on itself—discouragement might be thought of as an aching awareness of not being needed. The pain is there, "under your fifth rib," all right, but it can serve as a reminder that you are alive and a member of the human race, and able to contribute if you lift the weights from your "sandbagged soul," become vulnerable again, and see what words, or works, or ideas of your own are at hand, so that you can "put some back" in the form of meaningful employment resulting from a persistent job search.

Persistence

There's the word—persistence. Discouragement erodes it, under-cuts it, tries to smother it. Discouragement puts the fire out. The really discouraged person stops looking. The persistent person never gives up. Torrey Foster, founder of Job Seekers, a church-based support group at St. Paul's Episcopal Church in Cleveland Heights, Ohio, tells his clients, "You've got to be pushy." Lest they go too far, he tempers the advice by explaining that he is speaking of "diplomatic persistence."

I sat in on a 7:30 A.M. Job Seekers meeting on a snowy January Friday. ("We meet on Fridays to encourage them not to shrink the search to a four-day workweek," explained Torrey Foster.) Jim Piper had good news to share. "I was a victim of society," he said, referring to the downsizing phenomenon, "but now I've been reclaimed." The call came at 10:30 on the morning of Christmas Eve, he was happy to say. And to the others there who remained jobless during and after the holidays, and who had had to drive through snow to attend the meeting, he said, "Keep on spinning your wheels and eventually you'll get some traction." Persistence eventually pays off.

One of the Cleveland Heights job seekers, a metallurgist who moved into management only to move out on a downsizing wave, "got tired of looking," so he started his own business: Power To Go, an airport-based, traveler-oriented, battery-pack pickup service for travelers uneasy about the battery life in their portable computers. The portable battery package is ordered by phone, paid for by credit card, and returned after the trip for recharging by the company and deposit retrieval by the user.

The metallurgist-turned-entrepreneur explained to members of his support group why he started his own business: "It was better to do something than to slowly die." His business forecast was modestly confident: "Lots of little seeds get planted and 88 percent of them die; you hope for the other twelve." Regrettably, this new business seedling also died, so now his hopes are reduced to the remaining eleven possibilities.

Tom Peters, of *In Search of Excellence* fame, had something encouraging to say to this kind of initiative in an interview with *Psychology Today* (March/April 1993). The questioner commented, "Your ideas are remarkable in their compassion for failure." Peters replied, "Well, to not fail is to die.... If you are not pursuing some damn dream and then reinventing yourself regularly, assiduously, you're going to fail. Period." He further explained,

> In the world of dull, boring management, the essence to me of everything that one accomplishes in life, from the trivial to the grand, is failure. You don't ride a bike the first time. You don't play a violin the first time. The essence of experimental physics is to create experiments at which you fail; then along the way you eventually achieve some knowledge of something. It's hard to articulate because, for me, it's so damned obvious that the only thing worth pursuing is failure.

Peters has much respect for "the role of groundless courage" in an individual life.

One of the men in my study, a fifty-four-year-old manager of advertising and sales for a large tire company, left his job voluntarily because he chose, for family reasons, not to move to a distant state. When I met him, it had been fifteen months and he still had no job. "I tried to devote three to four days a week to employment seeking," he explained. "I went to support meetings, yet there were days and weeks that I gave up on myself and gave in to depression. I did nothing directed to job seeking. Pulling myself out of those bad days and weeks has been truly tough—for me and especially for my wife. If nothing else, this has been the greatest test of our marriage. So far, we're winning." Because he had given up on the search, he had not yet come up with a job. His spouse was holding him and their marriage together. The ground had gone out from under his career, and the will power wasn't there to summon up the "groundless courage" to keep his job campaign going.

I've been told that the painter Francis Bacon (b. 1909) used the phrase "exhilarated despair" to describe himself; he saw it as "a state where one's basic nature is totally without hope, and yet the nervous system is made out of optimistic stuff." I'm talking here about something that is even better. I'm talking about the importance of living in hope. In the words of poet George Herbert, "He that lives in hope dances without music." The job seeker has to keep on dancing to music from within, after the "background music" you get from your job stops. Another line from Herbert suggests the unappealing alternative: "He begins to die, that quits his desires." All of this is condensed in the experience of one manager, age fifty-one, whose severance pay was long gone and who had, after two years, no job prospects that looked promising. In describing this "most traumatic experience" in his life, he wrote in a letter to me:

> Unemployment has had a positive effect on my life in that it has made me a much more sensitive and caring person. I have been humbled and that is good. Last year for a time I was driving an airport limousine to make twenty dollars a trip (every little bit helps). On one occasion I picked up one of my former peers who still works at my last company. That was humbling! I keep telling myself that someday I will find financial security and I will look back with gratitude for having had the chance to become a better person. I remain hope-

*ful, but my trust is only in my own effort. I expect no help
and want (and deserve) no sympathy. My situation is the
result of the choices I personally made. I have no one to be
angry at, including myself. I am proud of my strength, but I
do fear despair. If someday I did lose hope, the result would
be final.*

Persistence can activate the optimism that lies hidden in the
inner person, somewhere in the nervous system, ready to spring.
By exercising persistence, you can experience the exhilaration and
reduce the despair. But you have to try it to become convinced.
You have to believe that the other side of every "out" is "in," and
that any exit is an entrance in reverse. Every ouster is the starting
gate for a comeback.

You also have to remind yourself that you are not alone. You are
experiencing just one dimension, admittedly painful, of the human
condition. For the musical *Closer Than Ever*, director and lyricist
Richard Maltby, Jr., penned a telling lyric for a song called "One of
the Good Guys." It is a musical portrait of the hard-working, faithful family man, troubled by doubt, but hanging in there as one of
the "good guys."

*Just between good guys
It's not which road you take
Which life you pick to live in
Whichever choice you make
The longing is a given
And that's what brings the ache
That only the good guys know.*

The ache is there. Having it does not at all disqualify you
from association with "the good guys" or marginalize your membership in the human race. You have to resist the temptation to
give in to the pain and begin thinking of yourself as a "yesterself."
Authentic yesterselves are not still around; you are, and you are
capable of drawing on your past education and experience to
carve out a new career.

Insisting that "my youth is not dead—yet," a sixty-year-old marketing manager gave me his reaction to the very discouraging "you're overqualified" response he had been receiving to job inquiries. "It really means you're too old, or your salary range is too high, or simply 'we don't want you.'" When you hear "overqualified," he said,

accept the fact that it isn't worth your while to pursue it, but don't give up; just point your pursuit in other directions. Maybe you are too old for a particular job. But look at it this way: If you needed brain surgery, who would you rather have operate on you—an overqualified surgeon, or someone less well qualified? Package the skills and experience that make you "overqualified," and sell that package, at a bargain price, perhaps, to someone who really needs it. Your job now is to find that someone.

Searching for that someone, even by telephone, is never going to be easy. The single-day experience of one man I spoke to will not necessarily be typical. He made thirty-five phone calls one day and did not get past the receptionists to one live voice; he deposited messages in thirty-five separate voice mailboxes. Needless to say, that can be discouraging.

When your job campaign brings you this close to the trees, the forest—the larger picture of life and its cycles and your place within them—recedes from view. A series of defeats can clamp your outlook into too tight a focus. You convince yourself that you've spent the first half of your life just warming up, and now the second half is being spent just wearing out. You should know that you are experiencing, unconsciously perhaps, something that runs deeper than the rejection of an unanswered phone call or a frustration in your attempt to get an interview. You are experiencing downside discouragement. You are probably experiencing it without examining the slope of the downside, its dimensions, its natural contours, and the appropriateness of your position there.

Don't Let the Arithmetic Get You Down

Chronologically, as you go through life, your position on the up-, top-, or downside can be arithmetically established by multiplying your age by two, then asking yourself how many people you know who are alive and active in careers at an age double your own. People over forty cannot come up with many names or impressive numbers. So do the multiplication and then admit it: You are on the downside. You are closer to the end than to the beginning.

Note, however, that the chronology of your working life did not begin to run until two decades or more after your birthdate. Multiply your working years to date by two, and look at that number. You will surely know many productive persons who had satisfying years of activity in the space that fits between the total number of your years at work and the target number you associate with your own expected retirement. Sure, you are on the downside, but there is a block of productive work time in front of you waiting to be filled, by you.

Some discover with regret that the old saying is really true: "In middle age, we become the person we always were." Others see this truth as pointing to a storehouse to be drawn from, a natural deposit to be mined, an endowment to be tapped. How well do you know the person you always were? Your search (in solitude, support group, or interspousal communication) for that person can open up avenues to reemployment and dampen down feelings of discouragement. Even if you think novelist Eugene Fitz Maurice had you in mind when he described a character in *The Hawkeland Cache* as "a man with little of life left before him, and nothing of value to be left behind," and that you are the Londoner he knew who "was a man of no depth and a negative position in intellectual reserves," your conversations with supportive counselors and friends will uncover genuine personal assets upon which you can base your job search and build your future. Just go ahead and do it!

In 1983, Dorothy Brier, then assistant director of the social work department at Manhattan's Lenox Hill Hospital, conducted a seminar there on "The Middle Years of Life." Her advice to participants:

> *Middle age has to be self-defined. It is a combination of your age, your psychological state, and how you feel about things. But if the issues you face are midlife issues (related to teenage children, aging parents, career uncertainties, health problems, and conflicts between spouses), then you have midlife problems—no matter what your age.*

No matter what your age (about which you can do nothing), there is a lot you can do about your psychological state and how you feel about things. One thing you can certainly do is keep hope alive in your mind and heart. As William Faulkner saw the choice, "Between grief and nothing, I'll take grief." But you've got to work at it; you've got to choose positively. This doesn't mean that you will feel great all the time. Nor does it mean that as you look back, there will be no regrets. But you should realize, as the famous trial lawyer and professional sports entrepreneur Edward Bennett Williams learned in his midlife years and always reminded others, "The two great culprits in the theft of your personal time are regret and indecision." They are also barriers on the road you need to traverse if you are going to get on with your life.

Mention of Washington lawyer Ed Williams, who was influential politically and also owned the Washington Redskins and the Baltimore Orioles, opens up a line of reflection for me that brings both athletes and politicians into view as I examine the way we humans manage discouragement.

Washington Post columnist Chuck Conconi wrote (Oct. 17, 1983):

> *Washington is a town filled with ghosts. Mostly, they are the ghosts of offices past. You can see them everywhere around town: at receptions and parties, at restaurants such as the Monocle, Duke's, and Mel's, and especially on Capitol Hill. They are the senators, representatives, and cabinet members*

who have the word former in front of their titles. They are the
senator who never goes back home; they are the defeated can-
didate looking for one more campaign.

One senator who did go home—to Texas to write a book—was
John Tower. He had resigned his seat and later lost, by three votes
in the Senate, a bitter confirmation battle to become President
George Bush's Secretary of Defense, which would have been the
fulfillment of his grandest ambition. Not surprisingly, when the
book appeared, the *Washington Post* sent a staff writer to Dallas to
interview Tower. Marjorie Williams spoke with him in his apart-
ment in "the kind of building to which wealthy widows and wid-
owers remove themselves as their lives contract." Her published
article (March 4, 1991) notes that the

> *triumphant experience of being nominated [to be Secretary*
> *of Defense] proved merely to be the apex of his life's parabo-*
> *la. From somewhere on the descending slope he has issued*
> *"Consequences," a memoir looking back bitterly on his career*
> *and its sudden, thorough end.*

Later in the long article, Marjorie Williams writes of Tower's

> *strenuous poise, formed of details: well-tailored British suits*
> *and formal cuff links and good posture and deliberate ges-*
> *tures.... But all the care he takes seems a form of armor, a*
> *grooming of the shell.... Inside the clothes, the man seems*
> *depleted.*

After his 1984 presidential defeat, Walter Mondale asked his
party's unsuccessful 1972 standard-bearer, George McGovern,
"When does it stop hurting?" to which McGovern replied, "I'll let
you know, Fritz."

Former Senator Tom Eagleton is remembered for his involuntary departure from the vice-presidential slot on McGovern's 1972
ticket in consequence of publicly acknowledging, "on three occa-
sions in my life I have voluntarily gone into hospitals as a result of
nervous exhaustion and fatigue." Once the press and the public
learned that he had bouts of "depression" and submitted to "elec-

FINDING WORK *without* LOSING HEART

tro-shock treatment," he was off the ticket. Twelve years later, in announcing his intention to retire from the Senate and return home in 1986, and not remain in Washington, Eagleton said in an interview with the *Washington Post* (June 20, 1984), "Having made the decision I wanted to get out of politics, I decided I didn't want to hang around the fringes. Occasionally I see a former senator in the corridors or maybe the steam room and, well, it's a little sad."

Two glum but insightful Washington maxims are "What goes around comes around" and "Inside every winner is a future loser."

Eugene McCarthy, the former Democratic Senator from Minnesota, often quips, "Being a successful politician is like being a successful football coach; you have to be smart enough to understand the game and dumb enough to think it's important." Of course he's not serious. It hurts to be "out," so why not joke about it?

Less well known are the political writers. They easily accept inflated estimates of their importance as their bylines meet hundreds of thousands of inquiring eyes searching for news and opinion. One of them recently wrote, "Our bylines reveal nothing. Our anonymity is complete, as a bylined friend discovered after retirement a few years ago. 'I have found,' he said, 'that I am not a has-been; I am a never was.'"

Sentiments like these abound in the athletic domain, where glory fades and people wear out early. An insightful high school teacher, Sylvester Conyers, himself a fine athlete and later a coach, sees it this way:

> *Very good athletes lead a different sort of life than most other people. At a very young age you're well known, you get a lot of publicity. It's almost like being in the womb, in that everything is given to you. But once the career ends, a lot of athletes have trouble adjusting to real life. They find out that nobody pampers them.*

The adjustment is easy if the athlete "never really had things out of proportion," says Conyers. "The adjustment is only tough when athletics is the biggest thing in your life, when you lived every day to be the star, to play the game, rather than taking care of your education." This is fine advice for the student athlete, but, omitting the reference to education, it also describes perfectly the typical life of the pampered professional athlete and points to the difficult days ahead after retirement.

Joe Gibbs ended his playing days only to begin a successful coaching career that took him to the top of the National Football League as head coach of the Washington Redskins for twelve years. He led the Redskins to three Super Bowl titles and an impressive string of wins. When no one else except his wife wanted him to quit, at age fifty-two, Joe Gibbs abruptly resigned for an array of reasons that related to family, keeping things in perspective, values, and a balanced life.

His decision prompted *Washington Post* sports columnist Tom Boswell to write (March 6, 1993), "Millions of people face the problem, not just Joe Gibbs. It is so basic that William Butler Yeats just called his poem 'The Choice.'" And Boswell lifted the line that fits the Gibbs situation as it applies to the rest of us:

> *The intellect of man is forced to choose*
> *Perfection of the life or of the work.*

As the sportswriter pointed out, "The best poet of the 20th century knew that the idea of 'having it all' was nonsense before anybody ever dreamed up such a fatuous phrase." Yeats saw the choice as an insoluble problem. "In luck or out the toil has left its mark," wrote Yeats. Those who put family and friendships first were left with "that old perplexity of an empty purse." Planning for a move like the one Joe Gibbs made will entail some provision for the purse. That was certainly no problem for him. Although it will not necessarily empty a person's bank account, a decision in favor of a balanced life will, in all probability, mean less income but more life.

The choice is always difficult. Sometimes it is compounded by accompanying guilt. You chose to move on, but now you feel adrift, out of control, and guilty. If someone else chose to move you on (or out, or down), it must have been because of something you did, or didn't do, right? Maybe right, maybe wrong. In either case you feel guilty, and in virtually all cases the guilt is without foundation.

Many discouraged job seekers have their backpacks loaded with guilt. Guilt, conscious or unconscious, can deepen the discouragement and push it toward despair. Listen to the wise distinction made by a client to a counselor (not the other way around); the counselor is a friend of mine who recalled for me his client's words: "'I made a mistake' is the admission of normal guilt; 'I am a mistake' is the expression of neurotic guilt, even despair." It was a personal struggle that produced this insight for a person who had been on a downward spiral that just about convinced him that he, not his action, was the mistake. Although unable to identify it, the president of a printing company said, "I struggled greatly with the 'failure' that must have been the reason for my termination." The struggle, he told me, was to maintain "self confidence and pride."

Even if you did make some mistakes that triggered your separation, that doesn't say that *you* are a mistake. You are the answer to someone's problem, and you will earn money and find fulfillment in solving that problem. You have to believe not only in yourself, but in the emerging fact that you will find another job eventually, and a very good one at that. You simply cannot permit yourself to fit the description of despair sketched out for me by the wife of an ousted trade association president. She was in the unusual position of doing personnel work for a federal agency and "feeling guilty" that she was interviewing candidates for employment but was unable to do anything for her husband. The problem was compounded because she felt she couldn't talk about her work to her unemployed spouse "because of the anger and pain it would cause him." She told me:

> It was especially painful for me to recruit at two job fairs where I was interviewing candidates for a variety of positions all day. Many of them were unemployed, and I saw (and identified with) their various stages of unemployment: denial ("I'll find something at the same salary or greater very soon"), panic ("I've been out of work for three months"), and despair (virtually catatonic with a look that said, "I don't know why I even tried to apply for the job; it is the same old story—no

*one wants someone as worthless as I"). I was quite depressed
after each of these events.*

But she was careful not to communicate that depression to her
husband; he was feeling bad enough.

Here is an excerpt from a letter Donald Nunes sent to his
daughter on the occasion of her graduation from college; it was
later published in full as an article in the *Washington Post* (April
27, 1993). He provided her with fatherly advice to carry away
from home and into her first job. One of his nine points deals
with failure.

*Of this I am absolutely positive: Over the course of your long
life you are going to fail. Many times. Miserably. Horribly.
There is no avoiding failure. If you don't fail, it's absolute,
pure, blind luck. And that's very dangerous. Because, while
failure enables you to grow, success just makes you cocky.
Arrogant. You learn nothing from success.*

*Obviously, failure teaches you what not to do again. But
that's not the most important thing about failing. When you
fail and you calm yourself down and make yourself examine
the reasons for your failure and then fix the problem or write
it off as a cross you'll have to bear, you grow personally. You
gain a sense of trust in your ability to handle the most difficult situations. You learn that you survive failure. From
those experiences comes self confidence. You only get that
when you fail and pick yourself up from calamities and have
at it again.*

*People sense it when others have that kind of deep, solid self-
confidence. It's the one thing that sets people apart. It makes
them leaders. Forget how much you know. If you have experienced failure and grown from it, it shows. That inner
strength is what I look for when I'm hiring senior managers.
Do they refuse to fold under pressure? There's always pressure. Are they not afraid to fail? They're going to fail a lot and
have to keep going. Do they know what they can do and what*

they can't? If they do, they'll make more right than wrong decisions.

Never, ever, be afraid of failure. Nobody wants it, of course. But, in the end, it can be your friend. It helps you develop a sense of what you can do and what you can't do. Success never teaches you that. (Emphasis in the original.)

If you take this perspective on failure, even if you do not view your separation as a personal failure, you will have the right disposition for managing the normal discouragement associated with job loss. You just have to pick yourself up, wounded perhaps, but wiser for the experience, and "have at it again."

The Choice Is Yours

How, then, do you deal with discouragement in that in-between time, during those days and weeks of waiting and uncertainty, during that ambiguous span of time with no end point in view? A female corporate attorney told me, "You have a choice—negativity or a positive attitude. Since a negative attitude adds neither value nor quality to your life, choose to be positive!" How does a fifty-nine-year-old former vice president of manufacturing, who has been out of work for two years, deal with discouragement? "I spend full-time at my job search. I get up at 6:00 every morning and start at 7:00, and work until 5:00 or 6:00 in the evening." This is consistent with the prescription offered by William Morin, the outplacement specialist, when I asked him about his advice to clients on dealing with discouragement: "You have to bring yourself to the realization—and this may be for the first time in your life—that you are in business now for yourself." And the business, of course, is finding a job.

You deal with discouragement by not giving up. You simply decide not to live your life "back there"; dredging up the past can be a real depressant. You decide to take life one day at a time. You ask yourself: What is most important in my life right now? And you know, as you look at your potential, your family responsibilities, and the economic realities of your existence, that the most important thing for you right now is getting a job. And so you act. You "keep going back," said the man who explained to me this strategy for dealing with discouragement. His expertise was corporate tax management. He had his priorities lined up correctly—God and family well ahead of work and income. But he knew that this particular crisis point in his career pushed work and income to the forefront of his personal agenda.

He knew his past achievements. He knew there were corporations that could benefit from his capabilities; he had researched them in *Value Line* and *Hoover's 500*. "Then, I'd call them up. That was hard. I'd look for reasons to avoid it." Why? I asked. "Who wants to be rejected?" And he went on to describe his relief when he called and heard the words, "He's not here right now." He would be advised to call back. "But I'd put it off." And, he said, "there is a real temptation to say, 'I always wanted to be a consultant; now is the time.'"

He overcame that temptation with his simple device for dealing with discouragement; he kept "going back." Not looking back with regret, but going or coming back with persistence to the points of contact, one of which would eventually lead to employment. He lost job one on October 15; he began working at job two on the following April 29. Discouragement could have turned the in-between time into a swamp capable of swallowing him up; persistence turned a painful experience into a successful job search.

Repeatedly, I heard unemployed executives say what a fifty-three-year-old ex-manager of research and development told me when I asked him to offer advice to other managers who were looking for work: "Be optimistic. Do what you have to do. Plan for the future. Focus. Keep busy." This is a formula for dealing with discouragement. A variation on that theme was struck by a technical manager in the chemical industry who decided to look upon his separation as a "graduation," an opportunity and a welcome change, not a problem to be solved.

Keeping busy will mean different things to different people. Whatever it means, it functions as an antidote to discouragement. "In addition to job hunting," a female manager told me,

I did lots of projects around the house, played golf, kept up on my walking regimen, took up a new hobby of painting floorcloths, did needlepoint, got lots of sleep, started writing articles for professional publications, investigated how to get a children's story I wrote published, read a lot, did all the sewing for a revamped room (curtains, cushions, pillows, etc.), and spent more time talking to friends.

She characterized the transition as "stressful," but she came through it, by her report, as a stronger person in a stronger marriage. Much more sparing in detail, a male manager explained how he "kept busy" during a nine-month transition by "catching up on projects around the house. I did things I had wanted to do for years. It felt good!" Others, however, warn that this sort of catch-up work can distract you from the central task of looking for your next job.

A marketing executive in Atlanta found that "the transition was the greatest time of my life. It was extremely difficult, but it was like a rebirth." How did he deal with the difficulty? He devoted all his time to building his network. "Most people simply want the pain to stop, but they do not seek an effective remedy—the right job. I spent my time using every conceivable technique to build my network of business associates. It is surprising that we don't build networks of business friends until we need them."

There will be times when the weight of discouragement will not fall easily from your shoulders (or, more accurately, from your psyche). You may want to see a therapist for a reassuring checkup. A male vice president for marketing and communications found himself on the street at age forty-three and had serious doubts about himself and his future. He noticed that he wasn't looking for help, so he decided that he might need some. "I visited a therapist once during the six-month transition period, to make sure I wasn't repressing anything." He was told he wasn't. "With that pressure relieved, I was less uptight and anxious. I found it easier to be with others, and others found it easier to be with me." When I asked him what advice he would have for others in similar circumstances, he said, "There is no way to recommend that people prepare for termination by saving money; having a relationship with God; going through therapy, as needed; having a loving and supportive spouse; or learning what it's like being terminated, but that's what it takes!"

An outplacement professional said to me, "When someone sits in here and cries, I say, 'That's good; go ahead and cry. But when you sit down across from a prospective employer, cut that out. Nobody buys weakness. If we can't steel you or get you to steel yourself, then go to a therapist and get some help.'" But the need for that kind of help to overcome discouragement is, in his experience, rare. Get it if you need it, but only if you need it. You are much more likely to be like the character in the cable-television comedy series *Sessions*, who is losing both hair and sleep, and laments: "I'm older and slower, and every day something new gives me gas." Get some exercise, watch your diet, go to bed at a reasonable time, and get cranking on your job search every day. Be like the painter Philip Guston, who told novelist Gail Godwin that he deals with artistic dry spells by going "to my studio every day, because one day I may go and the angel will be there. What if I don't go and the angel came?" What if you cave in to discouragement just when the object of your job search was coming into view?

The National Mental Health Association buys newspaper space on occasion to print the following checklist along with a phone number (1-800-228-1114) and a simple suggestion: "If this sounds like you, don't ignore it. Because your doctor can help." Here is the list:

- Feelings of sadness or irritability
- Loss of interest or pleasure in activities once enjoyed
- Changes in weight or appetite
- Changes in sleeping pattern
- Feeling guilty, hopeless, or worthless
- Inability to concentrate, remember things, or make decisions
- Fatigue or loss of energy
- Restlessness or decreased activity

- Complaints of physical aches and pains for which no medical explanation can be found
- Thoughts of death or suicide

"Sounds just like me on one of my better days," quipped a normal, healthy job seeker whose sense of humor under stress suggested that he could afford to forget the 800 number. Someone who should have called, and didn't, was a banking executive under extreme pressure in 1990, who was described by a friend as "so depressed, he just couldn't do anything." He simply "sat in his office alone at night, smoking cigarette after cigarette in the dark."

Patrick Nuttgens, writing in *The Tablet* of London (Jan. 25, 1992), recalled the "unusually profound" comments a friend of his would make on occasion. "I asked him one night if he had a good definition of happiness. No, he answered, he had not. But he had a good definition of unhappiness. 'Unhappiness,' he said, 'is the refusal to suffer.' He was the happiest friend I ever made."

The comment is, indeed, profound. It will take a bit of pondering to appreciate the connection between suffering and happiness, or, coming at the issue from the other side, the link between unhappiness and rejection of suffering. Viewers of the play, and later the film, *Teahouse of the August Moon*, received a hint of the resolution of this riddle in the suggestion that pain makes one think, thought makes one wise, and wisdom "makes life endurable." Many of the men and women I met in the course of this study simply remarked, "This, too, will pass."

Involuntary separation from any job, but particularly from managerial responsibilities, forces you to accept the fact that, as one outplacement specialist explained it to me, "You only rent a job; you don't own it unless you own the company. So don't ever let yourself be caught with your résumé down." Your separation puts you, he said, "in the same rowboat with many others in this monsoon called executive severance." He likened the experience to labor pains. And those kind of pains may well be the beginning of a working-world wisdom that can bring you an undefined, even undefinable, but no less genuine happiness.

So there you have a menu of metaphors to apply to your down-side situation. You've been "evicted" from that job you've been renting; you can find a better one. Or, if you don't like the risk of renting, think about buying—i.e., owning your own firm. Monsoons and labor pains pass; so will your unemployment—if you remain alert, flexible, and active.

If you were to ask the staff of the Career Initiatives Center in Cleveland how to cope after job loss, they would pass along to you these ten steps originally outlined by Cary Arden:

1. Find selective places to talk honestly about your feelings.
2. Knowledge is power, so gain knowledge of the job-search process.
3. Learn about what you can control—yourself.
4. Live each day fully. Have an attitude of gratitude.
5. Do something for someone else. Volunteer time to worthy causes or organizations.
6. Build your own support system. Ask for help.
7. Exercise and practice good nutritional habits. Keep a high energy level.
8. Do something creative.
9. Maintain hope. Set realistic goals.
10. Look for the larger meaning in life's lessons.

Not infrequently, the principle embodied in the fifth point on this list was articulated for me by persons who successfully overcame discouragement. "I found that an interest in helping and healing others worked to my own benefit. By helping others, I found a way to diffuse both anger and hurt. Helping others healed my own wounds. It boosted my morale and reinforced my ego; it also opened up sources for job leads and advice that were useful to me." Another person I interviewed for this study—a female corporate manager who eventually began her own business, thus giving herself "a sense of purpose"—provided pro bono services to organizations and did some volunteer work "to offset the isolation between assignments."

Point seven found expression during a forty-nine-year-old banker's transition in the form of competitive long-distance running. "It kept me in shape and released tension, and by winning my age-group races, I managed to keep my pride intact!"

One man in my sample, an experienced project manager, offers this helpful insight. Job loss leaves you with "feelings of confusion, anxiety, and depression." To offset these, you have to take immediate steps "to locate and make use of a resource that will help you begin to *plan* your personal approach to reemployment. There *must* be a sense of order and progress in your life to balance out the feelings of confusion, anxiety, and depression."

You can also cope with the feeling of discouragement by lengthening your timetable, giving yourself more slack, lightening up on the self-imposed tyranny of expectations you yourself have raised and those deadlines you yourself have set. Beware of the tyranny of the promises you make to yourself. This is not a polite way of saying "abandon hope." It is a practical reminder that you are in a human predicament and you can deal with it only in human—i.e., nonmechanical—ways. The human way is inevitably an imprecise way of more or less; of experimentation; success; failure; second, third, and fourth tries; and both pleasant and unpleasant surprises. Avoiding unrealistic expectations is both prevention and cure for normal discouragement. Be content with being human. And add your personal amen to William Faulkner's line in his Nobel Prize acceptance speech: "I believe that man ["woman" would, of course, be specifically included today] will not merely endure: he will prevail."

Chapter 4

THE LITERARY MIRROR

We read fiction, expose ourselves to its magic,
among other reasons, to learn what we may not
have noticed about ourselves and others.

—*William Carlos Williams*

John Tracy Ellis, the noted historian, was a man I much admired. The harshest criticism I ever heard him level against anyone was simply this: "He has stopped reading; he doesn't read anymore."

Job seekers cannot afford to stop reading. Nor can they content themselves with reading only the want ads, or the business press, or the journals that keep them up to date in their respective fields. They are human beings, and one of the delights of being human is the ability to enjoy good literature. Even if the literary merit is less than great, good biography, poetry, history, scholarly writings, and quality fiction can feed the spirit and stimulate the mind. Job seekers cannot afford to isolate themselves from good books, but they can be wasting valuable time if they use their light or heavy reading just to escape. "I read fiction to escape," a Cleveland executive told me. Her business card, like those of numerous unemployed managers, said "consultant," but she was still looking for permanent employment, and the escape into fiction was deflecting time and attention from the job hunt.

When I asked a displaced financial executive, president of a major New York bank, what reading he was doing while in transition, he replied simply, "None." He literally did not know what he was missing. An identical reply came from another banker, who offered the added explanation for not reading, "All I do now is worry and work (at getting my next job)."

Another interviewee, a displaced health-care executive who was perhaps the most angry person I encountered in the course of this study, told me he read *Ironweed* and *Coming Home* because "they are fairly depressing and they enabled me to see people in worse straits than mine."

From reading, from the reading habit, you can learn to read your life. Let Robert Scholes explain what I mean. Here is an excerpt from his *Protocols of Reading* (Yale, 1989):

> *Learning to read books—or pictures, or films—is not just a matter of acquiring information from texts, it is a matter of learning to read and write the text of our lives. Reading, seen this way, is not merely an academic experience but a way of accepting the fact that our lives are of limited duration and whatever satisfaction we may achieve in life must come through the strength of our engagement with what is around us.*

Explaining his approach to the actor's art, Charles Laughton once remarked, "People don't know what they're like, but I think I can show them."

Playwright Edward Albee put the matter this way in an interview with the *Washington Post* (June 23, 1991):

> *People don't participate in their own lives enough.... They drift. They end up at a certain point in their lives, filled with failure and regret, of things done and things not done. But to be a survivor, to be able to survive everything that life gives you with a certain humanity, is important. And all plays, all serious plays, show more how we should not behave than how we should behave. So you hold up a mirror to people and say, "Look, you're behaving like this. You don't have to. Try to change." So all art is corrective, therefore all art is useful.*

Another playwright, Arthur Miller, held his own mirror, so to speak, up to himself in a May 9, 1984 interview in the *New York Times*. Then sixty-eight, he said he could now see himself in the famous character of his own creation, Willy Loman. But when *Death of a Salesman* opened on Broadway in 1949, Miller tended to identify more with Willy's son Biff.

"When Biff's yelling at Willy now," he says, "he's yelling at me. I understand Willy. And I understand his longing for immortality—I think that's inevitable when you get older. It's not in terms of work. It's more a mystical sense. Willy's writing his name on a cake of ice on a hot day, but he wishes he were writing in stone. He wants to live on through something—and in his case, his masterpiece is his son. I think all of us want that, and it gets more poignant as we get more anonymous in this world."

Reflecting on the uneven course of his own career, Mr. Miller spoke of the need for a national theater in America; the experience of being "thrown back into the marketplace" whenever he brought a new play to production has been humiliating and unnecessary. Mid-career business managers who find themselves "on the street" know the feeling.

Miller's seventeenth play, *The Last Yankee*, opened simultaneously in London and New York in 1993, when the playwright was seventy-seven years old and still focused on the failure theme. "You want me to say I'm a failure," Miller's character Leroy Hamilton, a small-town carpenter and descendant of Alexander Hamilton, says to his wife: "I'll get a bumper sticker printed up: 'The Driver of This Car Is a Failure!'" In a radio interview when the play opened, Miller acknowledged a parallel with *Death of a Salesman*, but without the confrontation. "Here's a man who is a failure by the world's count," Miller said, "but he's got a grip on life."

Read Your Way Toward Clarity

The point of this chapter is not necessarily to exhort, and certainly not to direct the reader to become a patron of libraries and bookstores, although time there will certainly be well spent. I want to "hold up the mirror." George Bernard Shaw once said, "You use a glass mirror to see your face; you use the arts to see your soul." My purpose here is interpretative. I'm convinced that persons burdened with the stress of job loss can have their burdens lightened, if not lifted, by seeing themselves in the literary portrayals of persons and situation not unlike their own—descriptions and metaphors—crafted by fine writers and poets whose insights into the human condition are available to anyone willing to read. The return on the time invested in this kind of reading is personal progress in getting a grip on life.

A helpful figure of speech fashioned by Franz Kafka will help to make my point: "A book should serve as the ax for the frozen sea within us."

You may not think of poetry as the place to get help in tightening up your grip on life or cracking the immobilizing ice of discouragement, but poetry, as well as fiction and drama, can help. In his long poem, "Asphodel, that Greeny Flower," William Carlos Williams suggests that there is something in poetry that you might be missing:

> *It is difficult*
> *to get the news from poems*
> *yet men die miserably every day*
> *for lack*
> *of what is found there.*

To be thorough about it, you might want to go back to Homer, the poet of "the mind's dear clarity." Thomas D'Evelyn calls Homer "the poet of responsibility" and explains, in a review-article in the *Christian Science Monitor* (Sept. 9, 1987), that the "moral theme" of the Iliad is the question of why Achilles wouldn't fight. Unemployed managers who are ready to give up the fight and are tempted not even to get out of bed in the morning can profit from the poet's words, as rendered in Christopher Logue's translation. Achilles wakes:

> *Those who have slept with sorrow in their hearts*
> *Know all too well how short but sweet*
> *The instant of their coming-to can be:*
> *The heart is strong, as if it never sorrowed;*
> *The mind's dear clarity intact; and then,*
> *The vast, unhappy stone from yesterday*
> *Rolls down these vital units to the bottom of oneself.*

One of the participants in my study told me that he found himself falling back on literary snippets he retained in memory from humanities courses three decades earlier at Marquette University. During his search for work, said this financial services executive, "I kept coming back to a line from Chesterton's 'The Ballad of the White Horse.'" He remembered it as, "They harden their hearts with hope." Here is the line as Chesterton wrote it: "And Alfred, hiding in deep grass,/ Hardened his heart with hope." This executive explained that he understood those words to mean, "Don't tell me it's not going to work. I can do it." He had to fall back on that "hope" theme twice in situations of job loss, he told me, and he uses it often to encourage others in the executive search business he now owns. Another line, as he recalls it, refers to "the giant laughter of Christian men." "Here were men," he recalled, "ostensibly on the verge of being exterminated, and they were laughing! You can't afford to lose your sense of humor."

Novelist Jonathan Carroll says, "Any writer is organizing his chaos. My life has been sort of fevered in certain ways.... Most people have these [same] experiences, but they're busy trying to cope, whereas often the artist is taking notes." Because the writer not only had experiences like your own, but also "took notes," you can see yourself in the literary mirror he or she holds up to you on the printed page. In seeing yourself thus, from a fresh angle or in a new light, you can find clarity and illumination, understanding and insight; these can assist you in making your personal transition.

Hence, this is not a bibliographic chapter offering you information on "how to do it" or "where to find it" books. You will find here an assortment of literary specimens, or a writer's personal observations, capable of helping you get a clearer picture of yourself and your portion of the human condition.

The novelist's challenge, said Walker Percy in concluding a 1986 essay, "Novel-Writing in an Apocalyptic Time," "is somehow to humanize the life around him, to formulate it for someone else, to render the interstates, to tell the truth, to show how life is lived, and therefore to affirm life." The good novelist, despite his or her own misgivings, is both acute and reflective; otherwise he or she would be neither in print nor worth reading.

"Everybody knows more than the novelist," says Percy, "but what the novelist may be good for, despite his shakiness and fecklessness, or perhaps because of it, is to record what other people, absorbed as they are in their busy and useful lives, may not see.... [I]t is the novelist's business to look and see what is there for everyone to see but is nonetheless not seen." And Walker Percy wisely observes, "There is something worse than being deprived of life: it is being deprived of life and not knowing it. The poet and the novelist cannot bestow life but they can point to instances of its loss, and then name and record them" (*Signposts in a Strange Land*, 1991). The naming and recording can be a service rendered to the job seeker, if the person looking for work is willing to read along the way.

Confronted by good poetry or prose, the reader can come to know the experience described in "Draft of Shadows" by Nobel prize–winning poet Octavio Paz: "I hear the voices that I think,/ the voices that think me as I think them." You can hear yourself in the dialogue of the good novel; you can often see yourself in the situations the gifted writer constructs. And you can lift phrases from another's pen to express the situation in which you find yourself. Substituting "corporation" for "army," some will find Christopher Tietjen, a character in Ford Maddox Ford's *Parade's End*, speaking for them as he says, "The curse of the army, as far as the organization is concerned, was our imbecile national belief that the game is more than the player."

Dante's opening words in *The Inferno* suggest to me the utility of a compass, which this book hopes to be, for the mid-career executive suddenly faced with the challenge of a job search. Reading these few lines may help to convince the reader that the compass is more important than the roadmap at the beginning of the journey to reemployment.

> *Midway life's journey*
> *I was made aware*
> *That I had strayed into a dark forest,*
> *And the right path appeared not anywhere.*

Some see this as the first description of midlife crisis in Western literature. Anyone can imagine the "dark forest" as the unwelcome enclosure known to those unable to locate the "right path." The words were written in 1300 by a thirty-five-year-old who was frustrated over his inability to connect politically. As Robinson Jeffers once remarked, "In our world where all things are beautiful, it is the poet's business to choose what is abiding."

Writing in the *Washingtonian* magazine (September 1988), M. B. Howard asks: What is an adult? When do you become one? "Maybe to become an adult is to become familiar with dread—with that gnawing, uneasy fear that everything that seems to define you as an adult is in truth a house of cards, waiting for one hard wind to blow it down." Howard reinforces this point with lines from Coleridge's "The Rime of the Ancient Mariner":

> *Like one that on a lonesome road*
> *Doth walk in fear and dread,*
> *And having once turned round walks on,*
> *And turns no more his head.*

And then the author comments: "Maybe to become an adult is to learn not to turn around."

Comfort and encouragement, as well as clarity, are available to readers of *Motherwit: An Alabama Midwife's Story* (Dutton, 1989), an account by Onnie Lee Logan of her life in the South and her forty years practicing midwifery in Mobile and rural Alabama.

> *I let God work the plan of my life and I am satisfied at what has happened to me in my life. The sun wasn't shinin' every time and the moon wasn't either. I was in the snow and the rain at night by my lonely self.... It was rough, but you know what? I taken it with a smile and I enjoyed it.... I had my mind on where I was goin' and what I was goin' for....*

> *This book was the last thing I had to do until God said well done. I consider myself—in fact, if I leave tomorrow—I've lived my life and I've lived it well.*

To keep your mind on where you are going and what you are going for is one of the keys to success for both midwives and mid-career executives.

A Fictional Life

John Updike says that in fiction, "reality is—chemically, atomically, biologically—a fabric of microscopic accuracies." The penetration of his fictional descriptions and insights bears this out. Many executives will read their own unpublished (and unexpressed, even to themselves) thoughts in the musings of "Rabbit," the nickname John Updike's famous character Harry Angstrom carried throughout a life that spanned four novels. The fourth, *Rabbit at Rest*, won the National Book Critics Circle Award with a citation noting that the book "brings to a close a work which will stand as one of the major achievements of American fiction in the 20th century."

Harry "Rabbit" Angstrom appears to have learned most of what he knows about life from high school basketball—so much so that readers who follow him through his fictional life are never sure that there was, for Rabbit, any meaningful life after basketball.

"Give the boys the will to achieve," says Rabbit's high school coach some years later in explaining his approach to the game. "I've always liked that better than the will to win, for there can be achievement even in defeat. Make them feel the, yes, I think the word is good, *sacredness* of achievement, in the form of giving our best." "A boy who has had his heart enlarged by an inspiring coach," he concludes, "can never become in the deepest sense, a failure in the greater game of life." This is restaurant table talk in the first novel, *Rabbit, Run*. Harry, then twenty-six, had run away from wife and job and sought out his old coach for reassurance and advice.

Ten years later, in *Rabbit Redux*, Harry is concerned about what the future holds for his own young son. In a pensive mood, he

> *looks out the window and sees in dusk ... a basketball hoop on a far garage. How can he get the kid interested in sports? If he's too short for basketball, then baseball. Anything, just to put something there, some bliss, to live on later for a while. If he goes empty now he won't last at all, because we get emptier.*

While watching a minor-league baseball game, Rabbit reflects about

the players themselves ... each intent on a private dream of making it, making it into the big leagues and the big money, the own-your-own-bowling alley money; they seem specialists like any other, not men playing a game because all men are boys time is trying to outsmart.

Caught in a troubled marriage and a dead-end job, Rabbit describes himself in a candid conversation with his mother:

Just yesterday I was sitting over at the Blasts [minor-league baseball team] game thinking how lousy I used to be at baseball. Let's face it. As a human being I'm about a C-minus. As a husband I'm about zilch. When Verity [the company that employs him] folds, I'll fold with it and have to go on welfare. Some life. Thanks, Mom.

Autumn is walking time for just about everyone, even in those parts of the country where leaves don't change color and drop to the ground. Most job seekers find themselves walking a lot. One said to me, "You have to do something to relax and compose yourself alone. I spend time birdwatching on long walks through woods and parks." He could easily relate to this picture of Rabbit walking through fallen leaves and a midlife crisis as well:

There is that scent in the air, of going back to school, of beginning again and reconfirming the order that exists. He wants to feel good, he always used to feel good at every turning of the year, every vacation or end of vacation, every new sheet on the calendar: but his adult life had proved to have no seasons, only changes of weather, and the older he gets, the less weather interests him. How can the planet keep turning and turning and not get so bored it explodes?

Rabbit's young son has discovered soccer.

Afternoons, Harry comes home to find the child kicking the ball, sewn of black-and-white pentagons, again and again against the garage door, beneath the unused basketball back-

board. The ball bounces by Nelson, Harry picks it up, it feels bizarrely seamed in his hands. He tries a shot at the basket. It misses clean. "The touch is gone," he says. "It's a funny feeling," he tells his son, "when you get old. The brain sends out the order and the body looks the other way."

One of the executives I interviewed for this study, a displaced CEO of a large bank, told me that his son gave him needed encouragement by simply remarking, "Dad, you've just lost your fast ball, that's all; now you've got to start working on your curve." Sports metaphors crop up repeatedly in explanations business executives offer by way of interpretation of where they've been and where they are likely to wind up in their careers. A telecommunications executive, who had successfully "rebounded," told me that his involuntary departure from his previous position left him with a sense of "loss of camaraderie"; he laughed as he added, "you miss the smell of the locker room." On his office wall was a photograph of himself, thirty years younger, dribbling past a defender and driving in for a layup in a major college basketball game. Another experienced manager in my study, himself an author, advises those looking for new career opportunities: "Don't worry about home runs; until you assess some very basic issues, you'll never get out of the batter's box. Begin with an honest assessment of yourself." And a banker, who had been looking for nearly a year, told me he thought he was "rounding third," but realized he could be "thrown out" before scoring.

Sidelined managers—not those who manage baseball teams, but those who know how to run complex organizations—may want to look for the works of W. P. Kinsella on the public library shelves. "After delivering two fictional fast balls with 'The Iowa Baseball Confederacy' and 'Shoeless Joe' (the basis for the movie 'Field of Dreams'), W. P. Kinsella confounds his fans by throwing a change-up in 'Box Socials,'" remarks *New York Times* book reviewer Herbert Mitgang (March 25, 1992). "His new novel is more about small-town life than big-time baseball. It's a story filled with nostalgia about a time when the game was played on real grass and was called on account of darkness. But even more, it's about the everyday hopes of what it must be like for most people to play out their lives in the minors." Many displaced executives think of themselves that way; they are like Owen Browne, the protagonist of Robert Stone's *Outerbridge Reach*, who struggles with "old rages and regrets" and finds himself "in rebellion against things."

In *Rabbit Is Rich*, Harry Angstrom really begins to show signs that he is losing the contest with middle age.

> But a lot of topics, he has noticed lately, in private conversation and even on television where they're paid to talk it up, run dry, exhaust themselves, as if everything's been said in this hemisphere. In his inner life too Rabbit dodges among more blanks than there used to be, patches of burnt-out gray cells where there used to be lust and keen dreaming and wide-eyed dread; he falls asleep, for instance, at the drop of a hat. He never used to understand the phrase. But then he never used to wear a hat and now, at the first breath of cold weather, he does. His roof wearing thin, starlight showing through.

Naturally, somebody has to be at fault. "It was his wife's fault. The entire squeezed and cut-down shape of his life is her fault; at every turn she has been a wall to his freedom." Deep down, he knows the fault is not really hers; he needs her. "What more can you ask of a wife in a way than that she stick around and see with you what happens next?"

Rabbit recognizes that "his own life closed in to a size his soul had not yet shrunk to fit." His son Nelson, now married, is old enough to understand the situation:

> Dad doesn't like to look bad anymore, that was one thing about him in the old days you could admire, that he didn't care that much how he looked from the outside, what the neighbors thought ... for instance, he had this crazy dim faith left in himself left over from basketball or growing up as everybody's pet or whatever.... That spark is gone.

But Harry has his own view of the matter, as he explains to Nelson later in *Rabbit Is Rich*.

"The past is the past...you've got to live in the present.... It's the only way to think. When you're my age you'll see it. At my age if you carried all the misery you've seen on your back you'd never get up in the morning."

"Look, Nelson. Maybe I haven't done everything right in my life. I know I haven't. But I haven't committed the greatest sin. I haven't laid down and died."

"Who says that's the greatest sin?"

"Everybody says it. The church, the government. It's against Nature, to give up, you've got to keep moving."

Rabbit at Rest, the fourth and last of these tightly focused novels, opens with the self-absorbed protagonist Harry in Florida, where he and his wife Janice now spend half the year. In the airport, watching a

little guy, seventy if he's a day, breaking into a run, hopping zigzag through the padded pedestal chairs so he won't be beaten out at the arrival gate, Harry remorsefully feels the bulk, two hundred thirty pounds the kindest scales say, that has enwrapped him at the age of fifty-five like a set of blankets the decades have brought one by one.

Out on the golf course, Harry misses a putt. "Not his day. Will he ever have a day again? Fifty-five and fading." One of his golfing partners, Harry remarks to himself, is "at the other end of life's rainbow."

One of the more reflective participants in my study, a partner with executive responsibilities in a major accounting firm, found himself involuntarily "retired" at age fifty-three, long before his career plan called for subsidized inactivity. He was, however, unenthusiastic about returning to work, and there was no economic necessity for him to do so. "I was sick and tired of the struggle. I wanted nothing more than to pull up the drawbridge," he said, "move to Florida, buy a 'golf villa,' and do absolutely nothing." So he did. "Well, nothing worked the way I wanted it to. My wife was not ready to retire. She did not like Florida for most of the same reasons that John Updike gives in his last Rabbit book." She, he says, was "determined" to get out of there; he was "intransigent." He "gave in." "I would like to say that I changed my mind, but there is still a little resentment on my part from time to time. Perhaps it will dissipate in time. The joke is that we couldn't even make the six months residency requirement to qualify for Florida tax status." They returned to their home in Washington, D.C., where he is back in a business suit working as chief financial officer for a major museum, she is getting an advanced degree, and both are happily committed to a heavy schedule of voluntary service activities. Florida is not for everybody, even those who can easily afford it.

Up north again, in his home state of Pennsylvania, Rabbit thinks "everything has been paved solid by memory and in any direction you go you've already been there." He takes a drive through the old parts of his home town. "The city is quicker than he remembers it, faster on the shuffle, as the blocks flicker by, and buildings that he felt when a boy were widely spaced now appear adjacent." Sight of the downtown hotel where his high school class had its senior prom reminds him of Mary Ann. When "he went off to do his two years in the army," she "without a word of warning married somebody else. Maybe she sensed something about him. A loser. Though at eighteen he looked like a winner … [and] … felt like a winner, offhand, calm, his life set at an irresistible forward slant."

Eventually, however, he came to discover that "life is a hill that gets steeper the more you climb."

As Rabbit's story and life are running out, the reader who has followed him for well over a thousand pages can relate to this:

> Just thinking about those old days lately depresses him; it makes him face life's constant depreciation. Lying awake at night, afraid he will never fall asleep or will fall asleep forever, he feels a stifling uselessness in things, a kind of atomic decay whereby the precious glowing present turns, with each tick of the clock, into the leaden slag of history.

John Krull's interview with John Updike, "Hunting Rabbit," appeared in *Universitas*, the alumni magazine of Saint Louis University. "Few, if any, other writers," says Krull, who is an editorial writer and columnist for the *Indianapolis News*, "have captured so well the twin demons of middle-American life—the tremendous desire to get more out of life and the suppressed but overwhelming realization that life isn't likely to offer much more." It is helpful, I believe, for dislocated mid-career managers to have someone like Updike hold up a mirror in which they can see something of their own predicament.

"I was trying to write about the human predicament," said John Updike in a *Washington Post* interview (Oct. 28, 1990), "rather than the American predicament, but naturally being American you write in an American accent, as it were. Harry's continuing bind between wanting to do what you want to do and what you ought to do. Between the inner appetitive self and the social self, the self of obligations."

These snippets from four novels of one author illustrate the refractory potential good writing has in the hands of a reader seriously intent on sorting things out, searching for meaning, clarifying choices, seeing him- or herself through the fictional lives of others.

The job seeker who spends an inordinate number of daylight hours slumped before the television screen might have to plead guilty to the charge leveled by a European commentator: "People today watch television as a surrogate for the lives they have ceased to live."

Keep On Running

"When You Stop, You Die" is the headline *Commonweal* attached to psychologist Thomas J. Cottle's June 19, 1992, article on "the human toll of male unemployment." The title is taken from comments made to Cottle by a forty-seven-year-old former manager of a small tool company: "There's only two worlds: either you work every day in a normal nine-to-five job with a couple of weeks vacation, or you're dead! There's no in-between.... Working is breathing. It's something you don't think about; you just do it and it keeps you alive. When you stop you die." There is, of course, a whole lot more to life than work. But the absence of work can smother the spirit, if inertia sets in. The unemployed manager has to keep on moving, working the phones, developing the network, making the contacts. I like the image Flannery O'Connor uses in her short story "The Displaced Person." It is applicable to the job seeker, whose sense of loss differs a lot in degree, but not altogether in kind, from the despondency of a husband who has lost his spouse: "Whenever he thought of Mrs. Shortley, he felt his heart go down like an old bucket into a dry well." The job seeker has to fill that well with ideas, activity, and friends.

I admit to admiration for, but cannot claim any competence to offer an interpretation of, the novels of Walker Percy. I did, however, have underlined in my copy of *The Moviegoer* (1961) the same sentence Phil McCombs later quoted as an epigraph to his long profile, "Walker Percy and the Assault on the Soul," in the *Washington Post*, May 14, 1987: "The search is what anyone would undertake if he were not sunk in the everydayness of his own life." In the novel, Binx Bolling is the moviegoer and narrator of his own story. To the words just quoted, he adds: "To be aware of the possibility of the search is to be onto something. Not to be onto something is to be in despair."

Walker Percy did not write about job seeking, as far as I know, but he did write a lot about life, and discouragement, and social malaise. He often made the point that because the world is insane, his characters, typically at odds with the world, appear to be insane, precisely because they see things as they really are.

In *The Moviegoer*, Binx Bolling speaks of "my vertical search," which was completed

> one night when I sat in a hotel room in Birmingham and read a book called The Chemistry of Life. *When I finished it, it seemed to me that the main goals of my search were reached or were in principle reachable, whereupon I went out and saw a movie called* It Happened One Night *which was itself very good. A memorable night. The only difficulty was that though the universe had been disposed of, I myself was left over ... [so] now I have undertaken a different kind of search, a horizontal search. As a consequence, what takes place in my room is less important. What is important is what I shall find when I leave my room and wander in the*

neighborhood. Before, I wandered as a diversion. Now I wander seriously and sit and read as a diversion.

The search—vertical and horizontal—is an important part of being human and an indispensable part of being a successful job seeker. Writers like Percy can activate the search apparatus within the human spirit. Percy had the power, as Gregory Waldrop put it, "to bring readers to themselves in the dark wood of their own everyday existence, whether on Manhattan's Upper East Side or in 'Feliciana Parish,' La." Good writers can hold up the mirror, as Percy does in *The Second Coming* (1980):

> *How did it happen that now for the first time in his life he could see everything so clearly? Something had given him leave to live in the present. Not once in his entire life had he allowed himself to come to rest in the quiet center of himself but had forever cast himself forward from some dark past he could not remember to a future which did not exist. Not once had he been present for his life. So his life had passed like a dream.*
>
> *Is it possible for people to miss their lives in the same way one misses a plane?*

When he died in 1990, a few days short of his seventy-fifth birthday, Walker Percy was praised by the *New York Times* for having written brilliantly "about modern man's search for faith and love in a chaotic world." The obituary quoted Percy's own words to articulate the theme of his six novels: "the dislocation of man in the modern age."

Sometimes a single line of poetry is all it takes to set off a personal line of serious reflection. In his poem "Zeroes," Philip Booth muses that we may have "wired our lives to suicide bombs." That could prompt defense analysts to think about the applications of high technology to the protection of national interest; it could also nudge a job seeker to think about the life-giving or death-dealing potential of the personal priorities he or she is adopting and "wiring in" to career goals.

The discouraged job seeker might be nudged toward action by a line in John Ciardi's poem "In Place of a Curse," where the poet speaks of "the meek, who gambled nothing, gave nothing, and could never receive enough."

Remarkably, a student poet, Joelle Lamboley of Georgetown University, caught in a poem called "Love Song" much of what I tried to say in Chapter 2 about a job seeker's need for spousal support. Her poem, expressed in the woman's voice, focuses on the general relationship between man and woman, not on the special support a wife can give her unemployed husband. I present it here to illustrate how a sensitive young woman has full possession of an insight—"I cannot help it; I am a woman/ Who is constantly healing, understanding,/ searching, and letting go./ I know men like you"—that any woman who wants to shore up the spirits of a man in search of work needs.

> I know men like you.
> The injured bird who never
> Regains his ability to fly.
> Shrouded in uncertainty.
> The pain is a seduction technique:
> A means of provoking the nurse
> Or mother in every woman.
> Women do not shy away from instability.
> We try to milk it, to cure it,
> And once you are healed, another
> Bird comes in the window
> With broken wings, unable to
> Fly against the currents
> Of the lonely winter wind.
> And you fly away, feigning
> Injury, revitalizing the
> Claims that your father had
> Broken the ego inside your
> Red breast.
> I know men like you.
> The lonely hunter in the woods,
> Perhaps exiled from the court:
> Shooting arrows at birds and

Sleeping hungry because your
Aim is off.
No one understands you.
Your secrets dancing in your
Eyes like a dirty limerick.
I know men like you.
The world has done you
Wrong, the gods are not in
Your favor and libations are
Irrelevant.
You were born under the wrong
Sign, like Orpheus, and you
Sing your song to the delight
Of us all.
And I listen, intently, for
Clues to the key that unlocks
Your secrets.
I cannot help it; I am a woman
Who is constantly healing, understanding,
Searching, and letting go.
I know men like you.
Maybe I should move.

The thought that "maybe [she will] move," whether expressed or not, weighs upon the already burdened job seeker. The suggestion of a threat at the end of the poetic reassurance that she is there to listen, heal, and cure echoes the cynical saying that "next to the wound, woman makes the bandage best." Spouses should be talking to one another about wounds and bandages in the context of lost employment; poetry can open up the conversation. Reading aloud to one another is a pleasant way to pass the evening hours, or to shorten the time of long-distance drives.

Just Let the Phrase Sink In

Often, a phrase will come off the page that doesn't have to be shared with anyone, just pondered for purposes of a reality check on how you are dealing with life in your own particular job-seeking circumstances. Novelist John Gregory Dunne once described himself as "one of life's neutrals, a human Switzerland." Phrases like that can serve as wake-up calls for self-pitying job seekers.

And passages like the following from Edwin O'Connor's *Edge of Sadness* (Little Brown, 1961) are remarkably helpful in providing perspective on the tendency to let the realization of aging pull one's spirits down into a swamp of discouragement. The narrator has just caught sight of a longtime friend.

> *I realized that she was a* grandmother *and … this brought home to me the blunt truth that she and John and all of us who had been young together were young no longer, and that we moved steadily, day by day, to the once distant world of the old.…*
>
> *Which, as I say, is a foolish way to feel; obviously, no one ever grows closer to the cradle. But getting old is a strange business. It's happening to you every minute of the day, and you almost never give it a thought; then, one day, you catch a glimpse of an old friend, or you hear a phrase from an old song, or your eye falls on a solitary sentence in the daily paper, and suddenly, without being able to do a thing in the world about it, you seem to be for a moment outside your own skin, taking one good long look at yourself, exactly as you stand, exactly as you are. And at this point, no matter who you are, or what you believe, or who you may be, it sometimes becomes a little hard to give three cheers for the inevitable.*

Referring to another writer, Graham Greene, and another novel, *The Power and the Glory*, one of the participants in my study—a financial services executive who went through outplacement twice ("It was the pits!")—recalled drawing strength from this book. He read it, in fact, three times.

> *Here's this man that maybe shouldn't have been a priest in the first place. He was very weak, clearly has a drinking problem, sired illegitimate children. A "whiskey priest," I think they call him. And yet when this final call comes about*

*the person back in Mexico that wants to confess—he's rea-
sonably sure it's a trap, but he goes back. His physical
courage is so thin that he really has to get himself almost
intoxicated to overcome his fear. He certainly is among the
weakest links in the chain. Yet, when all was said and done,
he did what he had to do. And I think when you're hurting,
an image like that isn't all bad.*

That's the point of holding up the literary mirror—you can better understand and accept yourself in the images good authors
place before you.

Graham Greene once remarked, "The writer and the priest
never have a sense of success, because the priest feels he hasn't
been a saint, and the writer knows he hasn't been another Dickens."
Success and failure preoccupied Greene as a writer; that is one reason he is worth reading during a job-search campaign. He once
raised the rhetorical questions: "Isn't it the story-teller's task to act
as a devil's advocate, to elicit sympathy and a measure of understanding for those who lie outside the boundaries of … approval?
[The writer] stands for the victims and the victims change." One literary critic called Greene "a true magician in the words and spells
of authentic drama … who has found an instrument for probing the
temper and tragedy of his age, the perversions and fears that have
betrayed it, and the stricken weathers of the soul."

In teaching "Business and Society" or "The Social
Responsibility of Business" to college students en route to business careers, I invite them to select a novel set in the business context, read it carefully, and then, from the perspective of the narrator or protagonist, write a short essay under the title "On the
Possibility of a Full Human Life in the American Business
System." The assignment enables the student to "see" the business
world he or she will soon inhabit through the eyes of the protagonist or narrator, whose biases for or against the system will be
clear. The point of it all is to encourage a vicarious experience by
way of preparation for what might lie ahead.

This is an exercise that might be useful to the job seeker.
Consider, for instance, the premise Louis Edwards lays out at the

opening of his *Washington Post* (February 10, 1992) review of *Company Man*, a novel by Brent Wade (Algonquin): "What any would-be company man must acquiesce to is the submergence of some part of his identity (and probably the loss thereof). He must stand in his employer's shadow.... To commit blindly is to initiate a form of metaphysical (or is it merely, here, metaphorical?) suicide." Your local librarian (with whom you should become friendly when you are in transition) can provide you with a list of good novels whose characters live their lives in corporate settings. Try to "climb inside the skin" of one or more of these characters and view the world from their perspective. You will see things you haven't noticed before—about business and also about yourself.

The Bible is, of course, literature. As literature it deserves at least brief mention here because the Book of Job provides the archetypical example of the literary character with whom the discouraged, perhaps unjustly treated, job seeker can relate.

Shakespeare also has something to contribute to the literary mirror. In *The Tempest*, for example, you will meet Prospero, who was a failure as Duke of Milan when his daughter was just a child. When she is a young adult, Prospero has trouble telling her about this, and fears that she will esteem him less on account of it. "It is a humiliating moment—a trial which at some time or other comes to all parents when for the first time their children look at them frankly and critically," notes the Introduction to this play in G. B. Harrison's edited volume of *Shakespeare: The Complete Works*. Early in the play, Prospero explains to his daughter Miranda, now a young adult, that he was betrayed by his own brother, who promised to pay both tribute and homage to the king of Milan on condition that the king "Should presently extirpate me and mine/ Out of the dukedom." Prospero was ousted

> *in the dead of darkness*
> *... Me and thy crying self.... They hurried us aboard a bark,*
> *Bore us some leagues to sea, where they prepared*
> *A rotten carcass of a butt [a tub], not rigged,*
> *Nor tackle, sail, nor mast. The very rats*
> *Instinctively have quit it. There they hoist us,*

To cry to the sea that roared to us, to sigh
To the winds, whose pity, sighing back again,
Did us but loving wrong.

Miranda has no memory of this but presumes, "Alack, what trouble/ Was I then to you!" Quite the contrary, relates her father in language not unlike that used by several men I met in the course of this study, men whose daughters gave them affection and encouragement to ease the initial shock of job loss. Prospero replies to Miranda,

Oh, a cherubin
Thou wast that did preserve me. Thou didst smile,
Infused with a fortitude from Heaven,
When I have decked the sea with drops full salt.
Under my burden groaned, which raised in me
an undergoing stomach to bear up
Against what should ensue.

The point of directing your attention to the literary mirror is simply to suggest that what you see there may help you get the "stomach to bear up against" whatever difficulties you may encounter in a job campaign of unpredictable duration.

Chapter 5

NETWORKING

*Network, network, network, and let people know
you are out of work. They can't help you if they
don't know you need to make a change.*
—*Academic administrator, after a successful search*

In one of the many conversations I had with knowledgeable advisers during the design phase of this project, a good friend, who is also an experienced human resources professional, told me, "You're going to hear some harsh judgments leveled against corporations that let someone go 'just before Christmas.' It often happens that way, and when it does, the corporation could be doing the person a favor." He went on to explain that waiting until mid-January to break the news may appear to be more humane, but that would mean "depriving the person of the chance to take advantage of the many networking opportunities that the holiday social events offer." The parties and the social contacts tend to dry up in mid-January; that means fewer opportunities to tell the world that you are out of work and looking for a job.

"Networking, networking, networking," was the drumbeat reply I received from managers who had successfully negotiated their respective transitions. I asked, of course, what they considered essential for an effective job campaign. No one failed to stress the importance of networking. One of America's top corporate executives, who had been through a couple of involuntary separations, told me, "The only way you get a top job is from people you've met somewhere along the way." The people you meet along the way make up your network. A senior financial executive, adding his voice to the "Network, network, network!" chorus, added the homey reminder that you have to "kiss a lot of frogs to find a prince."

The term *networking* is self-explanatory. It means assembling an initial list of contacts and broadening that list continuously. One relatively young and very systematic job seeker told me that he simply placed twenty-six dividers (one for each letter of the alphabet) into a loose-leaf binder and then went back through his telephone logs for the past five years. He lifted all the names associated with calls placed or received, arranged them in alphabetical order, put them in the binder, and started to make the calls.

Others begin at home—with their Christmas-card lists and their high school and college alumni directories. At the office, often when cleaning out the desk, departing managers sometimes discover to their surprise that they have accumulated hundreds of business cards. Unmarked, unannotated cards offer mute witness to the no-longer working hypothesis that "it can never happen to me." If you had the foresight to make notes on the cards and arrange them in some kind of order by industry or geography, you will have given yourself a head start on the important construction project of building your network.

The outplacement firm Jannotta, Bray & Associates provides its clients with an "Executive Workbook," fourteen chapters of detailed and helpful information designed to facilitate the job search. An entire chapter is devoted to contacts, what I've been discussing here as networking. The higher a client's last salary, according to Jannotta, Bray, the more likely it is that the next opportunity will be identified as the result of a contact. Why? "Because only 20 to 30 percent of the available executive positions are ever advertised in a publication or listed with a search firm. The other 70 to 80 percent are frequently referred to as the 'hidden job market.'" You find your way around in the hidden job market with the help of friends, persons whom others are asking, "Who do you know who might fill this position?"

Jannotta, Bray has the most extensive memory prompter I've seen to assist a person in putting together a network. Here are the categories: friends (take a look at your holiday card list); neighbors (current and past); social acquaintances: golf, swim, tennis, social club members, PTA members; classmates: from any level of school; other college alumni (can you get a list of those living locally?); teachers: your college professors; your children's teachers; anybody you wrote a check to in the past year (tradesperson, drugstore owner, barbershop/hairdresser, doctor, dentist, optician, therapist, lawyer, accountant, real estate agent, insurance representative, stockbroker, travel agent); manager of the local branch of your bank; coworkers and former coworkers; current and former employees and bosses; relatives—even your in-laws; politicians (local leaders often are businesspeople or professionals in town and know everybody); administrative assistant to your congressional representative; local town council members; Chamber of Commerce executives in town; clergy; members of your church or synagogue; professional organization executives; trade association executives; other members of your professional societies; people you met at conventions; speakers at meetings you have attended; business club executives and members (Rotary, Kiwanis); other career transition clients and consultants; salespeople, customers, clients, suppliers you dealt with in previous positions; spouse's contacts; people whose business cards you have collected; others.

Phew! They advise that you arrange the contacts in order of likely effectiveness, but warn; "Be careful, however, not to eliminate people too quickly.... Often a fairly unlikely source may have a relative or friend, unknown to you, who can open that key door."

The point of it all is to find more and more potential contacts to potential employers. They are not likely to contact you first, unless those who know you well also know that you have been or are about to be separated. Few will be as fortunate as a very senior executive at one of America's best-known corporations who, shortly after learning that he had been bypassed for the chairmanship, received a call from a nearby university president, who told him, "I hear they're about to make a big mistake over there. I can't do anything about that and didn't call to discuss it. I'm calling to invite you to take a professorship here." This, of course, is far from the typical case. I should note, by the way, that when I spoke to this executive six years later and found him happily ensconced in a business school deanship at another university, he remained warmly appreciative of the call that came when he was "tired, disappointed, and in need of someone to verify my capabilities." We all know the feeling!

He also told me that his experience convinced him of the importance of having diverse interests while holding a top-level executive position. Executives who provide leadership in the local United Way campaign, for example, or who are involved with universities, hospitals, civic groups, the arts, and other forms of public or community service will be working with other influential volunteers who easily and naturally can become part of one's network. Pity the isolated, workaholic executive who remains aloof from outside involvements, only to find, when involuntary separation comes, that no outside involvements then means no outside contacts now. Even worse is the discovery that the inside, on-the-job contacts have vanished with the disappearance of the job. Those who have been there will tell you that outside involvements are in your personal as well as organizational interest. As an ex-IBMer told me, "Most businesses, and most positions within them, focus inwardly, despite their claims to be always 'scanning the environment.' Your contacts tend to reside within the business. These inwardly focused people are the least helpful when it becomes necessary for you to network in order to find a new position."

Constructing the network is a pencil-and-paper project that can begin immediately, even before you feel like talking to anyone. The computer enables you to do the job in a more sophisticated fashion. You can, of course, use a personal computer simply to compile and organize your list of contacts. Or, if you are capable of logging on to computer on-line services like CompuServe and Prodigy, you can utilize "bulletin boards" and on-line job banks for an electronic job search. The task, whether high- or low-tech, involves memory, records, and reaching out—not as a mendicant (although you should never be too proud to ask), but as a merchant of your own potential either to meet the needs of a potential employer, or match the strengths of a potential business partner, or find the investors you need to back you in a new venture.

In *Parting Company* (Harcourt Brace Jovanovich, 1991), William Morin and James Cabrera draw on their extensive outplacement experience (they describe themselves as "career continuation" specialists) to make two important points about networking. First, they know from the experience of their Drake

Beam Morin clients all across the country that networking—personal contacts—accounts for 70 percent of the success stories in finding new jobs. Second, before clients place any calls or send out résumés, they must "memorize the first two rules of networking: Never ask for a job; always ask for suggestions. Don't ask for favors; ask for advice." Asking for advice sounds to me a lot like asking for a favor, but I wouldn't strain over the distinction. The point to keep in mind is that you need network contacts to point you in the direction of jobs, not to provide you with the job itself.

People Like to Help

A "Job Search Skills Workbook" placed in the hands of clients by Jannotta, Bray & Associates points out that networking is "the fastest way to locate a good mechanic, a good doctor, *and a good job.*" And then these outplacement experts explain that networking is a request for information, not a straight-out request for employment. "Networking is asking for a small favor—some time, information, and advice." The workbook reminds the job seeker that asking straight out for a job in conversations with network contacts seldom works for two fairly obvious reasons. First, chances are small that an available job is there waiting for you, and second, people tend to shy away from job requests, even people who want to help you. They feel uncomfortable listening to your pitch when it is aimed directly at them. They do not, however, mind responding to a request for a "small favor." And it is safe to presume that just about anyone you know wants to help.

A woman of forty-two, who lost her job as corporate manager of communications, told me: "I was really burned out. I'd worked eleven-hour days for seven months. I took time off before I started looking, because I needed to recharge my batteries." When she was ready, she discovered that "networking is the way to go. It is the most effective job-hunting technique. It also gets you out talking to people; it keeps you sharp."

Networking works in an infinite variety of ways. A human resources executive who had personally benefited from networking resolved, in a spirit of gratitude, to make himself available to assist

others in the Tampa area, where he was then working. He received
a call one day from a woman he did not know; she had been
referred to him by a mutual friend. Just from talking to her on the
phone, he knew that she was really down, so he decided he would
call her about three times a week, around 9:30 in the morning, and
ask, "What are you doing today? How many people have you
called? How many résumés have you sent out? I'm going to call
you in a day or two and find out where you are." He did that three
days a week for about six months, and finally she found a job. She
thanked him, of course, but the two had never met face to face; he
did not know what she looked like. Nor did he know that the job
she got was in the same office tower where he worked.

Some months later the company he worked for was acquired by
another company, and he, along with three other top managers, was
let go. "I was lucky enough to be a top manager," he commented to
me. And he went on to say that somehow or other, the word of his
job loss got back to the woman he had helped. She called a friend
of hers in Nashville, who in turn called a friend in Tampa, "and that
guy called me out of the blue to say, 'I understand you're looking for
a job; so-and-so has recommended you, and I'm wondering if you
would like to come and talk to me.'" He still hadn't met the lady
whom he had helped and who was now trying to be helpful in
return, nor was he immediately inclined to go for the interview, so
he deferred. Continuing the story in his own words:

> Then at a Christmas party that I had not wanted to attend
> because I was unemployed, and low, and all that—you just
> have to kind of force yourself in those situations because it's an
> opportunity to meet people, that's why I went. She was at that
> Christmas party, and we met for the first time. She pressed me
> to follow up on the call I had received. I went for the job inter-
> view and learned that the job was way below my background.
> But the problem that the guy had was that they were selling
> the company and his director of human resources left in the
> middle because he didn't want to have to deal with laying off
> his friends. So when the job offer was made to me, I said, "The
> pay is about half of what I have made and would expect to

make, and you know the job will run only for a year, at best. Here's what I'll do. I'll consult with you three days a week and charge you an hourly rate that will amount to double what you are offering. Don't pay me any benefits; for the next ten months you need the top end of the job. You need communication, you need compassion, you need people talking to managers. I will attend to that as if I were your director of human resources, but I'm only going to come in three days a week. Let's sign a ten-month contract and see where that goes. At the end of ten months, you won't need me any more."

They agreed; he had two days a week for other pursuits—"and that was the beginning of my consulting business."

The most valuable part of the consulting, he told me, was the personal reassurance. "Instead of being on the street, I was in an office where somebody cared about what I said, and I was earning good money during a ten-month job search." He interviewed on Mondays and Fridays and was working Tuesday through Thursday, and "feeling a lot better" about himself.

The network linkage to the person in Tampa he hardly even knew gave him the consulting job. The firm for which he was consulting was bought by Cigna, a Philadelphia company, which had a job they couldn't fill in Philadelphia. "I had lived in Philadelphia for forty-three years before moving to Tampa," he said. "When they came to me with an offer, that conversation was over in fifteen minutes and I soon found myself back in Philadelphia in a major job." It all began with one link in a network chain.

Since consulting was part of that story, this is as good a place as any to pass along advice offered by a communications executive to persons in transition who write "Consultant" on the top of their résumés: "Never say you are a consultant, unless you are. And if you can't say, 'I'm consulting for …,' a corporation you can name, don't say anything at all about consulting."

Those who believe that "consultant" sounds impressive should talk to a friend of mine whose son injured his leg during a family skiing vacation. When the father took his son to a nearby hospital emergency room, an admitting clerk asked what he did for a living.

"I'm a consultant," said the father. "Is anyone in the family employed?" the clerk inquired. He had Blue Cross/Blue Shield coverage, but the hospital would not take it. He had to put the charge on his (verified) VISA card.

A health-care executive, who turned to consulting in New Jersey while hoping to return to permanent hospital-based employment, told me he found the work to be "like Mexican stoop labor; I now feel very close to the asparagus cutters."

Enough for the moment about consulting; one additional Christmas story is worth repeating. It involved me personally and illustrates how networks function.

For many years, during the week after Christmas, I've been joining about a half dozen of my close friends from college days, and their wives, for a dinner party. Many years ago, as one of those pleasant gatherings was breaking up, a classmate took me aside, pulled some folded papers from his pocket, and, out of both sight and hearing of the others, asked if I would take his résumé with me and keep him in mind if I heard of an opening for someone with his background and experience. He had liquidated a successful automobile sales-and-service operation about a year before, thinking he would have no difficulty finding something new and challenging to do. One of the reasons he decided to get out of the automobile business was the very high interest rates then prevailing; the "floor plan" offered by banks to dealers squeezed profit margins excessively. That and other pressures convinced him that it would be a good move to get out of automobiles. He had been out for about a year.

As we spoke, I glanced at the résumé and noticed that it was not possible to estimate his age from the information summarized there. When I commented that if a career summary raises questions instead of providing answers, it could hurt more than help, he replied, "Who wants to take a look at a guy who is fifty-one?"

The very next day, in another city at a Sunday brunch hosted by a bank chairman on whose board I served, I found myself seated next to a man in the oil business. Someone at the table commented on the high interest rates that showed no sign of breaking and were hurting business. I mentioned that I had just been talking to a friend who was a "refugee" from the automobile business because of high interest rates, among other things. The oil man expressed interest and inquired about my friend's identity. When he heard the name, he asked if there had been a leasing business attached to the sales-and-service operation. It turned out that he knew my friend slightly, was aware of his reputation, and wondered if I could obtain for him a copy of my friend's résumé! He had a friend, a major manufacturer of gasoline service-station pumps, who was looking for a general sales manager. My classmate got the job.

Your network should not be limited simply to what I've referred to earlier as functional friends, those you meet on the job or get to know through your work. Special links in anyone's network will be those close friends to whom you can turn when you want to talk and need advice. A construction company executive put it succinctly: "Networking works—keep up those contacts at all times." Expanding a bit on that, he made the point that you should "talk to everyone, and from those conversations you will learn what your main assets and talents really are; then you can devise your marketing strategy. Your hardest sale is selling yourself."

A fired company president, the one whose chairman thought he ought to get all his bad news on the same day, told me how he had been supported by many good friends. Two, he told me, "were fantastic." One was the first he called when he lost his job. They went for a walk together and had an hour's conversation before the ousted executive went home. After several consulting jobs and the erosion of his savings, he met with this same friend again and disclosed his plans to move in with relatives and rent out his home. "No way," said the friend, "I'll pick up your mortgage payments." Another friend simply gave him an envelope containing a letter of support and a check for $20,000, which the surprised and grateful recipient eventually returned. More important to him, he said, was the reassuring support of personal friendship. After talking it over with close friends, this job seeker decided to remove "president" from his résumé. He didn't attempt to disguise the fact that he had been with that particular company, but he had come to see the company that fired him three weeks after giving him the largest salary increase he had ever received as dysfunctional, and thought it better to describe himself as a person having "ten years of sales and executive experience." Through another friend, a financial and legal consultant to a company that was being sold, he was invited to join that organization as a senior sales and marketing executive.

In the same vein, a corporate communications executive found that "friends were not only key in terms of personal support, but also key proactive network enlargers. In fact, a friend uncovered for me the job I now hold." A repositioned personnel director told me, "Support from friends and business contacts was overwhelming to me; they kept me afloat and helped me retain my self-worth and dignity, and—above all—my hope."

"Given my search experience, I'd say forget replying to classified ads even in local publications," said a college vice president and treasurer who lost his job as a result of "personality differences." "Network, network, network, and let people know you are out of work. They can't help you if they don't know you need to make a change." He went on to relate an interesting story in tracing the help he received. "I have a friend whom I was able to help when he was a student and whom I later employed on my staff. Eventually, I had to terminate him in a staff-reduction situation, but I brought him back as a consultant. By the time my termination was at hand, his business was flourishing. He provided me with a base from which to operate, encouragement to keep me going, and an opportunity to get some health insurance when I was out of work." Your network can become your safety net!

Some Thoughts About Outplacement

I've mentioned outplacement, the professional service aimed at facilitating career continuation, at various points in this narrative. It is a service I knew little about as I began working on the book; it is one I've grown to respect a great deal as I've met men and women who are its beneficiaries. Strictly speaking, outplacement counselors are not part of your personal network. But they assist you in building a network of contacts, and they normally become so supportive and helpful in motivating you to pursue your job campaign that they become significant reference points on that 360-degree circumference of your personal job-finding compass. In effect, that circumference traces out all your network contacts, so that you find yourself thinking of your outplacement counselor as part of your own personal network. A general manager, out of work at fifty-one after thirty-three years with the same company, found outplacement services so valuable that he now says, "If you don't have outplacement counseling provided to you as part of your severance, it may be wise to pay for it yourself as an investment for the future."

Outplacement amounted to a "life raft" for one of my respondents; it enabled him to feel secure while being "forced to think of what I really wanted to do." A less appreciative and far less optimistic viewpoint is reflected in another's comment that the outplacement office is "death row—where the living dead get buried." I also heard an in-house outplacement center like the Hawaiian Room you read about in the Foreword to this book referred to as "the silver bullet room." A corrective to that viewpoint was provided by a former industrial executive, bypassed for the chairmanship of his manufacturing company and now a consultant and provider of outplacement services. I interviewed him in the conference room of his office suite. "We hold the wake," he said, "here in this room." And with a sweep of the hand, he added: "We take care of hanging the crepe; we then help the client get on with the business of life."

On the wall of her New York City office, outplacement counselor Rose Begnal, of Jannotta, Bray, has a print of the familiar Norman Rockwell painting of himself in front of an easel and mirror, doing a self-portrait. Imposed on the print, for Rose Begnal's purposes in working with clients, are the words: "Every job is a self-portrait of the person who did it." She assumes, she told me, that her clients bring with them good reputations or "portraits" from past employment; the trick is now to project that portrait into another setting. "I try to put a tourniquet on the negativism," she said, "so that it doesn't bleed into the job search." She begins by asking them what they would like to say to the person who fired them. With that out and on the table, she tries to frame the problem as a business decision, the result of downsizing or relocation, to explain why the client is sitting there. And then she asks, "Now look, are you going to be fun to work with?"

Dr. Robert M. Hecht of Lee Hecht Harrison, Inc., another top outplacement firm, explained to me the three elements of outplacement: (1) one-on-one counseling and advice about what to do next; (2) the provision of support services—secretarial, phone, fax, research; and (3) providing office space, a base to work from, a place where clients can interact with job-seeking peers as well as with professional counselors. (One executive in my sample related to me how important it was for him to get out of his house each working day because the house, in those daylight hours, had become for him a symbol of his personal failure.) The employer usually pays for this as part of the severance package; a typical fee would be 15 percent of one year's cash compensation for continuous outplacement service until a job is found, although fees and length of support service vary.

Recently, outplacement firms have become active in "job development" initiatives; they call around and inquire about openings that can be brought to the attention of their clients, but responsibility for "going out to get the job" remains with the individual client. This "job bank" is typically updated every few weeks.

Periodically, Lee Hecht Harrison circulates among potential employers at no cost and with no fee for use a "Directory of Executive Talent." It lists clients by number code along with a four-line profile of their skills, experience, and most recent compensation levels. Interested potential employers can fax requests for the full résumé and then followup as they wish with the job seeker.

In these days of mass white-collar layoffs, these firms are doing group outplacement, running seminars and offering related counseling on the employer's site for employees who have been or soon will be told that they will be released. (Lee Hecht Harrison's brochure advertising its group services offerings reads: "Plotting a steady course through untroubled waters is challenging enough ... but holding steady in the winds of change that accompany a corporate restructuring requires an expert at the helm." The message is enhanced with photographs of sailboats on both calm and stormy seas.

Bob Hecht tells anyone willing to listen that it is essential "to keep your network up." He adds, "The worst thing you can hear as an outplacement counselor is 'I don't know anybody.'"

A woman who was at first "devastated" by loss of her executive position told me that someone advised her to sit down and "make a list" of everyone she knew. "I don't know anybody," was her response to that suggestion. But she was pressed to do it and eventually produced a list that ran fifty-six pages in length! She later found herself advising others who were looking for work to "tell everybody; tell absolutely everyone you need a job." When she finally found her new job, she told me, "I had to go all over the place to spread the good news—the pet store, the shoe repair, the Chinese laundry, the liquor store; all those people knew I was looking for work." The day she got her new job, she made ninety-two phone calls to people in her network. "And this is someone who didn't know anybody," she said with a smile.

An outplacement counselor told me that he thinks women are better than men at networking. Men have more of a problem, he said, "because of the macho thing." One of his clients did exactly what millions of moviegoers saw Jack Lemmon do in *The Prisoner of Second Avenue*—he went six weeks without even telling his wife that he had lost his job. This real-life macho later realized, "I denied her the opportunity to mourn with me." He should also have known that the job quest goes better and faster when the spouse is involved in the process.

Richard Hanscom, a vice president for production at a large bakery corporation in Cleveland, lost his job and was given outplacement assistance. He found it unsatisfactory and in the process came to see a need for something better for unemployed managers in the Cleveland area. So he wound up running the not-for-profit Career Initiatives Center (CIC). His own separation taught him how important it is to "constantly network." He adds:

When no actual job interviews are coming your way, you can always network. When doing your job search, you have to get out of the house and go to an office facility with people around. From that kind of base, go anywhere that jobs are being discussed. That kind of activity, together with research, occasional interviews, regular exercise, and building your network contacts, amounts to a full day's work, and that's exactly what you need in those difficult days in between jobs.

He estimates that about 80 percent of new jobs are obtained through networking.

At the CIC, Dick Hanscom defines "networking" for his clients this way: "Meeting people who you have selected to get you into your target companies, or referrals you get from 'advice/referral interviews' that can introduce you to opportunities in the hidden job market." An advice/referral interview is a method for enlarging your network. You ask to see someone, a person who has, or is close to one who has, the power to hire; you want to see that person not to ask for a job, but to get advice. You thus gain more accurate and current information about the workplace. You get help in defining or redefining your job target, and, in the process, you keep your interview skills sharpened for the real thing.

CIC clients who need to be convinced are presented with a sheet listing a dozen reasons why they should network:

1. To identify unadvertised jobs
2. To obtain names of company contacts and bridge contacts
3. To identify and learn about specific hiring agents
4. To come face to face with potential employers
5. To demonstrate visibility and availability
6. To increase list of target companies
7. To identify changes and needs in the workplace
8. To stay current with economic and industry information: competition, markets, products, services, trends, developments, changes, and technology
9. To learn about specific companies: markets, competition, organizational structure, people, culture, and needs
10. To create a new position (your job)
11. To determine market salary range for positions
12. To develop a relationship with networkers and to meet someone who may recommend you for an open position

In the view of one of my respondents, a systematic, highly technical person, today's job seeker is confronted with a terribly inefficient system within which to look for work. "As crazy as it seems, we really do have a paleolithic job search/connection process in this 'high-tech' country. Personal networking, which has been done for centuries, still yields most job contacts—70 percent or so, by most accounts."

For a development officer who experienced a long stretch of idleness between jobs at a university and a health-care foundation, "networking was the key. Every friend, associate, acquaintance, et al. was part of the network." Once the phone numbers and addresses are lined up, he said, you should "try to set up three appointments every day. I spent too much time alone. In one hour of idleness, I can put myself in a negative-thinking mode for a day—or longer." A publishing executive, who has been through all this himself, now spends a lot of time helping others through support groups. He remarked, "You have to have something to counter the loneliness; being unemployed is like having leprosy."

A creative form of networking was devised by a dislocated manufacturing manager who belonged to a Chicago support group of unemployed white-collar executives. At first, he declared himself to be a "consultant" and had a business card—his name "& Associates, Management Consultants"—printed. Not an uncommon step for ousted executives to take as part of a rebound strategy. It then occurred to him to form a "firm" with four "partners," all four being out of work and members of the same support group. The firm's name, derived from the first initials of the four founding partners' last names, appeared on an attractive business card; an informative brochure made the rounds of potential clients known to the partners from their previous bases of employment. As engagements came and went, so did partners, who were free to follow any employment leads the consulting opportunities produced. As partners rotated in and out, new business cards were printed up. The firm served as a mini-support group and a locus for the exchange of ideas and encouragement, not to mention occasional consulting fees.

The First Move Is Yours

Although networking, by definition, requires interest and activity on the part of many other people, it depends entirely on you to make the first move. You have to find someone who is willing to serve as a point of entry, a contact. You cannot expect that person to find a job for you; you simply want that person to open a door or make an introduction or a discreet inquiry. You have to be ready to help that person by putting into his or her hands a one-page résumé to pass along or send, with a cover letter, to someone else. That third-party cover letter, sent to someone your contact knows well, should take a simple, direct, noncoercive approach: "This will serve to introduce you to...." Some highlights of your education, experience, and interests, together with a comment on why your job search is in progress, make up the next paragraph. "If you know of anything that looks like a good match for these credentials, I'd be grateful if you would give him (or her) a call. If not, thanks for taking the time to review the résumé."

End of letter. Opening, perhaps, of the door to your next job.

Your contact made it clear that the recipient of the letter (or the call) is expected to act if, and *only* if, that person chooses to act; otherwise, he or she is "off the case." No one objects to receiving a letter like that; many recipients of such inquiries will respond if they have any way of being helpful. The résumé provides the information needed for getting in touch; it is also something visible and tangible that can jog the recipient's memory and trigger subsequent action. Networking rests on the assumption that people like to be helpful; they want to help. The problem for the job seeker is getting up the courage to ask for help and finding someone to broker the contacts.

Chapter 6

THE RELEVANCE OF RELIGION

*In his anguish [Job] reaches out for God; God
eludes him, but Job still trusts in his goodness....
This is the book's lesson: faith must remain even
when understanding fails.*

—Introduction to the Book of Job
in The Jerusalem Bible

"I'm an agnotheist," explained a technological management consultant, formerly a full-time manager in a high-technology firm. "You are what?" I asked. "An agnotheist. On the good days, I say I can't know God. On the bad days, I say there is no God to know. It's just like my job search—on a good day, I'm convinced that there is a job out there; I just can't find it. On the bad days, I'm convinced there is no job to be found."

During World War II, it was often remarked that "there are no atheists in foxholes." During the corporate downsizing of the late 1980s and early 1990s, I ran into only this one "agnotheist," but I found a diverse group of atheists, pietists, devout believers, secular humanists, and religious pragmatists occupying their isolated foxholes and observation posts in the campaign for jobs. For the most part, the job seekers I met are men and women of faith. Most of them identify with and find support in organized religion. Some, however, while classifying themselves as believers, look upon religion as a faraway, stained-glass abstraction with which they did not connect in the past and to which they do not care to relate in their present job-seeking circumstances. They fail to see any connection or potential benefit. But they do believe in God and turn to God in the midst of their present troubles associated with job loss.

Often, the word *spirituality* drew a response where *religion* failed to trigger an affirmative nod. As a female executive who describes herself as Episcopalian/Christian but does not attend church services put it, "I have a relationship with God that works for me. I had a difficult childhood and youth and went to church a lot until adulthood. With that background, my 'conversations' are important and settling for me. If I didn't have this relationship with God, life would be harsh." A Catholic transportation CEO, who had been through three transitions in his career, told me, "My advice to others would be to pray frequently and do whatever is necessary to posture oneself closer to God."

As one with a personal anchor in faith and a professional identification with organized religion, I wondered about the relevance of religion to those caught in the uncertain, often frightening, mid-career "no-job land" that became familiar territory to so many dislocated white-collar workers in the 1990s. I assumed that religion would have relevance for many, if not most job-seekers, and found this to be the case—approximately two out of three persons in this study. I also assumed that ministers of religion would, in the main, feel unequal to the task of helping executives and upper-level managers through the ordeal of a job search, and found, on the testimony of job-seekers themselves, that this assumption was also, in general, correct.

I further assumed that organized religion had not adequately recognized the ministerial opportunity it has to serve the spiritual needs of men and women whose faith in themselves and in God is threatened when the bottom falls out of their workaday world. Their familiar reference points are lost. Their self-esteem is diminished, if not altogether shattered. Their economic future is in doubt. They fear for themselves and for their families. They wonder if they will ever work again. They were thus, it seemed to me, prepared, although not by their own choosing, for the reassuring response organized religion can provide. In order to respond to this need, however, ministers of religion must have a "feel" for the trauma these people have known, and a vocabulary to speak to them in terms they can understand and appreciate as relevant to their stressful circumstances. As one of my respondents expressed it, "I just don't know how to find my way down the road with God." Another said, "I just didn't feel my pastor could relate to my situation." Organized religion, although trying in many places and many ways to be helpful, has not yet translated its traditional spiritualities into words and images that address this human need, nor organized its services effectively to meet these people where they are.

To their credit, the churches were there to support union-organizing efforts in the 1930s and remain supportive of organized labor today. Men and women on the other side of the hyphen that separates labor from management are now also in need of help, even those whose ouster was cushioned by a "golden parachute." A new kind of ministry is needed to widen the range of support the churches provide to men and women in (and trying to get back into) the workplace.

There is an important place for organized religion in the essential network that job seekers are encouraged to build. The church or synagogue is both a place to go and an assembly of people to meet. Even more important is the faith-based support that religion and spirituality can provide.

A woman who lost her job as chief administrator of a hospital told me: "Organized religion per se—i.e., church and pastor—is unable to conceive of the needs of and is not structured to respond to or support people like me. My experience is that the church does not embrace single, professional women as such—practically or conceptually in normative terms—so when someone like me is in a situation of change and stress, there is no response from the church." She did indicate, however, that "prayer, belief in the goodness of God, a deepening of self-knowledge, and getting to know my own potential through reflection and meditation proved to be critical in my becoming a person." And she added that during the job transition, "A belief system is critical; it may well help you grow toward new insight." Another woman, a Protestant, said, "I don't consider myself a particularly religious person, but I find my religion and my faith act like a backbone when I'm really down—they seem to give me strength I didn't know I had."

A fifty-six-year-old Episcopalian expressed his estimate of the critical role of religion in these words:

If I had not had faith in God, I don't think I could have made it. Sometimes I needed to pray to have the strength and courage to pick up the phone to make employment calls. I prayed before interviews. It was a horrible time in my life. Loss of job is cruel and demeaning to a person; it is an example of man's inhumanity to man. If employers understood this better, they might be better managers.

Another Episcopalian, age forty-nine, told me that religion had always been a part of his life. He was convinced that "spiritual growth came with adversity." He also found that "religion provided structure—ritual and spiritual. A faith that works kept me on solid footing emotionally and spiritually when life became chaos." He acknowledged, however, that before the crisis, religion for him had been "an untested support system." During the transition, "I embraced a program of spiritual growth based upon God as the center of life and not religion as an adjunct. Loss of the job was one facet of a period of enormous change in my life. Without the spiritual focus, I do not believe that religion—as I had known and employed it—would have sustained me." Still another Episcopalian, a fifty-year-old New Yorker, took "quiet time" for prayer during the job search and liked "to stop by a church during a busy day in Manhattan to gain a sense of solace and comfort."

Speaking of men whose careers crumble, psychologist Steven Berglas notes: "When their sense of power is pierced, these individuals often try to recapture it through very inappropriate means." The altogether appropriate means of religion is sometimes not taken, I believe, because before the crisis, religion was not central to the individual's life, and after the separation, ministers of religion are not there to offer assistance. The inappropriate remedies are obvious and available, and all too often taken without a thought to the possibility of turning to religion instead.

Alfred North Whitehead defined religion as what a person does with his or her "solitariness." Solitude, as I noted earlier in this book, is a chosen form of isolation and thus different from loneliness. There is a good deal of loneliness associated with the job search; there is also time for solitary reflection, with all the positive benefits such reflection can bring to the inner person if the person freely chooses to take this route. The chief executive of a London-based consulting group, a member of the Church of England, experienced a voluntary separation and transition at age fifty-five and now runs a company called Future Perfect—Creating Opportunities for Life. He told me, "I have found in our workshop activities, when helping people to plan for the future, that Christians generally tackle the issue far more positively than nonbelievers. They seem to be more used to looking at themselves, and are less apprehensive about dying." With reference to his own personal transition, this man said: "My faith has been an instrumental part of the process, and I see my new role as being a Christian commitment in a pioneering venture."

The wife of a high-level executive-in-transition brought this "Modern Day Twenty-Third Psalm" to the attention of her husband:

The Lord is my Pace-Setter, I shall not rush;
He makes me stop and rest for quiet intervals,
He provides me with images of stillness,
which restore my serenity.

He leads me in the ways of efficiency through
calmness of mind,
And His guidance is peace.
Even though I have a great many things
to accomplish each day,
I will not fret for His presence is here,
His timelessness, His all importance, will
keep me in balance.

He prepares refreshment and renewal in
the midst of my activity,
By anointing my mind with His oils of tranquility.
My cup of joyous energy overflows,
Surely harmony and effectiveness shall be

the fruits of my hours,
For I shall walk in the pace of the Lord
and dwell in His house forever.

Religion does indeed have a role in the business of the typical job campaign. It enables many to endure the stress of the job search. It can help a person deal with the loss-of-control anxiety that is so well known to the displaced manager. Religious reflection and counseling can assist with the essential self-assessment that is preamble to any successful reconnection for the dislocated executive.

The prefix *re-* is used in ordinary conversation by just about everyone every day. But the *lig* in "religion" is virtually always etymologically ignored by persons cut off from gainful employment. It is the same *lig* that carries the meaning in *ligament*—a cord, a connecting line, a tie-in to something strong, firm, and permanent. Religion reconnects a dislocated creature to the Creator. The disconnected executive can be helped enormously by religious faith—the human decision to entrust oneself to God, no matter what. Blind faith can see through the human condition. It sees redemption in the face of failure. Faith illumines self-worth to the point of suppressing self-doubt. "I believe in God, and I believe that God believes in me" is a good prayer for anyone with doubts about his or her ability ever to reconnect in the job market.

As a priest, I have had many opportunities to assist people in distress. Often, I have found a reflection from the pen of John Henry Newman to be effective in lifting the drooping spirits of persons who have faith, but are burdened with confusion and self-doubt. I will quote that reflection below. Occasionally, during the course of this study, I met persons who, I thought, might like to have these words, so I sent them to them, but that did not happen often. I did not approach anyone I interviewed with the expectation that they wanted to hear anything about religion from me. I made it clear that I was simply curious about the relevance of religion to them. To the question on my survey instrument about the relevance of religion, one respondent just wrote, "None. Sorry!" When I interviewed her later and remarked that there was nothing to be sorry about—no offense to me—she replied, "But I am kind of sorry, you know. My father was Jewish, my mother Unitarian, and I'm nothing. I wonder about my daughter; she has no religion now, and I can only hope it works out better for her."

The Shield

In reviewing Alvin Kernan's *Printing Technology, Letters and Samuel Johnson* for *The Christian Science Monitor* (March 4, 1987), Thomas D'Evelyn makes note of Kernan's observation that Johnson's bouts of depression, and his anomie, would sometimes yield to the activity of reading and writing books. For Johnson, Kernan says, "books and the larger world of letters" served the same purpose as "religion, sermons, and prayers"—"to shield him from nothingness."

Here is the "shield" Cardinal Newman would put in the hands of the dislocated manager or any believer who is in distress and in need of help:

> *God has created me to do Him some definite service; He has committed some work to me which He has not committed to another. I have my mission—I may never know it in this life, but I shall be told it in the next.*
>
> *I am a link in a chain, a bond of connection between persons. He has not created me for nothing. I shall do good, I shall do His work. I shall be an angel of peace, a preacher of truth in my own place while not intending it—if I do but keep His commandments.*
>
> *Therefore, I will trust Him, whatever, wherever I am. I can never be thrown away. If I am in sickness, my sickness may serve Him; in perplexity, my perplexity may serve Him; if I am in sorrow, my sorrow may serve Him. He does nothing in vain. He knows what He is about. He may take away my friends, He may throw me among strangers, He may make me feel desolate, make my spirits sink, hide my future from me—still, He knows what He is about.*

Newman often said, and really believed, that "we succeed by failing."

Faith, for those who have it, reduces the pain, and becomes within them an all-consuming trust. No one can explain it fully, but anyone who talks to enough job seekers will see faith-as-trust at work as a sustaining force in the lives of many. "Without religion," an auto executive told me, "I would not have been able to endure the pain." A fifty-two-year-old engineering executive said, "Without the support of religion, I don't know how I would have survived mentally; losing my job was a real crisis for me." Another respondent, a Presbyterian health-care executive, commented: "The tenets of religion that relate to the dignity of the person, the belief that everyone has value, and God's purpose being served—even if we don't understand it—provided me with the foundation for getting on with the next phase of my life." Those words, of course, reminded me of Newman. But the respondent went on to say that his financial severance package made it "more palatable," since "the notion that 'God will provide' does not incorporate one's mortgage payment." He described the burden of having to deal with the possibility of losing his home as "onerous."

A self-described Baptist fundamentalist, out of work as a vice president for systems at age forty-nine, described the relevance of religion to his separation with a simple assertion: "God is in control! All things work to good to those called according to His purpose." Another Baptist, an African-American corporate tax director, age forty-seven, spoke of religion as enabling him "to survive without various material things; possessions have not been the basis of my happiness."

An experienced outplacement specialist, a partner in one of the top firms, thought about this issue and reflected on his experience in counseling clients. "I've not heard much talk about faith and religion from people I see; I just don't hear it. They believe *they* have to make it happen, and they believe in *luck!*" But he then began to wonder whether some significant thoughts and feelings were going unexpressed in the conversations he had been having with clients over the years.

One participant in my study, a Catholic, certainly didn't talk about religion much during his transition because, he said, "I had a difficult time going to Sunday Mass; it was a tough time to sit and contemplate a week of frustration and futility. My prayer to God was, 'Hey, when are you going to do something for me?'" It was different for a forty-six-year-old accounting executive who lost his partnership in a major firm: "During the transition, I attended Mass three or four times a week other than Sunday. I gained a sense of peace at Mass." Still another Catholic in the survey group said, "Religion gives you the strength to move through the process with an optimistic attitude; it helps you avoid pessimism."

For a Presbyterian perspective, here is an international personnel director, age fifty-six, still in outplacement: "My faith in the future and in divine intervention keep me moving toward new situations and not dwelling on the past." As one who has "always felt that religion is the source from which I draw my strength," a regional sales representative who is Methodist observed, "After a person has gone through the full range of emotions associated with job loss (and they will), there is no other answer that fits as well as God's word. He has been faithful to me as He promised, and I shall always be faithful to Him."

A Jew who had lost a research management position in a university, and who was still out, spoke to me of the relevance of "faith," rather than religion:

> I lost faith in me and had to find faith in something or Someone. Once over the "why me?" aspect, my attendance at services did not really increase, but my intimate little "conversations" with G-d did. No voice from a burning bush was expected, but self-questioning and self-examination sessions were helpful. The old saying of "G-d helps those who help themselves" became more self-evident. This helps me become focused and develop the confidence to continue searching.

A twice-severed health-care CEO carried on a dialogue with God and described it for me in terms of direct appeal to God—"They're your children too, You know, and You've got to help me take care of them. I accept Your will, whatever it is for me, but I'll never stop pleading with You to take care of my kids."

A fifty-four-year-old lawyer, separated from his firm and looking for a corporate position, viewed his "ongoing (almost two-year) experience as a spiritual journey with a profound meaning for my life." He experienced, he said, "a conversion—a total commitment to Jesus Christ. I realized that all that I had in power, authority, prestige, and money did not fill the void in my life and that materialism and items associated with it were meaningless." His experience was not so profound, however, as to prevent him from enclosing the following for the amusement of readers of this book:

A MEMORANDUM

To: Jesus, Son of Joseph, Woodcrafter Carpenter Shop, Nazareth 25922

From: Jordan Management Consultants, Jerusalem 26544

Dear Sir:

Thank you for submitting the résumés of the twelve men you have picked for management positions in your new organization. All of them have taken our battery of tests. We have not only run the results through our computer, but also arranged personal interviews for each of them with our psychologist and vocational aptitude consultant.

The profiles of all tests are enclosed, and you will want to study them carefully.

As part of our service and for your guidance, we make some general comments, much as an auditor will include some general statements. This is given as a result of staff consultation and comes without any additional fees.

It is the staff opinion that most of your nominees are lacking in background, education, and vocational aptitude for the type of enterprise you are undertaking. They do not have the team concept. We would recommend that you continue your search for persons of experience in managerial ability and proven capability.

Simon Peter is emotionally unstable and given to fits of temper. Andrew has absolutely no qualities of leadership. The two brothers, James and John, the sons of Zebedee, place personal interest above company loyalty. Thomas demonstrates a questioning attitude that would tend to undermine morale. We feel that it is our duty to tell you that Matthew has been blacklisted by the Greater Jerusalem Better Business Bureau. James, the son of Alpheus, and Thaddeus definitely have radical leanings, and they both registered a high score on the manic-depressive scale.

One of the candidates, however, shows great potential. He is a man of ability and resourcefulness, meets people very well, has a keen business mind, and has contacts in high places. He is highly motivated, ambitious, and responsible. We recommend Judas Iscariot as your controller and right-hand man. All of the other profiles are self-explanatory.

We wish you every success in your new venture.

Not for Everyone

The range of responses to my inquiry about the relevance of religion moved from blank space on the questionnaire to a curt "not relevant," up a step to this kind of neutral zone: "I consider myself a religious person, but religion did not play a greater or lesser role in my life during the period of severance and job search," and then up another notch to a guarded "my strong inner faith and a belief in a higher being lending me support convinced me that I would eventually get back on track and find employment." There were, of course, examples of very high religious commitment and total dependency upon God, expressed in words like these from an out-of-work California banking executive, a Roman Catholic:

So there I was at home scared almost out of my wits. What to do? On Marge's dresser there's a crystal statue of Mary with

Child. I simply got down on my knees and with arms out-stretched I prayed the most fervent rosary I knew how. When I finished, I felt somewhat at peace. I stood up and headed to the bathroom to get dressed. I took two or three steps and the phone rang. It was the CEO of a bank in New York. We had talked a month before, but it looked like a failure was at hand, and so we broke off discussions. Now he wanted to know how soon I could join him in the rescue effort. I was there in a week and there was joy in Mudville. Did Someone intervene? I'm comfortable with my answer to that question.

Another high-commitment response, this one also from a banker whose transition took him out of the industry into another as vice president for administration, took this form:

I am blessed with having good faith. This faith and my close association with my parish and pastor were very instrumental. I used my pastor to cry on more than once. I talked often to God and to my Dad, who passed away in 1986. I am convinced that God was listening and my Dad was up there lobbying on my behalf. I truly feel my faith is stronger for having gone through this experience. I feel my bond with my family is stronger as well. It was a sobering experience that forces you to reflect upon your priorities of work and family.

A Catholic lawyer, forty-three, whose career was corporate with a specialization in taxation, would, from his résumé, be assumed to be cerebral and reserved in the realm of religion. Not so. I will let him speak for himself:

If you define religion as my relationship with God, it was very important to me. At all times during the transition, I felt that God was in charge. I was willing to do whatever came, including a change of life. I put my life and my family in God's hands.

I have found that daily prayer makes me a nicer person. Under these trying circumstances, prayer was all the more important, especially in helping me not to get bitter or take

*offense at criticism. When I did take offense, prayer helped
me to forgive very quickly.*

*The summer before I received the news of my severance, I
was on a lake fishing late at night in conversation with the
Lord. I had been having a running dialogue with Him for
years. I felt that He wanted me to keep a written record of the
lessons He had taught me over the years. It was an irregular
effort on my part—mostly in journal form—that would start
and stop with my changing moods. After admitting my recent
laxness in writing, I heard, clear as day, "What do I have to
do—take your job away?" I had long ago stopped making
deals (that I knew I wouldn't honor) with the Lord. I simply
said, "Why do that? I'll try to write more."*

*When I was told of the decision two and a half months later,
I was immediately, mentally, back on the lake: "OK, but I
need to support your grandchildren." There was no animosi-
ty, and I am still not as faithful to the writing process as I
should be.*

After reading that, you will not be surprised to learn that during his transition, this job seeker began each day "with prayer—
especially for myself, my family, and the individuals for whom I
used to work."

The briefest and, possibly, the most positive response I
received regarding the relevance of religion came from a senior
broadcast communications executive for whom religion was, in his
one word, "everything" during the separation crisis.

More typical and more Main Street traditional was this reply:

*Our religious roots, combined with the loving support of
family and friends, were most important during this time of
stress and change. Our faith that "this, too, shall pass" and
that God has a plan into which all this will fit was our foundation of hope. It is my responsibility to work hard and smart
in forming an action plan to pass through this employment
transition.*

A savings and loan executive who lost all retirement benefits when his institution was forced to close in 1991 told me:

Religion was very relevant to me when I experienced the severance from the job. The callous way in which the severance was handled by a major corporation was devastating. If I had not had a strong faith in God that I would be fine, that He would see me through it, and that I would in fact be a better person for having experienced it (humility), I would not have been able to focus so strongly on a job search. I sought and obtained a position with a not-for-profit organization that has provided me with more job satisfaction than I ever experienced previously.

A woman who described herself as being for many years "agnostic or atheistic," noted that the severance experience provided her with "more faith that there is a guiding hand assisting me." She had become a Unitarian in 1984 and developed an interest in Eastern religions. When she lost her job in 1992, she "reframed the experience on a spiritual level, realizing that I should have left this unhealthy workplace long ago; because I was afraid to leave, I got a 'nudge' and an opportunity to change." Years earlier, she said, she had "been prone to anxiety and worry." When job loss occurred, "Amazingly, I felt very little anxiety or worry; rather, I felt a sense of freedom and anticipation of a more fulfilling lifestyle. Even though my income [as a private consultant] is way down now, I consider myself happier and more relaxed than ever." Another woman personalized both her religion and her response this way: "My spiritual communication with my God became more honest and more clear, as I was being more true to myself at my essence where I experience my God." A Catholic nun, who found herself unceremoniously separated by a lay-religious board from the CEO position at a large hospital, later reflected: "As I prayed for peace and less anger, I knew in faith that this action was a part of the Lord's larger plan for me. It was difficult to understand why those religious women in authority would not stand up for justice, so I had to work through that. However, as time passed, I became more independent and secure in who I was as a result of meeting some beautiful people along the way." She is now happily at work in another hospital in another part of the country.

A sales executive in California who identifies himself as Christian-Presbyterian suffered an employment setback at age fifty-four. Three years later, when asked to put that experience in religious perspective, he said,

> I have been justified and sanctified—the Lord Jesus Christ died for me. He will deliver me, but I must put forth every effort to reach my goal. But I recognize that I cannot do anything without Him. My mother died during this time, and I was reminded by my best friend (a pastor in a distant city) of my mother's favorite hymn—"Life Is Like a Little Mountain Railroad." Time with him before and after her memorial service was valuable.

When released from the presidency of a beverage company, a Catholic in my study found that his religion enabled him to "feel like I was being taken care of and protected." An evangelical Christian, once an academic administrator and now a consultant, said, "I have always been able to trace God's hand in everything that has happened to me vocationally." A transportation CEO, a Methodist, discloses something of his approach to religion in this comment: "Since the separation experience was not traumatic or disheartening, religion was no more or less relevant than under normal conditions." A self-described Christian, age thirty-nine, had been a vice president and project manager for a construction company, but was unemployed when he related the following to me: "Recovery in a twelve-step group led me to a spiritual conversion and then to a personal Christian conversion in 1982. These experiences laid the foundation for a personal faith that has sustained me with a sense of hope and a belief that I will fulfill His plan for my life."

"I believe in the power of prayer," said a corporate communications director who found new employment in health-care public relations. "It is, and was, a source of great comfort. I feel that God gave me the tools to build a life, and that the results are up to me.

Religion and faith provide for me the ethical context for decision-making." A similar view was expressed in slogan fashion by a marketing executive: "Let Go and Let God." He added, "I put my life and my will in the hands of God, and I trust Him."

Jewish participants in my study tended to be more taciturn in matters of religion. For some, their declared religious commitment, like that of some of their Christian counterparts in the study, had little relevance to the job-search process. Others, like this former executive vice president, said simply: "I have always felt that G— does things or has things happen to you for a reason. Therefore, this situation occurred for a reason, and we must face it and make the best of it." Another Jew, a successfully repositioned vice president for human resources, noted, "You have to put your faith in G-d that something good will come out of this situation."

For the person of any faith, religion has a reassuring answer to Elie Wiesel's question, "What is man? Hope turned to dust, or dust turned to hope?" Hope fuels the fight against discouragement; it keeps a focused job search moving forward. It enables the job seeker to "dance without music."

A voluntary separation experience, and what proved to be its disappointing aftermath, had an unanticipated religious repercussion in the life of a fifty-five-year-old executive. "Externally, I went out with grace—head high; but the symbol of victory, a golf villa in Florida, proved to be unsatisfying to my wife." So he sold it and they returned north.

I've been oriented to achieve, to "declare victory." I approached religion in the same way—emphasis on the victory, not the process. I'm not as comfortable as I used to be. I always assumed that I could lean back on religion, but now I find it to be less of a crutch and more of a challenge. I used to think of it as a bank where I could make deposits and withdrawals. Now it is making demands of me. It's fuzzier now. I'm angry with this Christ person who seems to be asking too much.

For this man, religion in the sense of "wrestling with God" is more of a factor now. He thought he was going to "pack it all in and enjoy the victory." He remains strongly faith-committed but uneasy about where the faith journey is taking him. (The image of the believer as wrestler reminds me of Walker Percy's words, "Life is a mystery, love is a delight," an expression he elaborated upon as follows: "I don't see why anyone should settle for anything less than Jacob, who actually grabbed aholt of God and wouldn't let go until God identified himself and blessed him.")

In a similar deposit-and-withdrawal vein, another participant in my study explained,

My religion has always been my foundation for my life. This trial [involuntary separation] was no different from other trials in the sense that I depended on my faith to strengthen me. As always, it did not fail me. I believe you get out of it what you put into it. If you remain faithful to God and to His laws, He will be faithful to you. So far, this compact has been kept on God's side very well.

Typical of the religious reaction of a lot of couples—all Christian—where one or the other lost a managerial job is this comment voiced by a successful executive of sixty-two who was forty-nine at the time of involuntary separation: "God has always been an important part of our lives, and we have been risk takers. We had confidence in ourselves and included God in our plans, but we didn't expect Him to provide." One risk taker decided not to look for another job but to head off "in another direction"— making personal investments in small companies. "My religious experience gave me the strength to believe it would all work out."

"The loss of status, the insult to my ego, the fear and uncertainty actually caused me to think of death and dying," disclosed a fifty-seven-year-old Christian who did not attend any church services regularly and still does not. But with the loss came a "spiritual awakening that helped me put my relatively minor problems in perspective." He turned to the psalms, the Book of Proverbs, and the gospels, and appears to be content in his present capacity as consultant to venture capitalists. He keeps his distance, however, from formal religion. Because he and several others mentioned the psalms as sources of help, I decided to edit a "user-friendly" version of the psalms for job seekers; it has been published by Sheed & Ward under the title *Take Courage; Be Stouthearted: Psalms of Support and Encouragement.*

"Does the Book of Job Have My Name on It?"

One of the most depressed and certainly the angriest person I encountered in the course of this study lost his marriage as well as his job, and twice came within a whisker of taking his life. He is, relatively speaking, back on track now ("I reserve the right to hate my former boss") in another industry and occupation. It was his religious background (Roman Catholic), he told me, that prevented him from committing suicide. "I just knew I could not face God; I thought He'd destroy me." He had for years, he said, "intellectualized God; now the relationship is pretty raw." Given his religious background, he said, he expected that "people would treat me fairly." "I always wanted to make a positive contribution—that phrase kept returning while I was down, and out of work."

Like several others in this study, this troubled job seeker mentioned the Book of Job; identification with Job was easy for him. He used to argue with God, he told me, and recalled walking down the street one day, both jobless and optionless, and saying to God, "You don't think I can take this, do you? Well, make it tougher!"

Interestingly enough, the phrase from the Book of Job that rang deep and true for him was, as he repeated it, "No one asked his counsel." He found this to be, he said, "so true when you are out of work, and this really hurts." The reference in the text, however, is to God, not to Job. "Yet he himself [God] had filled their houses with good things, while these wicked men shut him out of their counsels" (Job 22:18). In any case, this man thought of himself as "a target for [God's] archery" (16:13) and he took to heart the Lord's words to Job to "brace yourself like a fighter" (38:3;

40:2), the stance he chose to take for his complaints and conversations with God.

The reader of the Book of Job is alerted in the prologue to the fact that Job's troubles were not of God's doing, but the work of Satan. The religious message of the book is that God's ways are mysterious—the mystery of a God of justice who permits good people to suffer. Job's faith and faithfulness are being tested. As the introduction to this book in the Jerusalem Bible puts it: "In his anguish he reaches out for God; God eludes him, but Job still trusts in his goodness.... This is the book's lesson: faith must remain even when understanding fails."

Another man I interviewed said he had found himself ten years earlier asking himself, "Does the Book of Job have my name on it?" He was in outplacement for nine months. Without in any way wanting or deserving it, he was also in "the Disaster-of-the-Month Club." He had six months of family and financial problems: an unmarried daughter became pregnant; ten days later his wife's only sister died unexpectedly while awaiting brain surgery on her husband; one month later his father died; in April, "the IRS came after me big time"; and he then discovered that his father, a physician, had been covering his mother's Alzheimer's disease, which was now evident to all and provisions had to be made. "I didn't have any dogs licking my sores, but Job and I had a lot in common!"

A very reflective and resourceful person, a former CEO who describes himself as taking a "liberal view of religion, as seen by my Unitarian affiliation, although I was raised a traditional Lutheran," said he used "the church process" to "reflect on my life, values, and desires for responsible accomplishments" while going through transition. But "I did not push the process any more or less than normal while going through the change."

When asked about the impact of his Catholic religion on his job-loss situation, a Philadelphia banker said, "What impressed me the most was not the solace I found in my religion, but how deeply religious the people were who provided the most support to me. People with deep religious beliefs do reach out to help." Another banker explained his personal belief that "my talents are a gift" and it is his responsibility to use them well. "Most of my spirituality comes from 40 years ago," he said, "not from any recent influences."

After acknowledging to me that his religion was "very important in terms of support, spirit-lifter, solace, hope," a senior vice president in advertising who had made a successful transition, went on to say: "Four years ago, I was out of a job and hurting. I vowed then to help others when I found a job." He kept the promise by hosting, in a corporate headquarters auditorium, a monthly support group of 50 and providing one-on-one assistance whenever he got a call. He makes himself available as a speaker to church-sponsored support groups in the New York area, so much so that an admiring observer describes this volunteer work as "a ministry."

Needed: More and Better Help from the Churches

When the forty-four-year-old chief financial officer of a Denver-based oil company was separated from his job, he asked the company to provide "testing that will force me to rethink my life." He received professional outplacement assistance and in that setting "saw people who were totally crushed. It was a tense period for me." I had asked him about the relevance of religion in his life at that time, and he replied, "None. And it's a damn shame." His Baptist church disappointed him, he said, in two ways. First, it has teachings and scriptures it fails to use to help people deal with rejection. Second, it spends a lot on outreach through programs like Alcoholics Anonymous, but does not address the unemployment problems of white-collar workers. "If I didn't have sores and scabs, they didn't want to help me. They ignore people in three-piece suits carrying attaché cases. I think assistance to people in career transition—at all economic levels—should be the number-one outreach program of all churches." He did indeed mean "at all economic levels," but he and most of the displaced managers I talked to did not see themselves as in the same boat, much less in solidarity, with the lower-skilled, lower-income unemployed.

Many, however, emerge from the experience more sensitive than they otherwise would have been to blue-collar victims of both cyclical and structural unemployment.

A highly paid chief operating officer of a large publishing operation saw his company sold out from under him and, for the third time in his life, found himself, at age fifty-four, looking for work. Religion was critical to him in each of the searches, he told me— so critical that he thought the churches in his affluent northern New Jersey suburban community should be doing something to help the many displaced executives who were "hiding" in the pews on Sundays, unknown and invisible to others in the congregation who were gatekeepers to jobs. He decided to get personally involved. With the pastor's permission, he recalled, "I got up one Sunday, went into the pulpit, and literally demanded that these people crawl out of their closets and come to see us." He also appealed to employers in the congregation to post job openings. He set up an outplacement service on his Catholic parish property (Most Blessed Sacrament Church, Franklin Lakes, N.J.), but he is quick to point out that "it serves a client group that is Catholic, Protestant, Jewish, and unchurched." There are "a lot of people out there waiting to take advantage of the unemployed," he told me. "We don't charge a dime, and they get suspicious about that because they've been running into a lot of people with their hands out who offer help with the résumé, with selling the house, and that sort of thing." Some lawyer-members of this affluent parish provide pro bono assistance in obtaining delays of mortgage foreclosures for about a year. Several foreclosures had occurred, he discovered, because people were hiding and neither neighbors nor parishioners were aware of the problem.

The parish sets aside 10 percent of its weekly income and puts it into a fund created to help those in need. Permission was obtained to apply those funds to the needs of both parishioners and nonparishioners who participate in the weekly outplacement sessions. Disbursements, based on a private discussion between the pastor and the person in need of help, take the form of grants, not loans.

The prime mover in the support-group activity in Franklin Lakes is himself a person who has had to deal with involuntary separation. He urges attendance at church (any church) as an expression of gratitude upon those who participate in the parish program. And, he claims, there is abundant evidence that the job search brings people back to regular church attendance.

In another city, it happened this way for a nonpracticing Catholic who found in the local Episcopal church "a weekly job support meeting which I attended." He went on to recall, "While attending the weekly meetings at St. Martin's Episcopal Church, I felt a strong attraction to the nave and sanctuary. In retrospect, I am certain that this was due to God's grace—in the form of a swift kick—and the presence of the reserved sacrament on the altar. I started attending church there and was married there two years later."

Curiously, another participant in this study, who also founded a parish-based support group for unemployed managers, had preferred to go it alone some years earlier when he lost his executive position. "While I had a strong faith and commitment to my church, my strength during the transition was more private. I did not reach out for support through church activities or spirituality groups." He is Episcopalian. His experience was not unlike that of a Catholic telemarketing executive who drew from his religion "peace of mind in a time of high anxiety."

A different experience is reported by the former manager of international corporate finance for a large bank; he moved into life insurance with the help of Episcopal church–based friends and later recalled, "Nearly all the friends to whom I turned for help in my networking effort were members of our church. Ultimately, I found my current job through an acquaintance at church." His advice: "Be active in your church; it will help you realize how fortunate you are. It is all relative. Count your blessings. Try to do good. Get on with your life. Don't harbor grudges. Keep your friends from all your old jobs."

The Career Initiatives Center (CIC) in Cleveland evolved in 1987 from a Presbyterian congregation's "Samaritan Network Program," founded in 1984 as a peer-support group for unemployed managers and professionals. The Samaritan program was based at Fairmount Presbyterian Church in Cleveland Heights. CIC now has close links with Job Seekers, an ongoing support group at St. Paul's Episcopal Church in Cleveland Heights. Those responsible for the program at St. Paul's decided against beginning their weekly sessions with a prayer because, they explained, they welcome persons from all religions or no religion at all, and they do not want to make anyone feel uncomfortable or excluded. Religion is not emphasized, but, I'm told, the power of prayer and the importance of divine guidance are often mentioned by members in open discussion. The focus of the meetings is on peer support—moral, practical, and often spiritual—of persons searching for employment. Similarly, CIC has no explicitly religious elements in its program, although reference to its church-based origins are included in all descriptive literature and an obvious faith-based inspiration motivates those who now run the program. The fee schedule suggests church-related origins and some operating subsidy. Membership dues are $10.00 per week for the first thirty weeks and $5.00 weekly thereafter. "Graduates" contribute a minimum of $100.00 within two months of successfully landing a job. Additional support comes from the Cleveland business community, civic organizations, churches, and individuals. Start-up funding in 1987 came from BP America, Ameritrust, the Episcopal Diocese of Ohio, and Fairmount Presbyterian Church.

All across the country there are church-based support groups for unemployed managers and professionals. They differ with regard to the integration of prayer and religious practice into the support process. For the most part, prayer is absent; any stepped-up frequency or intensity of religious practice is a private matter. In the vast majority of cases, clergy are not directly involved with the program, although they are supportive in providing space and some financial subsidies. Lay participation could easily be widened to include persons other than those looking for work and the enthusiasts, two or three typically, who spearhead the parish effort. Under the acronym EARN (Employment Assistance & Resource Network), a Yorktown Heights, New York, group, based at St. Patrick's Parish House, announces in a brochure that the group's "primary support will come from individuals in our own community who are willing to volunteer their time and energy in order to extend a helping hand to their neighbor in need." The support, provided free of charge, includes (1) providing encouragement and emotional support to both the job seeker and his or her family, (2) identifying and encouraging participation in job search training, (3) publicizing both job opportunities and the names of those looking for work, and (4) channeling resources from within the extended parish community to meet practical needs associated with the job search.

The potential for volunteer service focused on this one area of need is great. Church-related volunteer activity is not as extensive as one might expect. This could be because potential volunteers fear invading the privacy of those who are unemployed; these support groups do take on the character of an Alcoholics Anonymous chapter. Sadly, some shy away from the unemployed as if they were carriers of an infectious disease. But most, I suspect, are uninvolved because they have not been asked and have no idea how helpful they can be.

In Chicago, within a few blocks of the Loop, stands Old Saint Patrick's Church, home to the Crossroads Center for Faith and Work. Center founder John Fontana established, at Old St, Pat's, a support group for unemployed white-collar workers. I visited this group several times and was impressed with the gentle insistence by the volunteer facilitator, Tom Prost, a retired human resources executive, that guest presenters—HR people, executive recruiters, psychologists, and other experts—limit their talks to about twenty minutes in order to allow time for each of the forty or so members of the group to say not only a word about their employment goals but a few sentences about the strengths they bring to the table, based on their past training and experience. It is important, in Prost's view, to encourage participants to identify and focus on their positive attributes, not simply to point to their need for a job.

Churches and synagogues in virtually all parts of the country, some cooperatively, are trying to assist unemployed executives to get their bearings and find new jobs. I had noticed less of this kind of activity, relatively speaking, in the Jewish community, and asked a well-known rabbi for an explanation. He pointed out that many Jews are employed in family-owned businesses, and they have other means of resolving business differences and networking reemployment connections. There were, I noticed, Jewish participants in the several Christian church support groups I visited; there are also synagogue settings in the major cities where this kind of activity goes on.

In any case, it would be good, I think, for those who want to bring the institutions of organized religion closer to the problems to hear these comments from one of the more articulate participants in my study. He is a fifty-five-year-old Episcopalian who lives and works in the New York metropolitan area. He spoke of a Christian Career Development Workshop established by a group at a Presbyterian church in Greenwich, Connecticut. The workshop moved from church to church in the New York suburbs. "I first attended it at St. Catherine's Roman Catholic Church, and then I ran it for about a year at the First Presbyterian Church in Stamford. Aside from space, the churches contributed nothing to the workshop." He went on to say,

> The workshop did help me to believe that there was a path for me to discover, and it gave me support as I sought out that path. But the organized churches, as such, were useless in terms of help, possibly because they had bought into the "your job/your identity" syndrome. Many had good intentions, but not a clue in terms of practical help. Interestingly, the churches were cool to the idea of supporting or even publicizing our Christian Career Development Workshop because of a vague feeling that "it does not fit with our ministry." That has changed greatly in the past five years. Now many churches have career support groups—some useful, others only self-pity wallowing pits. Incidentally, I quit the Christian Career Development Workshop after about a year of leading it, when it was taken over by some charismatics who felt the message should be "Believe in Jesus and He will find you a job."

An equally articulate Catholic, a former trade association president, spoke with similar candor:

> *I believe that there is too little connection between what a parish pastor does day to day and the realities of the business world. In particular, the parish to which we officially belong [suburban Washington, D.C.] was headed at that time by an individual who followed the charismatic movement and believed it was more important to hold hands at Sunday Mass than to get down from the pulpit and deal with the realities of disenfranchised executives such as myself. I personally knew three other individuals who were in similar circumstances and wondered where the Church was at their time of need.*

He had a lot more to say along these lines, most of which he summarized in a closing comment: "My point in stating all of this is simply to suggest that the Church needs to become more involved in presenting some kind of message to the professional who does not currently have much of a connection with his church other than Sunday Mass and the weekly contribution."

What I saw in the course of this study verified that there is a widening opportunity for a response from religion to the plight of managerial men and women who are unemployed. The pain of every jobless person should, of course, be the concern of organized religion. Recent circumstances have made me aware of all the wilted white collars around these days, and I've noticed that large numbers of sidelined executives go to church or synagogue services with fair regularity, even though the institution does not speak immediately to their need. Significant numbers of unemployed managers say that the church has little to say to them about the meaning and purpose of life, particularly in the troubled circumstances of transition through "no-job land." And here again the distinction between religion and spirituality comes into play. As a fifty-two-year-old former manager of corporate price policy, now an independent consultant, put it, speaking for himself and his wife, "We are not 'religious' in the sense of any association with any organized religion; that is something we both consciously reject. We are, however, highly 'spiritual' in terms of our personal relationship with the Creator."

One critic, a forty-nine-year-old former public affairs executive, calls himself an "Episcopal-Catholic." In his view, "organized religion has failed miserably in this area. I can't help but think that this is not simply an isolated failure, but one that may be systemic in nature." He explains what he means by noting that

> for at least the past twenty years, organized religion—especially the mainline Protestant and Catholic traditions—has experienced dramatic decreases in active membership. This would seem to indicate that overall, organized religion is not meeting the basic spiritual needs of its members. The failure to respond to the unemployed is probably just one symptom of a far larger problem.

Others, without intending to (because it seems never to occur to them to do so), present a challenge to organized religion through comments like these, made by a Catholic woman, age forty-nine, who was let go as a corporate division manager and was just entering the transition: "Religion is not important to me. Spirituality is. As I'm moving toward this change, I often ask what would God want from me. How might I better serve my purpose in life as I develop a new business?" Good questions. Organized religion would be wise to become more involved in developing the substance of a response and the vocabulary to convey it.

Representatives of organized religion can often assist troubled but believing job seekers by explaining to them the distinction between the positive and the permissive will of God. Too often, good people think God is punishing them with misfortune, or if not punishing them, at least abandoning them in their troubled circumstances. Somehow or other, God "wills" their present hardship. In this case, religion has both the substance and the vocabulary for a helpful reply.

Here is how I attempted to explain it to a mixed group of Christian and Jewish job seekers when the question came up in a group discussion I had with them at the Career Initiatives Center in Cleveland. Maybe it is God's will that you lost your job as you did, or maybe it isn't. You have to distinguish between the positive will of God—what God really wants—and the permissive will of God—what God *permits* because He respects human freedom and refuses to impose His will on yours or anyone else's, including the person who may have treated you unfairly. Any one of us can choose to do something evil or just plain foolish, but we cannot say that God wills the result. God wills that we be free and wants us to use our freedom wisely. But God will not suppress human freedom and force anyone to do good. Nor will God reverse the laws of nature and suppress the human consequences of human acts or the natural consequences of natural forces—the law of gravity, for example, or the laws of learning and of natural growth and decline that affect all living beings. Miracles, of course, can happen, but God does not ordinarily suspend the laws of nature. Nor does God prevent unjust people from doing unjust things—even, perhaps, to you. What faith enables you to assert with certitude, however, is the conviction that God is always with you, at your side, protecting, helping, and loving you, no matter what.

In another setting, I sketched out these ideas for a fifty-one-year-old whose full-time employment as a senior marketing executive had ended three years earlier. As a younger man, he told me, he had begun "to question the seeming conflict between the concept of an almighty and all-loving God on one hand, and the existence of so much pain and suffering and evil in the world, on the other." He went on to say,

> I resolved the conflict in my own mind through what I call the concept of noninterventionism. Simply stated, the concept is that since the death of Jesus Christ, God has chosen not to intervene in the affairs of men. It follows, therefore, that prayer, in the sense of asking for God's help and influence, is futile. This is not to suggest that God does not care about man, only that he does not intervene.

He then remarked that his concept of noninterventionism may have some similarities with my notion of God's permissive will. But the experience of unemployment, he said, has had a negative impact on his Catholic faith, "the message of Job notwithstanding."

Ministers of religion and others associated with institutional religion can learn a lot from those whose faith sustained them through the ordeal of unemployment, although it is not to be assumed that this will always be the case, as the "noninterventionist" conclusion suggests. Here is the testimony of a thirty-seven-year-old Catholic, a vice president for finance who lost a $145,000-a-year job and was, when he wrote this to me, still looking:

> *My faith plays an important role in defining my values and priorities. I know that it allowed me to leave my position with great dignity and respect. It also provided a basis for establishing what would be important in my next job. It allowed me to face the severance with perspective on how "traumatic" this really was. I found myself praying that I allow myself to be open to the changes and challenges that would be coming, and that I accept them well. I also wanted to look to my faith to provide a long-term perspective on the decisions I would be making.*

> *I think the severance/reemployment experience has a bit of the "dying-resurrection" theme to it. My optimism about the opportunities that the "resurrection" could bring helped allow me to accept the "death" of severance. I also began to redefine what security and satisfaction really meant to me.*

If laypersons looking for work can speak like this in the vocabulary of organized religion (and many of them can), ministers who want to help should not be hesitant about opening up the conversation. When it comes to a discussion about the relevance of religion to the job-loss situation, both parties to the exchange—the job seeker and the minister of religion—have more of substance to bring to the conversation than they probably realize, and they also have, perhaps without knowing it, the vocabulary to make the conversation productive.

Men and women of faith are out of work and in need of help. Many of them (in my experience most of them) will welcome whatever help the ministers of religion can provide.

Chapter 7

THE NEW CORPORATE CONTRACT

*Whether the companies emerging as the new stars
of corporate America will add jobs as quickly as
some of the old-line giants are shearing them is
doubtful. But a certain amount of turmoil is part
of the natural renewal cycle that is inevitable and
ultimately healthy in a market economy, though it
is undeniably painful for the workers affected.*

—Stephen Lohr

"It used to be that you had a contract, now you're virtually working on a per-diem," said a displaced senior vice president of one of the major broadcasting companies. He and I were in a three-cornered conversation with another ousted executive from the same network. "We used to have careers, now we settle for jobs," said the other man. The first speaker continued, "The contract with corporate America is a thing of the past. If you're joining the corporate ranks today [1993], you have to understand that you won't be with one company more than ten years. Your guiding concept has to be: The corporation doesn't get me; I get them. There was an innocence about it in the past; now that innocence is gone." This man is probably the most cynical person I encountered in the course of this study; he was not burned out, just burned up as he exited the executive suite.

I asked him what advice he would give his son if that young man were entering the corporate ranks today. "Fake the niceties, feign the loyalty, and keep your eye on them because they're going to take you out!" In the matter of compensation, his counsel would be, "Go for as much as you can get at the front end, and don't count on much being there for you at the back end." There was a substantial amount for him at the back end of his own corporate career, however. Given that security (full benefits based on thirty years on the payroll) and the fact that he was just fifty-five, he became actively involved in television production ventures. "I feel good, whatever I'm doing now is me, not the network."

At the beginning of his career in the 1950s, this "organization man" had a contract and the expectation of orderly progress up the ladder, with increasing responsibility and compensation along the way. It was a contingent contract, of course, with no guarantee of permanence. But that was never really made explicit; at least, it was not at the forefront of the consciousness of either party to the contract. Both sides took the long view. They just assumed they would grow old together.

This was particularly true in banking. Many bankers I met spoke of the normal expectation of "womb-to-tomb" security in that industry. Their own American Bankers Association sponsored a book, published in 1992, that would have been unthinkable when the organization men settled into banking careers several decades earlier. Its title: *Career Alternatives for Bankers: How to Use Your Background in Banking to Find Another Job.*

What was once presumed to be a long-term "relational contract" can no longer be relied upon to sustain an uninterrupted employment relationship over time. What brings managerial employees and their employers together in corporate America is now more of a transactional contract; the transaction and the concomitant employment may be short-lived. Both parties to the employment transaction (the new corporate contract) negotiate the arrangement in a new way. The manager, wanting to be hired, says, in effect, "If you hold me contingent, I'll hold you contingent." He or she will settle in, but not too comfortably; other options will always be explored, front-end financial considerations will be more important than they were in more stable times, and severance packages will be filled and neatly wrapped before the job begins. Not only will other options be considered as the ink is drying on the new employment contract, but actual offers will be entertained at any time, although this, too, will be negotiated by many opportunity-seeking managers in a new way.

The broadcast executive I quoted above explained the new way of proceeding. First, he said, wherever you are working, be serious but quiet about building up your own skills bank. Then, at any time,

> *when expressions of interest come your way, act surprised and flattered. Regard the inquiry as an invitation to dance with the prom queen; you've always wanted to dance with that girl. It doesn't make any difference if you want the job or not, just make up your mind to get it. And once you get it—a bona fide offer—then sit back and ask yourself if you want to take it. Be careful, though, and look both ways—to the source of your present paycheck and to potential employers outside. Your body throws off vibes; people smell that you are thinking about moving on. But don't be too cool, and coy, and laid back about it, or you'll lose the offer. Let them think you'd kill for the job. Only when you get it, then decide if you want to take it.*

Free Agency Attitudes

Another term for this approach is free-agent management, an idea borrowed from baseball and used as the title of an article by Paul Hirsch in the *National Business Employment Weekly* (May 29, 1988). "Whether they lost jobs or watched others lose theirs, smart workers from the CEO down to the clerical staff, are investing less ego and self-esteem in any company or position," writes Hirsch.

> *These managers are now thinking like free agents. They're beginning to look out for themselves, find out how much they are worth and consider offers from other teams.... Free agents make it a point always to know their alternatives, to have a clear idea of where they could jump if unexpected roadblocks arise in the present job. They work*

*hard at their current jobs but never take them for granted.
They direct much of their energy toward shaping and
securing their futures.*

The free agent will not jump unless a safe landing is assured;
he or she is well aware that the best way to get a new job is to be
effective, and appear to be content, in an old one.

The change in the corporate contract, which left countless
managers jobless as the calendar closed out the 1980s and opened
up the decade of the 1990s, reflects shifts in the corporate culture
in America. As defined by the theologian Bernard Lonergan, culture is "a set of meanings and values informing a common way of
life, and there are as many cultures as there are distinct sets of
meanings and values." Anthropologist Clifford Geertz views culture as a "pattern of meanings embodied in symbols." There is a
new search for meaning in business; there are also new symbols
defining the business environment.

Cultures change as values change, as convictions shift about
the meaning of life and work. Symbols change too; this becomes
noticeable, for example, when bosses are called by their first
names and casual dress creeps into and around the executive
suite. Values like participation change the composition and style of
the typical business meeting when they begin to dominate a given
business culture. And when they do, management styles shift
toward more delegation and away from tight control.

Loyalty is a value that means different things to different people these days; it is now expressed differently or not at all in corporate America. Under the old contract, loyalty went from the
employee to the employer; no one questioned that. Security was
received in return, but those who did not own the enterprise seldom thought of this security in terms of the company's being loyal
to them, but in terms of its being fair to them. The company, like
Gibraltar, was just there—dependable, reliable, predictable.
Employees at all levels were loyal. Employers, some of them
unapologetically paternalistic, were simply there.

One of my respondents, an executive in a small consulting
firm, saw his situation as "somewhat unique, although it seems to

be happening more and more." He was part of a small enterprise that was downsizing,

> when all of a sudden, a very senior person—in order to save himself—decided to leave the company. The other loyal employees and shareholders decided to do what was best for those who remained. After a period of analysis, the decision was made to wind down the firm and seek new opportunities.... Our former partner and CEO decided he would be more secure elsewhere. We were left holding the bag. However, life goes on and so do we.

He viewed this as "morally wrong and shameful conduct on the part of one individual toward his partners and employees."

It is not unique, however. It is happening in large and small organizations, throughout the employment ranks—top to bottom—and has become, regrettably, a sign of the times. At the corporate board level, there is little evidence that this sign is being read. Few if any board committees have exclusive oversight responsibility for the organization's human resource function; I know of no board committee whose chief concern is human dignity and human values within the corporation.

Another participant in my study, a chief operating officer who turned successfully to consulting after his ouster, explained:

> My view is that corporate America—and all industrialized countries—will face a new revolution as the "corporate contract" disappears. Loyalty is a vanishing commodity. When the employer has no integrity or sense of responsibility, then the employee merely works and doesn't give any loyalty in return. This failure of mutual commitment will continue to reduce our industrial giants to has-beens. What effective, innovative people will continue to work in a culture like this? What kind of employee will agree to exist in this environment?

He sees this, however, in terms of "a generation of change. The whole thing will resettle in the form of smaller companies, not so impersonal." Smaller companies, nimbler managers—this appears to be the wave of the future. The old corporate battleships are yielding to new, more maneuverable corporate cruisers, with corresponding adjustments in crew.

One of the participants in my study, a forty-four-year-old president of a small technical services company, warns that managers should be alert to early signs that a separation is on its way.

> *I was actually more concerned about the company than the owners were. The owners, only concerned about themselves, were all too ready to sell the business. Early signs—in my case, character problems with ownership—are real warnings to get out. Several years before I was fired, I knew my long-range plans did not include this company.*

"Be loyal to yourself first" is the free-agent mentality. Downsize and outsource when the numbers (shrinking margins and earnings declines) tell you to is the corporate mentality; be willing to outplace managers, and don't think you have to carry them when they are no longer adding value or carrying their own weight.

Many middle managers are finding that top management really regarded them all along as conduits; they are now being replaced by better information systems. They are also the victims of downsizing and delayering strategies that spread their work over fewer remaining people. Repeatedly, middle managers told me that they will never again put the company's interest ahead of their own; they join in a chorus of rejection of the notion of company loyalty. One of them said that he would advise any manager, "Don't turn down an opportunity to put yourself in front of a CEO; you never know where it will take you." Another added: "The days of forty-year, one-company careers are over. If you stay with one company, you will not have a broad enough range to take the top job. The one constant in the workplace today is change."

The Economist of London used the headline "The Death of Corporate Loyalty" on an article (April 3, 1993) reporting that "big firms are shedding jobs not merely to cut costs, but also to change the very way they are managed.... [These firms] are tearing up the implicit contract they have always had with managers and other professionals: security of long-term employment in exchange for dogged loyalty." The *Economist* sees this crumbling of the contract and erosion of loyalty happening throughout corporate America and in Europe as well. And no new contract, particularly no new psychological contract, is emerging to humanize the relationship, to set the ground rules that might reduce uncertainty and clarify expectations between the company and what we used to call company men and, more recently, company women.

Why the Change?

The change in management style that has made the axe a prominent management tool is not easily explained. In part, it is a move toward delegating authority, granting autonomy, and fixing responsibility at lower levels. The discovery that "half our management team is writing reports for the other half to read" strengthens the will of those who think that a weight-reduction program for the elimination of middle-management spread may be overdue. They are willing to try it to see what happens.

Delayered managers, or "redundant executives," as they are known in England, have to wait to see what happens from an observation post on the outside. Something could happen that would reengage them, although not reemploy them, with the former employer. Once you are out, it is a short attitudinal step, but a large one entrepreneurially, to stop thinking of yourself as an outsider—a former employee—and to begin seeing yourself in an "outsourcer" capacity (one who supplies resources to the company from the outside); you become a new entrepreneur who can provide a needed service to the company for which you used to work. You can, in fact, provide from the outside the service you used to provide from within, as an employee. Now you do it for a fee. Your former employer "outsources" the need; you meet it— for a fee. You do it for other firms too. This is your new business. The firms pay you more on a per-diem basis but less in total compensation (since you receive no benefits) than they would if you were on their payroll. You make it up on volume and take care of your own benefits. You also have independence and the challenge of being your own boss.

For well over a decade now, most of the job creation in America has occurred in small businesses, and most of these businesses are in the service sector. If you are at work today in a large corporation, said one of my respondents, "you should have an exit strategy." He was the victim of a hostile takeover; he now runs a small company for less than he earned heading a division of a large publishing conglomerate. His advice to the young MBA just entering the employment market: "Think small and think services. Realize that an employment offer is just an invitation to take your first job. Don't trip over yourself in negotiations because this is just the first in a series of jobs you will hold. Get this one, but go into it with full knowledge that you will be moving on."

One of my respondents, a former CEO just over fifty, is my guide to the new world of downsizing and outsourcing, and the new opportunities for self-employment in an information-based, service-driven economy. His separation from his last formal tie with an organization—chairman and CEO of a medical management corporation—was not really involuntary; at his recommendation, he and his partners liquidated the company. Nor did he lose his earlier chairmanship of Diners Club, a subsidiary of Citibank; he left it. His career, says James R. Emshoff, has never been "the standard corporate stuff." He has blended the academic (Wharton School faculty) with business (notably Campbell Soup and Diners Club) and the consulting world, where he now works (from his home in the Chicago suburb of Lake Forest, Illinois). Author of *The New Rules of the Game: The Four Key Experiences Managers Must Have to Thrive in the Non-Hierarchical 90s and Beyond* (Harper Business, 1991), Emshoff writes "to help middle managers through tough career decisions." In order to advance and hold onto their positions in the 1990s, says Emshoff, middle managers will have to show evidence of "people relationship skills, customer orientation, leadership, and risk-taking." He is very big on the idea of getting close to your customers, a concept that can be applied within large organizations by top management, who should regard those at work on lower levels in the same organization as "customers" who should be seen, known, talked to, and heard from on a continuing basis. Wisely, Emshoff warns senior managers that they have one important quality that is absent in the ranks of middle management, namely, "enthusiasm for your job and a commitment to your company."

Whether retaining or replacing middle managers, top managers are dealing with free agents, or at least with elements of the free agent mentality. This idea should not be too difficult for them to grasp because more and more senior executives are showing signs of free agency themselves—witness the lineup of CEOs willing to be considered to replace John Akers as chairman of IBM in 1993. Although some who were approached declined, it is clear that other fully employed, highly effective, and apparently satisfied executives were ready and willing to make the move.

It would be a good thing for both parties to the new corporate contract, whatever form it takes, to regard the exit mentality as symptomatic of a new and acceptable way of corporate life. Both sides should plan for it. Employers should encourage it. Managers in particular should acknowledge, at least to themselves, that there is something wrong with them if they have no plans at all for future moves.

Another way of imagining what the corporate culture will be like in years ahead, as free agency spreads and the entrepreneurial spirit is embodied within managers who work for large organizations, is to look at the Congress of the United States. Just for purposes of illustration, imagine that there are 250 Democrats in the 435-member House of Representatives. Absent meaningful campaign finance reform—i.e., no change in the present necessity for never-ending, personal, political fund raising in order to be reelected every two years—we have 250 individual political entrepreneurs who call themselves Democrats, instead of 250 members of the Democratic party who view themselves as Representatives, working together in the U.S. Congress. They are individualists. They owe their loyalty not to the party, but to those who support their reelection efforts. And this kind of loyalty may or may not coincide with what is best for the nation the Congress is there to serve.

Imagine now the large business corporation. Even though the large corporation now exists in an era of consent—large organizations exist because others allow them to—the shareholders cannot be relied upon, as they could be in an earlier era of proxy passivity, to keep top management securely in place. Nor can boards of directors be controlled by the *primus inter pares* who holds the combined office of chairman and CEO. Outside directors are now a force to be reckoned with. In one week in early 1993, newly assertive boards of directors in three of this country's major corporations—Westinghouse, IBM, and American Express—invited their chief executive officers to pursue other interests. General Motors led the way in 1992, first by announcing a massive restructuring plan and then by ousting the chairman. Too big, perhaps, to be taken over by hostile suitors, these corporations are not too big to be immune to pressure from major institutional investors, chief among them the California Public Employees' Retirement System (Calpers).

There has always been turnover at the top of American corporations; however, it has become more frequent and thus more noticeable. Now, also, when turnover occurs, it is presumed that new leadership will follow a "lean and mean" strategy, cut costs by reducing employment, and bring a smaller, more efficient organization into closer contact with its customers. "The Axeman Cometh" was the headline over a feature in the *Economist* of London when Louis Gerstner replaced John Akers at IBM on April 1, 1993.

Managers in America, therefore, are living in a new corporate world. At the very top, they are less secure, although they are much more generously compensated. At lower levels, managerial men and women are less inclined to rely on the corporation for their security, more inclined toward entrepreneurial behavior within the corporation (as are partisan politicians within Congress), and always open to new opportunities that match their developing ensemble of managerial skills. This is a new entrepreneurial age *within* well-established corporations, not to mention the creation of new entrepreneurial opportunities outside the old corporations that now turn to outsourcing as a necessary, post-downsizing business strategy. If you are inside and cannot show that you are adding value, you will not be there long. If you are outside, ready to meet outsourcing requests but unable to deliver value to the downsized corporation, you have a new business idea that is going nowhere. In this new world, the managerial posture of preference, inside or outside the large organization, is "Heads up!" and "On your toes!"

An interesting perspective on this is taken by an executive manager for systems, who was separated involuntarily from a large computer manufacturer at age forty-six. He still thinks that "you should make a substantial commitment to your employer, because without that commitment you cannot expect career and compensation progression." "However," he adds, "you should always leave a piece of commitment for yourself. This will ensure that you are properly postured and have the resources, contacts, and skills necessary for a change of jobs or a career transition." You should at all times in this manager's view, "be at least semipositioned to change employers, so that you can hit the street running when and if it becomes necessary."

When I discussed these changing attitudes with Jim Herget, then managing director of Korn/Ferry, the executive search firm, in his Cleveland office, he commented that top executives should make a point of empowering their employees and staying in touch with their suppliers. And, as for a manager's personal stance in the new corporate environment: "Be highly flexible around an inflexible set of core values—God, family, country, job." Persons looking for security and long-term satisfaction in the corporate world will often be disappointed, said Herget; the organization of the future will be "smaller, with more rolling, contingent relationships." He reminded me that today's young adults are more hesitant and cynical in approaching the corporation because of what they have seen happen to their fathers. This explains much of their interest in benefit negotiations, a matter often taken for granted in days gone by.

As I indicated above, I learned a lot from Jim Emshoff, to whom I was introduced by Ted Jadick, a veteran executive recruiter with Heidrick & Struggles. Much of what I learned relates to the new corporate contract and changes in corporate culture.

For openers, Emshoff pointed out that

the 1980s turned out to be a decade when American companies made a 180-degree turn in their operating philosophies. The "bigger-the-better" principle that drove conglomerate growth at the start of the decade is dead. Today's downsized company is focused on niche markets with a "good-things-come-in-small-packages" orientation.

He sees new options opening up for the delivery of management services. Outsourcing is the way to go for supplies and services once delivered from within the corporation. "Properly managed independent suppliers are generally more effective than in-house functions," in Emshoff's view. He visualizes a time "when companies won't have any infrastructure functions; they will be replaced by very flat operating units that are supported by variable cost suppliers of management services." These, of course, represent new business opportunities, and those best positioned to respond to the opportunities are often the persons who once delivered the services from within. They and their function may now be "out" as a result of downsizing, but the function is still needed, and someone will have to provide it. Why not the person who knew both the function and the company well before downsizing rearranged the players in this game?

Mr. Emshoff has begun a new company, based at home. The name of the venture, IndeCap Enterprises, Inc., is a contraction of the services he can provide, namely, helping companies develop *Inde*pendent *Cap*ability *Enterprises* to serve the parent company but stand alone as profit-making independent businesses. He sees downsizing as only a partial solution to the broader problem of corporate restructuring; by itself, downsizing does not produce better financial outcomes for a company. "The danger is not that we will overshoot the restructure target, but that we will use only one tool—the downsizing hammer—when there are many other options available. My fear is that when we see poor returns from a particular downsizing program, we will inappropriately conclude we've gone far enough and freeze off any other strategy options for restructuring." What he sees as certain is a movement away from traditional functionalized organizations separated by rigid communications barriers. Some of those functions will be spun off into independent enterprises, but the barriers to communication will have to fall first, if this is going to happen with the most efficiency and least pain. Typically, spinoffs will retain some relationship to the parent company. But as outsourcing becomes a more normal business practice, new, completely independent and autonomous firms, established by the new entrepreneurs, will emerge to meet market demand.

I first heard the term *outsourcing* many years ago in the context of automobile parts production. Now, according to Jim Emshoff, "there are legitimate outsourcing options for every in-house function." That may sound like an exaggeration, but after reading "How Continental Bank Outsourced Its 'Crown Jewels'" (*Harvard Business Review*, January–February 1993), I'm not convinced that it is. Richard Huber, vice chairman of Continental, explains in the article that his organization is in the banking business, not the business of managing information systems. Therefore, it made sense for Continental Bank to give up complete internal control of its information technology and enter into a ten-year contract with the Integrated Systems Solutions Corporation.

The operative concept here depends on an accurate identification of your "core competency," followed by a determination to become world class in the practice of that competency. And instead of thinking in terms of vertical integration, the corporation should be thinking of forging customer-supplier linkages—horizontal networks of business partnerships.

Mr. Emshoff now writes, edits, and publishes the *IndeCap Newsletter*, which, in Issue No. 2, 1992, outlined the IndeCap position on outsourcing, noting that it will play a positive and rapidly increasing role in corporate restructuring strategies. "Functions that would never have been considered as candidates for Outsourcing will be evaluated as a Make or Buy decision on very pragmatic grounds—'Can I support the *success of my core business capabilities* better through a captive or through a purchased supplier relationship in each non-core function?'" The IndeCap position is that when such evaluations are made objectively, "purchased services will mushroom from today's levels." The future looks good for outsource suppliers. Companies, meanwhile, will be separating out what Emshoff calls their core competencies from their in-house support functions, and mentally classifying their internal support functions "as winners or losers if they had to compete for the internal business and sell services to external clients."

If outsourcing is to become a tool for restructuring the American corporation, downsizing is the reduction-in-force lever that, once thrown, makes outsourcing indispensable for the maintenance of services and functions needed to operate the core business of the downsized corporation. The restructuring question as it affects the future of the corporate contract is: With whom will the downsized corporation contract to supply the function, service, or even material previously provided from within? The supplier may be a more entrepreneurial, quasi-independent group within the corporation, now functioning as a supplier to other divisions or groups in the corporation while "competing," at the level of price and quality with any and all outside suppliers who may want the business. Or, the supplier could be an outside group, founded or strengthened by displaced employees of the downsized corporation. In either case, new, entrepreneurial energies will be prerequisite for success. And, in either case, entrepreneurship will involve risks and rewards that were not part of the old corporate contract.

The Change Is "Discontinuous"

During his own transition from corporate payroll to self-employment, Jim Emshoff was influenced by the British management thinker Charles Handy, whose *The Age of Unreason* (Harvard Business School Press, 1990) rests on the assumptions that discontinuous change is now affecting corporate life, that changes in the organization of work make a big difference in the way we live, and "that discontinuous change requires discontinuous upside-down thinking to deal with it, even if both thinkers and thoughts appear absurd at first sight" (pp. 5–6). Among the many propositions produced by "upside-down thinking" is one that suggests that "we should stop talking and thinking of employees and employment" (p. 25). Organizations are going to have fewer, but better qualified, people inside, and more people outside "who are contracted, not employed" (p. 52). The book is well worth reading.

Organizations are changing shape, says Handy; they are taking on a shamrock configuration. The first leaf represents core workers, the essential people. The second leaf represents work contracted out (the outsourcing solution). The third leaf is "the flexible labor force, all those part-time workers and temporary workers who are the fastest growing part of the employment scene" (p. 93). Since services cannot be stockpiled as factory products can, the preponderance of third-leaf activity will be in the service sector, and the come-and-go providers of those services will often be highly skilled professionals. In the good old days of employment contracts, these workers would have been on corporate payrolls as full-time employees. Now they are flexible, self-employed freelancers, paid in fees, not wages or salaries, who can draw little comfort from Handy's observation: "Self-employed people cannot by law or logic be unemployed, only broke."

If the organization man carried an attaché case into corporate America and remained there for full careers in decades past, Handy sees "portfolio people" (those on leaf two and leaf three of his shamrock) moving in and around corporations in the decades ahead. The "work portfolio" will not be filled with just one thing, the Job; rather, it will have compartments for wage and salary work, fee work, homework, gift work (pro bono, community service), and study work. "As more and more people move their paid work outside organizations, or are moved, they are pushed or lured into becoming small independent businesses. They are paid in fees, not wages, and have to develop their own portfolios of customers and of activities." And unlike the organization man of the past, who was handcuffed to his attaché case and wedded to his job, these new-age managers will demonstrate a higher regard for leisure.

Call it free agency, freelancing, being in business for yourself, or being the manager of a personal portfolio filled with (1) pay-check-related work, (2) fee-for-service work, (3) consulting-contract work, and (4) a mixed assortment of entrepreneurial risks and rewards—whatever you call it, you are talking about the other side, the new-age side, of the corporate contract.

Other changes will have to accompany this shift in corporate culture, this new configuration of the corporate contract. Prominent among them will be some form of universal health-care insurance coverage that is not directly linked to an employment relationship, and complete portability of pension benefits from one job to another.

In order to retain some semblance of psychological stability amid the uncertainties of this new corporate context, managers will have to become accustomed to, not threatened by, change. They will have to be self-starters, committed to productive activity that matches their interests and talents, rather than being committed to a particular corporation for both employment and self-identity (they will no longer depend on being "with the XYZ Corporation" for purposes of easy self-identification). As Paul Hirsch put it,

> *Whether they are ball players or corporate managers, free agents' satisfaction is rooted in what psychologists call their "internal locus of control." Their motivation is not controlled by a coach or boss they wish to please. Even though they may work at a company for many years, they always retain some emotional distance from the office ties that bind and potentially blind them to better opportunities elsewhere. In this sense they act like free-lancers, even if they are based inside the corridors of a particular corporation.*

Within the flattened corporation, there will be more of the entrepreneurial spirit animating the managers who continue to work there full time. It's not that thousands of individual entrepreneurs will be pitted in competition among themselves under one corporate roof, rather, there will be teams, competing units, guided by competing managerial groups, all under the same tent and all with an eye to the outside, not so much to discover "what the competition is doing" as to survey the landscape of opportunities for them "out there." And from time to time, teams will break away together to form new business organizations.

It should surprise no one to discover that the emotional distance between the corporation and its managers, now emerging in the wake of the death of corporate loyalty, goes both ways. "Never let yourself become emotionally dependent on an employer," said a manager who had done just that with IBM. "An employer may in good conscience seem to offer lifetime employment and benefits, but that will only last while the margins allow it," he told me. "Employer loyalty decreases in direct proportion to lower margins."

Calling the late-1992, early-1993 turmoil in corporate America "healthy but painful," Stephen Lohr was prompted by the upheavals at IBM, Westinghouse, Sears, Boeing, McDonnell Douglas, and other corporate icons to write in *The New York Times* (Jan. 28, 1993):

> *Whether the companies emerging as the new stars of corporate America will add jobs as quickly as some of the old-line giants are shearing them is doubtful. But a certain amount of turmoil is part of the natural renewal cycle that is inevitable and ultimately healthy in a market economy, though it is undeniably painful for the workers affected.*

I saw a lot of that pain in the course of this study. The best form of pain relief, of course, is a new and satisfying job. Some readers of this book are men and women who wonder if they are ever going to work again; they are still in pain. Others will be managers pausing from new employment routines to read this—some motivated by standard reader curiosity, some just interested in seeing their own transition experience in a better interpretative framework. The danger for repositioned managers in the forty-to-fifty-five age bracket is that they will think they are starting over again in a familiar corporate world. If their new surroundings are so familiar and predictable as to give them cocoonlike comfort, they have probably hitched their careers to the wrong corporate engines. Things have changed. Where life in corporate America appears not to have changed, there is a good bet waiting to be taken by those who are sure change is on its way.

> A *new generation of workers, inside and outside large organizations, with a different view of organizational life, is about to confront the realities of doing business in a new America.*
>
> *The new America is an environment of economic uncertainty, global competition, and managerial myopia. In the new America, old answers no longer suffice. In the new America, the economy remains at risk; the false gods of management still stalk the landscape; foreign competitors continue to outperform and outsmart us.*
>
> *Whatever the problems of the nations and whatever their causes, they will not be solved by the organization man. The organization man's watch is about to end.* (Paul Leinberger and Bruce Tucker, The New Individualists, *Harper Collins, 1991, p. 412.)*

For more on the implications of all of this for managers, consider what Susan Cohen has to say in "White Collar Blues," *Washington Post Magazine* (Jan. 17, 1993). The article appeared as the nation emerged from the only recession in the past thirty years in which there was more white- than blue-collar job loss, and where many of those white-collar jobs would never be seen again. Prompted by a special interest in middle managers who are, for the first time in their lives, experiencing a sense of economic vulnerability, the writer attended a monthly meeting of the Washington chapter of Forty Plus, a nationwide support network for over-forty out-of-work managers and executives. One of them, age fifty, told her that there had been a "social contract" between members of his generation and the corporations where they thought they would be employed for their entire working lives. "There's an awful lot of people who wanted to put their life and loyalty into something and were willing to take less money for the security—it doesn't exist [anymore]"; the contract has been broken. The article goes on to report:

Middle-class people are not just losing jobs. They're not get-
ting equivalent ones back. When they find employment after
being displaced, it's usually at lower pay, and often ... it's
part-time or contractual work. Temporary workers tripled
from 1982 to 1990, according to the Bureau of Labor
Statistics, which also reports that some 6.3 million people
who work part time really want to work full time.

This is the situation Charles Handy explains as the third leaf
of his shamrock organization. These people probably should get
used to the idea that they will not be working for any single
employer full time, which is not to say that they will not be fully
engaged with meaningful work in a diversified work portfolio.

In her *Washington Post Magazine* article, Susan Cohen passes
along advice from Richard Koonce, who runs the Washington office
of EnterChange, an Atlanta-based outplacement firm. "When his
clients are ready to listen," writes Cohen, "Koonce advises them on
how to make their own opportunities but with smaller, newer firms.
Or with self-employment." Here is what he says:

We're seeing people making transitions into contractual
employment, interim assignments, working on a trial basis
for a year or two, consulting, self-employment—more cre-
ative solutions. Any job-seekers who limit themselves to
thinking about full-time permanent employment are going to
have a hard time.[This kind of arrangement] can be lucra-
tive. It's virtually full time. There are some real advantages.
Working as a contractor gives you some freedom and flexibil-
ity. We're seeing more and more professionals do this in bank-
ing, law, telecommunications.

Koonce admits that this is not for everyone. It is chiefly for
people between thirty and fifty who have "the ability to live with
ambiguity." It is for those "who are willing to hustle," he says. "I
think that's the name of the game now, being willing to hustle."

Energy and Answers from Within

This is another reminder to the job seeker that self-assessment is crucially important. Before beginning a job campaign, an individual has to know how strong the traces of passive dependency are within his or her personality. Is there sufficient energy from within for independent, entrepreneurial activity? Is there tolerance for both risk and ambiguity? Is there enough resourcefulness to put together a work portfolio that will deliver the income, satisfaction, and fulfillment that match the goals the individual sets for his or her working life? It is also important to have the right ensemble of skills and to be able to post an honest account of achievements. But these questions, which only you can answer, and the answers to which have to come from within, are the ones that will be on the minds of those who may be thinking of hiring you full time, contracting with you for services needed, or having you stand by for well-compensated short-term work that you can fit into your portfolio along with additional work you are doing for other purchasers of your services, or maybe doing just for yourself in this new corporate culture. In the sprightly language of *Time* magazine (March 29, 1993),

> *This is the new metaphysics of work. Companies are portable, workers are throwaway. The rise of the knowledge economy means a change, in less than 20 years, from an overbuilt system of large, slow-moving economic units to an array of small, widely dispersed economic centers, some as small as the individual boss. In the new economy, geography dissolves, the highways are electronic. Even Wall Street no longer has a reason to be on Wall Street. Companies become concepts and in their dematerialization, become strangely conscienceless. And jobs are almost as susceptible as electrons to vanishing into thin air.*

To focus on the "who is getting laid off?" question is interesting, but perhaps more important is the question of why layoffs are happening. Market forces are at work, of course, often in the form of foreign competition. But technological change may be the key variable for explaining what is going on (and off) in the American economy. In explaining "Why Job Growth Is Stalled" (*Fortune*, March 8, 1993), Myron Magnet notes that the "technological revolution includes all the ways that computer and communications technologies have changed economic life." He lists examples of computer-controlled manufacturing processes with large labor displacement effects, and quotes Peter Drucker's view that "the labor content of manufactured goods, which has been going down since 1900, is going to keep on going down, not so much because of automation but because the new growth products require less and less labor and raw material." Magnet then writes: "Consider microchips, the preeminent product of our era: Compared with the auto, the hallmark product of the preceding age of manufacturing, these electronic components derive a much higher proportion of their market value from intellect than from either material or labor."

There's the key: the primacy of intellect over both material and labor as a source of value. As I mentioned earlier, the availability of computerized management information systems has led top management to conclude that many middle managers are little more than conduits that can be replaced by new systems. Magnet points out that these new systems are powerful enough to knit "global corporations into unified wholes," and he notes that Milton Friedman sees this technological revolution as making it "possible to produce a product anywhere, using resources from anywhere, by a company located anywhere, to be sold anywhere." This is why U.S. corporations find it desirable and managerially feasible to export not just jobs but factories overseas, and why American labor is deeply troubled by the prospect of more blue-collar job erosion.

There will be job growth in the domestic U.S. economy, but at moderate rates and mainly in service industries, not in manufacturing. The application of intellect will always be needed in a technological society, and the application of technology to services will be the road taken by successful new businesses and expanding small businesses. Moreover, providers of human services and managers of human effort will always be needed. Those most likely to succeed in meeting the new managerial challenges will, in my view, be persons committed to their own continuing intellectual and personal development; those who are human, confident, ambitious, and flexible; those who are sufficiently open to get along well with others in a more democratized, less hierarchical business culture. As one of my respondents insists, and I will let him speak for himself in Chapter 9, where job-seeking strategies are discussed, you should build your employment future on what he calls your "scar tissue," your past education, past experience, and present skills—being careful to nurture the continuing development of all three all the time.

What all this means to the job seeker is summed up by one who has been through it himself and volunteers a lot of his time in counseling others: "There is nothing wrong in considering yourself to be a 'product' or 'service' that has to be marketed. Look at bosses as if they were your customers or clients. Establish your own personal R&D program to keep yourself current. And no matter where you are working, always act as if you were a self-employed entrepreneur." These are the words of Torrey Foster, who says that they describe the new reality of employment in America today.

This must not, however, be permitted to remain a one-sided responsibility, looking only to an employee's need to stay flexible. There are responsibilities on the employer's side, too. If met, they will create a new form of corporate loyalty as part of the new corporate contract. Enlightened corporations will put a higher priority on shared goals—i.e., a sharing of vision, values, and objectives with employees, especially managerial employees. It will, in my opinion, become a characteristic of the "good" corporation that it provides career enrichment programs that help employees, including senior management, identify and develop their marketable skills, thus enhancing their employability elsewhere. Whether employees do this on their own or with the assistance of the corporation, those who are openly considering or even seeking other opportunities will not be labeled disloyal, just aware of the new corporate realities. We are not there yet in the world of work, but that's the way it will have to be if the new corporate contract is going to work.

If continuous employment in a given corporation cannot be guaranteed, it is wise and responsible activity on the employer's part to encourage those who could become victims of downsizing (and that includes just about everyone) to maintain their employability and marketability.

There was a time when the question, "Are you interested in transferring?" within an organization could not be taken at face value as a clear signal that certain advancement lay ahead; it was often just a test of loyalty. The only safe answer was a noncommittal, "I'm always interested in challenges." Things are changing. True, employees have a personal responsibility for their own career development, with or without help from their employers. But forward-thinking companies are now acknowledging a new responsibility to give their employees the tools to expand their employability, even though those tools may become tickets to opportunities elsewhere.

Good employers will provide the tools. Wise employees (all of whom are potential job seekers in this contingent employment universe) will use them well. Actual job seekers will find jobs faster and remain reconnected longer if they appreciate this new understanding of loyalty in the new corporate culture.

Chapter 8

GUIDING
PRINCIPLES

*View the transition as a rebirth that has to come
from within.*

—*A Reemployed Marketing Manager*

Principles are initiating impulses; they are internalized convictions that produce action. Principles direct your choices and guide your activities. Principles are beginnings; they originate the proceedings that lead to hoped-for outcomes. In matters of personal choice, your principles provide a definition of who you are, what you want to do, and where you want to go.

In talking with managerial men and women who are, or have been, in transition from one job to another, I learned that a variety of principles operate as directional signals or guidelines to help them make their way through "no-job land" to reemployment. Sometimes these guidelines function as guardrails to help keep job seekers and their search on track.

This chapter lifts from their experience those principles they would recommend to others. I am functioning here as a kind of editor and processor of the directional ideas that influenced them, not as an originator of the principles being articulated.

A Philadelphia banker, for example, took to heart advice given by Lee Iacocca to a mutual friend: "Don't make the same mistake I did; don't waste time trying to get even." Many guiding principles will be negative phrases stated for a positive purpose. On a positive note, this same person told me he would advise others to "take time to understand who you are, not what you do." That principle is operative within his own family, where, he reports, "the members are appreciated for who they are, not for individual achievements; we are not afraid of failure, nor do we hide from it."

Many job seekers borrow principles articulated by others and hold them up for their own guidance and introspection. For example, John Henry Newman's often-quoted reflection appeals to some: "In a higher world it is otherwise, but here below to live is to change, and to be perfect is to have changed often." "These days," said one person in this study, "change is not something you manage, it's something you do."

Many transitioners I met adopted a principle "not to dwell on the past" or "not to look back." Poet Samuel Hazo provides them with a rationale for this when he asks, "Can days of making sense/ of days that make no sense/ make sense?" Most executives in transition eventually conclude that no, it doesn't make sense to dwell on the past, but they have trouble getting rid of the anger. For most, the anger and resentment never completely disappear.

When Steven J. Ross, the controversial and highly compensated chairman of Time Warner, died in 1993, a group of family, friends, and associates paid for a full-page advertisement in the *New York Times* to reprint a poem by Emerson that Ross "carried as his talisman":

To laugh often and much;

To win the respect of intelligent people and the affection of children;

To earn the appreciation of honest critics and endure the betrayal of false friends;

To appreciate beauty, to find the best in others;

To leave the world a bit better, whether by a healthy child, a garden patch or a redeemed social condition;

To know even one life has breathed easier because you lived.

This is to have succeeded.

A talisman, your dictionary will remind you, is a special object, often engraved, thought to act as a charm. I didn't hear that word often, but I did hear *mantra* used to describe sayings that offered support and guidance for the advancement of a job campaign. One executive calls them "keepers," sayings to be kept in mind and in the card file. More often, I heard "words of wisdom" as a descriptive phrase to label home-made or hijacked maxims that helped job seekers stay on target and remain serene throughout the search. Under each maxim lies a value that can be internalized.

In a Chicago kitchen, while conducting interviews for this study, I was given a coffee cup with a "Words of Wisdom" imprint (and a Hallmark copyright) over the following sayings that literally covered the outer surface of the cup:

- The journey of a thousand miles begins with one step. (Chinese Proverb)
- Do what you love. (Anon.)
- Believe you can and you're halfway there. (Anon.)
- The only one who never makes mistakes is the one who never does anything. (Theodore Roosevelt)
- There is nothing permanent except change. (Heraclitus)
- This above all: to thine own self be true. (Shakespeare)
- The important thing is not to stop questioning. (Einstein)
- Tomorrow belongs to those who fully use today. (Anon.)
- In the mountains of truth you never climb in vain. (Nietzsche)
- If we did all the things we are capable of doing, we could literally astound ourselves. (Edison)
- No bird soars too high, if he soars with his own wings. (Blake)
- Courage is the best gift of all. (Plautus)
- Dare to dream great dreams. (Anon.)

These sayings, and others like them, work their way into the consciousness of persons who, in the circumstances of a job campaign, can draw strength from them and use them to shore up their drooping spirits and focus their minds on the task at hand—finding a job. After a job is found, the principles remain operative in many cases. One manager, for example, adapted the "journey of a thousand miles" saying for use on the job: "Always think one step

ahead of where you are in your career." This is a readiness principle that can serve an abruptly terminated manager well—he or she
has already been scanning the opportunity horizon and planning
for the next move. In effect, the first step has already been taken.

Reading Shakespeare might force a discouraged job seeker to
say, "In me thou see'st the glowing of such fire,/ that on the ashes
of his youth doth lie." Other "words of wisdom" heard along the
way can help a person focus on the fire, not the ashes, and fan the
embers to get the flames that will fire the enthusiasm needed to
keep moving toward the goal.

One of the women with whom I discussed transitions, hers
and those of executives she knows well, gave me this untitled,
anonymous verse that contained helpful principles for her:

> *After a while you learn ...*
> *that company doesn't mean security, ...*
> *And you begin to accept your*
> *defeats with your head up*
> *and your eyes open, with*
> *the grace of an adult and*
> *not the grief of a child.*
> *And you learn to build all your roads on today*
> *because tomorrow's ground*
> *Is too uncertain for plans and futures have*
> *A way of falling in mid-flight....*
> *So you plant your own garden*
> *and decorate your own soul*
> *And you learn that you really can endure ...*
> *That you really are strong*
> *And you really do have worth*
> *And you learn and learn ...*
> *With every goodbye you learn."*

Lessons Learned

I asked participants in my study to tell me, so that I could tell you,
what they learned. Here are some of those lessons, in the form of

guiding principles. There is wisdom here; there are also trite banalities. No one quoted the Boy Scout oath, but if anyone had, I would have listed it in what follows. The point is to let you see and judge the articulated principles that influenced others, before you put the searchlight on yourself and attempt to articulate your own guiding principles. You have to question your core and come up with some solid answers from within. Here's what others told me:

"Confucius is supposed to have said, 'A fool on a mountaintop can sometimes see more than a wise man in a valley.' Even I was smart enough to notice that you should strive to maintain outside interests and learn new fields while still in the top job. Because I did that, the interval between jobs for me was quite short" (president, advanced technology).

"If you focus on the congruence between your values and your business procedures, including the pursuit of profit, you will redefine success" (vice chairman, accounting).

"Your personal worth transcends the 'job.' When you wrap things up before departure, do it in the best possible fashion. You'll feel better, and you will leave on a positive note" (senior vice president, health care).

"Don't be too hard on yourself, or set too many demands; this, like everything, will be resolved one way or another, sooner or later" (vice president/operations, health care).

"Expect rejection; don't take it personally" (president, savings bank).

"Be positive and work hard at the search (a new job won't just happen). Although I have accomplished a lot, I am still fully capable of more accomplishments" (president, advertising).

"Go after what you enjoy most and do best" (partner, executive search).

"Don't ever turn a job down until after it is offered" (senior vice president, human resources).

"While in transition, although you should have been think-ing this way all along, commit yourself to the reality that your job now is to get a job" (corporate director of compensation, information systems).

"Before charging forward to conquer new worlds, choose to stay out a little longer so that you can make more considered decisions" (senior vice president/operations, air transport).

"Help others when they are in transition; they will likely be there for you when you need their help" (director of research and development, brewing).

"Don't take rejection—i.e., not making the cut in searches—personally. Be patient with search consultants and potential employers when they don't return phone calls or keep to timeliness" (president/CEO, health care).

"Keep a positive attitude and stay busy; success does not come to those who wait, but to those who do" (production manag-er, manufacturing).

"Let your pride push you rather than hold you back" (senior vice president, development corporation).

"If you are a Christian, make the Christian perspective your own: the Cross as part of life; the impermanence of wealth and power; true identity in Christ; faith as the basis for hope" (vice president/administration, real estate holding company).

"Let your values (as well as your conscience) be your guide" (partner, law firm).

"Be intent on helping others and you will find yourself being helped" (president, beverage company).

"Keep balance in your life—work, family, religion, friends, sports, hobby—so that when one goes 'pfft!' there are others to keep you going" (chairman, food company).

Drawn from a favorite passage in the Letter to the Romans (8:26–34): "We know that in everything God works for good with those who love Him, who are called according to His purpose" (vice president/production, baking company). (Several other participants in the study specifically mentioned Romans 8:28 as a guiding principle.)

"Take charge of your life" (senior vice president, communications).

"Don't ever give up!" (director of human resources, high-technology manufacturing).

"Soldier on!" (sales manager, computers).

"You are not simply what you do, and you should realize that the job revolution has resulted in people being out who have done nothing wrong" (chairman/CEO, banking).

"Never let yourself be isolated; never assume 'it cannot happen to me'" (general manager, manufacturing).

"Don't worry about what you can't control" (vice president/systems, distribution company).

"Don't live up to the limits of your income so that you are always prepared for any adjustments, even if the adjustments are mainly psychological" (president, money-center bank).

"Don't attempt a search on your own. Seek out a support group; it will keep you focused" (vice president/general manager, publishing).

"There is always something I can do to earn a living" (director of personnel, pharmaceuticals).

"You have to work your own way through the stages of loss to acceptance. But first you have to realize that your identity is not with your profession or company; it is tied into your personality, the kind of person you are. You also have to realize that most people will patronize you and cannot understand what you are going through. Come to terms with all of this and you'll have an operating principle to direct your search" (president, manufacturing).

"You are not what you own or your title" (vice president/ marketing, chemicals).

"Be patient; be selective. Don't leap at the first opportunity if it isn't right" (president/CEO, transportation equipment).

"A friend prevented me from rebounding too fast and taking the wrong position by cautioning me, 'You don't want to do that job, you just want to get that job.' I'd advise others that really wanting to do the job is a good principle of selection" (senior vice president/taxes, food conglomerate).

"Being positive or negative is your choice; choose to be positive" (corporate attorney, manufacturing).

"Never, ever believe your job is secure" (vice president, construction).

"View the transition as a rebirth that has to come from within" (vice president, marketing).

"Those you most expect to be of help many times are not; those from whom you least expect help and support often provide it" (vice president, human resources).

"Maintain a routine—gym, the search, family, social life; job loss initiates a normal passage or transition in life" (executive vice president, banking).

"Keep moving to stay motivated" (corporate manager, communications).

"Stay focused on the search" (manager of research and development, manufacturing).

"If you close yourself off, opportunities will pass" (administrator, health care).

"If you don't learn from your past mistakes, you will find yourself repeating them" (research manager, higher education).

"*Depend on nothing and no one except yourself; have a Doomsday Plan and keep it current,*" (vice president, health care).

"*Refuse to make negative comments about your former employer; do not encourage others, even by silence, to knock the mental or professional capabilities of the chap who fired you*" (foundation executive).

"*If you know it [the separation] was not your fault, believe it was not your fault, and don't ever let yourself begin to think it was your fault*" (vice president/human resources, trading group).

"*When you are overwhelmed, you tend to lower your standards. Acceptance of life and reliance upon God can protect you against that tendency*" (director of planned giving, higher education).

"*While working, plan for your next move and develop alternative skills. When looking for a job, pray as if it all depends on God and work as if it all depends on you—your efforts, your abilities, your talents*" (vice president/litigation, insurance).

"*Rely on direct, personal experience to check out views expressed by others and published job descriptions; the principle here is 'show me,' experience it first hand*" (vice president, manufacturing).

"*Don't rush into any commitments*" (president, financial services).

"*Set a reasonable daily pace—competitive with others—for your job search, and stick to it*" (director/human resources, insurance).

"*Even if you are on the right track, you'll still get run over if you just sit there*" (chairman and CEO, consulting—with due attribution to Will Rogers).

"*Only a positive attitude will propel you into a good job that is the right job for you*" (president, transportation).

"Give other people the chance to help" (CEO, financial services).

"It is all a question of character: yours—so be in touch with it; and your potential employer's—so learn how to read it in others" (president, technical services).

"Have your network in place before you ever need it" (vice president/information systems, communications).

"Always be open to new career paths—the principle of flexibility" (president, computer software).

"Look before leaping; don't rush into a new employment situation that could be as bad as or worse than your last one" (senior consultant, accounting).

"Make 'doing what you like to do' the principle of selection for your next job" (analyst, financial services).

"I don't want to do anything unless it is helping other people—affirming them, helping them discover who they are and what moves them. This is a new direction for me, based on the recent discovery that my résumé is not me" (former sales executive, office products).

"In the quest for reemployment, remember that the 'perfect' can be the enemy of the 'good'" (chairman, money-center bank).

"Less can be more—it is possible to live on much less income and improve the quality of your life" (assistant director, environmental research).

"If, while in transition, you go out of your way to do something for others, you will find it easier to accept the fact that it is not you but the economy that is responsible for the delay you are experiencing in finding a new opportunity" (vice president/human resources, technical services).

"Hang in there!" (executive vice president, advertising).

"Maintain and exercise your sense of humor; always have a plan, even in transition" (vice president/communications, food distribution).

"Action is your character in motion; you will feel good when you act" (vice president/marketing, insurance).

"Image your reconnections, imagine your opportunities, and then go for the realization of your imaginings" (technical manager, chemicals).

"Never let yourself get to the point where you have all the answers" (chairman, regional bank).

"Anyone who leaves a CEO position unwillingly is just about certain to leave a large chunk of self-confidence behind" (CEO, banking).

"Trust no one, except your family" (vice president, automotive services).

"Know your attributes and your targets first, and then begin to talk to persons on your list about reemployment" (vice president/sales, communications).

"Nothing is forever. Things change; people change—especially at the higher levels within corporate America" (president/COO, telecommunications).

Echoing this last idea, an ousted trade association president told me that he and his wife always "knew that the position could end as quickly as it began. We never permitted ourselves to be engulfed by the role of the office. We used to joke that flying first class would not last forever." Many men and women I met in the course of this study expressed guiding principles that prompted them not to become "too comfortable in the job" or "too used to the perks," and many would say that they "always had a plan for the next move."

One of my respondents, an information systems technical services manager, estimates (and others verify) that he produced $6 million in annual savings for his company one year before he was fired. He had reconfigured the entire information management system as part of a companywide downsizing strategy. He told me that there was one principle that did *not* work for him. He had always "really and truly believed," he said, "that if you worked hard for the company, the company would take care of you; if you gave it an honest effort, it would treat you fairly." He discovered that it doesn't work that way; at least, it did not work that way for him. "You have to look out for yourself, and it's terrible, I think, that you have to say that about American industry, but it's true." Now doing similar work in another industry in a distant state, he says, "My operating principle now is that I will never put the company's interests ahead of my own. It is my continuing assumption that the company will not look out for me."

A man whose previous employment had been as vice president of a bank holding company told me that he had no "words of wisdom" to pass along to others because "nothing properly prepared me for this experience." Similarly, a woman fired from a college presidency said simply, "It has been pure hell; no wisdom whatever emerged from this experience."

For what it's worth, I noticed that those who had no success in articulating guiding principles often tended to be those who had nothing to report when I asked them what books they had read that proved helpful in the transition. In the next chapter, I'll mention titles of books that respondents singled out as helpful and influential during that difficult in-between time for which very few managerial men and women find themselves adequately prepared.

Write Them Down

Jotting down your operating principles can be something of an intellectual game; it can also be a pastime. Simply note and later reflect upon what you find in unlikely places—in detective fiction, for example. A character in Colin Harrison's *Break and Enter* (Crown), Peter Mastrude, a seasoned divorce lawyer, has a business card that introduces him as "Counselor at law, Practicing Primarily in Family Law and Domestic Relations, No Charge Initial Consultation, Fees Available on Request, Compassionate

Advice Humbly Offered." This prepares you for his short list of "The Eternal Truths":

1. *This is it!*
2. *There are no hidden meanings.*
3. *You can't get there from here, and besides, there's no place else to go.*
4. *We are all already dying, and we will be dead for a long time.*
5. *Nothing lasts.*
6. *There is no way of getting all you want.*
7. *You can't have anything unless you let go of it.*
8. *You only get to keep what you give away.*
9. *There is no particular reason why you lost out on some things.*
10. *The world is not necessarily just. Being good often does not pay off, and there is no compensation for misfortune.*

Of course, cynicism pervades this set of principles, but wisdom is also present there. These maxims, like all the others presented in this chapter, are intended to be illustrative and thought-provoking. You are the one who has to assemble your own personal set and let them work for you.

One man, not yet forty, lost a corporate vice presidency when a large hotel chain downsized. While still looking for work, he composed for himself this set of five propositions with an eye to shaping the attitude he needed to sustain him in the search:

- Putting things in true perspective. Considering how good other aspects of life are and how God has blessed me in so many other ways.
- Ensuring that my life is a balanced one. Work is only one piece of it, and it does not define me or my personal worth.
- Considering this to be an opportunity for positive changes and positive outcomes.
- Recognizing that the environment that I am leaving is not a healthy, growing, stimulating one.

+ Recognizing and rewarding my personal strength and character.

It was a woman who directed my attention to an operating principle, phrased in an all-male vocabulary, that appeared as an epigraph accompanying an article entitled "Is There Life After Unemployment?" in *Black Enterprise* (February 1993). The author, Donna Whittingham-Barnes, answers that question, "Yes—if you're willing to stay flexible, acquire new skills and take some risks." The words of the epigraph are James Russell Lowell's: "No man is born into the world whose work is not born with him; there is always work and tools to work withal, for those who will." As a principle of action for the unemployed manager, this idea will drive him or her to do the self-assessment that identifies talents possessed and preferences held. Once that is done, another principle comes into play. It is expressed in the title of Marsha Sinetar's widely read book: *Do What You Love, the Money Will Follow* (Dell, 1987). That is a principle for the stout of heart, for the flexible person, willing to take some risks—the type of manager in demand to run operations and organizations in the new corporate culture.

The next chapter will focus your attention on strategy, the steps you have to take to reach your employment goal. The guiding principles outlined here are impulses or driving forces that keep your strategy moving; they are reference points that serve to remind you of who you are and where you want to go. Many people in all walks of life keep statements of principle in print and in view—framed on the wall, tucked into the wallet, inscribed on a bookmark. When I interviewed Bill Morin, chairman of Drake Beam Morin, the outplacement firm, I noticed that he had a set of principles framed and hung on the wall behind his desk. They are listed under the heading "My Values":

+ To be honest—with sensitivity.
+ To think of the other person's motivation, needs, and desires first, before making judgments or even offering an observation.

- To concentrate on providing quality services or products with my work and leisure time, rather than self-serving activities.
- To take responsibility for all my life's challenges and not blame my family members, friends, peers, the job, etc.
- To persevere for the common good, no matter what the cost.

Shortly after the death of former Washington Redskins coach George Allen, *The Washington Post* ran an appreciative article: "The Death of George Allen: 'When the Sun Comes Up, You'd Better Be Running.'" The quotation is from a sign on the wall in his last coaching office at Long Beach State University, where he returned to coaching at age seventy-one. Allen was fond of signs. This one read:

> *Every morning in Africa, a gazelle wakes up. It knows it must run faster than the fastest lion or it will be killed.*
>
> *Every morning a lion wakes up. It knows it must outrun the slowest gazelle or it will starve to death.*
>
> *[So] it doesn't matter whether you are a lion or a gazelle. When the sun comes up, you'd better be running.*

You should try your hand at reducing your own principles to writing, or, at the very least, writing down principles that appeal to you and fit your circumstances, even though they may have been articulated by others. If not in open view, your principles should be kept in your mind's eye for both guidance and inspiration.

Here are ten original principles, composed by a female member of a support group for unemployed white-collar workers in New York City. The author assembled these guidelines under the title, "How to Love Yourself," and gave a copy to each member of her group; one of them passed along a copy to me:

1. *Stop all criticism.* Criticism never changes a thing. Refuse to criticize yourself. Accept yourself exactly as you are. Everybody changes. When you criticize yourself, your

changes are negative. When you approve of yourself, your changes are positive.

2. *Don't scare yourself.* Stop terrorizing yourself with your thoughts. It's a dreadful way to live. Find a mental image that gives you pleasure (mine is yellow roses), and immediately switch your scary thought to a pleasure thought.

3. *Be gentle and kind and patient.* Be gentle with yourself. Be kind to yourself. Be patient with yourself as you learn the new ways of thinking. Treat yourself as you would someone you really loved.

4. *Be kind to your mind.* Self-hatred is only hating your own thoughts. Don't hate yourself for having the thoughts. Gently change your thoughts.

5. *Praise yourself.* Criticism breaks down the inner spirit. Praise builds it up. Praise yourself as much as you can. Tell yourself how well you are doing with every little thing.

6. *Support yourself.* Find ways to support yourself. Reach out to friends and allow them to help you. It is being strong to ask for help when you need it.

7. *Be loving to your negatives.* Acknowledge that you created them to fulfill a need. Now you are finding new, positive ways to fulfill those needs. So lovingly release the old negative patterns.

8. *Take care of your body.* Learn about nutrition. What kind of fuel does your body need to have optimum energy and vitality? Learn about exercise. What kind of exercise can you enjoy? Cherish and revere the temple you live in.

9. *Mirror work.* Look into your eyes often. Express this growing sense of love you have for yourself. Forgive yourself looking into the mirror. Talk to your parents looking into the mirror. Forgive them too. At least once a day say: "I love you, I really love you!"

10. *Love yourself ... Do it now.* Don't wait until you get well, or lose the weight, or get the new job, or the new relationship. Begin now—and do the best you can.

I ran across a number of people in the course of this study who profited from reading Stephen Covey's insightful book *The Seven Habits of Highly Effective People*. Mention of that fact need not wait until I list in Chapter 9 some of the books my participants found helpful. The book's subtitle, *Restoring the Character Ethic*, suggests that much of what Covey has to say relates to principles of action. When I interviewed a senior manager who was separated from a large advertising agency and asked him about the principles that were guiding him in his transition, he simply handed me a list of Covey's seven "habits," a set of internalized fundamentals or habituated principles that direct responsible and effective adult behavior. Culled from the Covey book, here are the principles this man chose to wrap in his own words and make his own:

> Habit 1. *Be Proactive*—the habit of individual responsibility, the principle that while we can't always control what happens, we can choose our response: we need not feel powerless, trapped, or victimized.
>
> Habit 2. *Begin with the End in Mind*—the habit of personal leadership, of discovering a personal mission and living out of a sense of purpose.
>
> Habit 3. *Put First Things First*—the habit of personal management, of operating from priorities that flow from mission, roles, and goals.
>
> Habit 4. *Think Win-Win*—the habit of interpersonal leadership and mutual benefit.
>
> Habit 5. *Seek First to Understand* (and then to be understood)—the attitude and skill cultivated by all successful professionals, as it is a key to influence.
>
> Habit 6. *Synergize*—the habit of creative cooperation that comes from exploring constructive alternatives, valuing differences of opinion, and seeking objective feedback.
>
> Habit 7. *"Sharpen the Saw"*—the habit of self-renewal, of implementing a daily total fitness program that rejuvenates the mind and body and enhances capabilities.

The person who adopted these principles for guidance during his search had a personal reference point articulated in words borrowed from William Butler Yeats and rendered in attractive calligraphy for desktop reference. The words help to explain his remarkable serenity and his availability, to a greater degree than anyone I encountered in the course of this study, to assist others in looking for work. "We can make our minds so like still water that beings gather about us that they may see, it may be, their own images, and so live for a moment with a clearer—perhaps even with a fiercer—life because of our quiet." His "quiet" attracted other job seekers to him, not because he could give them employment, but because he could give them hope, as well as sound advice for developing "clearer" objectives and "fiercer" strategies.

I have often thought it strange that we speak frequently of fierce competition, but rarely, if ever, think of fierce cooperation as a strategy, or refer to fierce adherence to a plan as a way of describing personal persistence. Have no fear of imposing fiercer standards on yourself and your strategy in the pursuit of reemployment. This surely does not mean walking over others to get to your goal. It does mean holding yourself to the plan you adopt to guide your job campaign. A successful plan will be a principled plan. So put your principles in writing—take time out to do that now—and consult that written page often as you articulate your personal mission statement and lay out the details of the job-search strategy that you will, I hope, want to write after reading the next chapter.

Chapter 9

YOUR JOB-SEARCH STRATEGY

A job search does not mean that you are starting all
over again. You are simply changing. To live is to
change. You do, however, have a blank page in
front of you that requires immediate attention.
Consider yourself an author. The strategic plan is
your story outline; get it down on paper.

—*Words from this chapter's final paragraph*

Winston Churchill's comment about Americans in general applies often to displaced managers searching for reemployment: "You can always get them to do the right thing, after they've exhausted all the other possibilities." Time wasted in pursuit of "all the other possibilities" will be shortened significantly by simply having a strategy for your job campaign. Strategies for individuals or organizations presuppose a sense of purpose, a statement of mission, a goal. Another prerequisite to strategic planning is strategic thinking; "Think before you plan" is as important a guiding principle as "Look before you leap."

Strategic thinking begins with the question, "What sets me (or us, or this specific organization) apart"? The answer to that question is a statement of your comparative advantage. You are wise to build on your differences—those advantages you have over others—which serve both to set you apart and to enhance the strengths you may have in common with others.

It all begins with you and ultimately depends on you. Although you will need the help of others, you can, if necessary, "outplace yourself," to use the title of Charles Logue's book, which is subtitled *Secrets of an Executive Outplacement Counselor* (Bob Adams, 1993).

There are many good books that can assist you in the step-by-step detail of building your strategy. Several that I would recommend are *Knock 'Em Dead: The Ultimate Job Seeker's Handbook*, by Martin Yate (Bob Adams, 1994); *In Transition*, by Mary Lindley Burton and Richard A. Wedemeyer (Harper Business, 1991); *Parting Company: How to Survive the Loss of a Job and Find Another Successfully*, by William J. Morin and James C. Cabrera (Harcourt Brace Jovanovich, 1991); and *What Color Is Your Parachute?*, the best-seller by Richard Nelson Bolles (Ten Speed Press) with a new edition appearing virtually every year since 1970. A note in the 1993 edition indicates that more than 4.4 million copies of this "practical manual for job hunters and career-changers" have been sold over the past two decades.

These books are loaded with good advice, drills, and diagrams. They will work best for you if you work through them in the company of others—in reading and discussion groups of two or three or in weekly support groups, which can be found almost anywhere in America today. If you read them in isolation (normally not a good environment for you, except during your reflective, self-assessment stage), you are likely to become bored, confused, and perhaps discouraged; you will be tempted to skip some strategic steps and go on to prove Churchill right again. You should read at least one of these or other practical, how-to-do-it manuals before you write out your own personal goals statement, followed by your own step-by-step strategy—your personal business plan for getting back in business again.

As I indicated at the opening of this book, my intention is to put a compass, not a road map, in your hands. The books I've just listed are more like road maps; they lay out the practical do's and don'ts of résumé writing, networking, telephoning, interviewing, and negotiating. And they are written by experts whose advice is worth heeding, and whose assessments of the relative worth for you of alternative job-seeking strategies will be helpful.

What I want to do in this chapter is relay to you strategies recommended by men and women who have been there before you, the participants in my study. I will also let you know what books they found helpful during their own transitions. And I will be dotting the landscape of this chapter with some suggestions of my own, derived from my own reflections on what I've learned in the course of this study. From here on, you have to think and act strategically.

Step 1—the first thing you have to do—is a personal, written statement of who you are. Step 2 is a description of what you want to do. If both of these are to be sure-footed steps, they must be taken with care, and they will surely take time.

Reflection on who you are will be difficult for those who have succumbed to what I labeled back in Chapter 1 as the great American heresy: What you do is what you are. And you will recall the unfortunate conclusion drawn from that proposition by many who lose their jobs that doing nothing means that you are nothing (and the whole world now knows it!). Step 1 requires that you write a simple statement of who you are without reference to what you do, have done, or may do. Here you will have the opportunity to do what several people I mentioned earlier in this book did, namely, identify a closely held personal value and use that value as a searchlight and criterion for selecting your next job. If you find it difficult, at first attempt, to reduce to a sentence or two a statement of who you really are without reference to what you do or have done, try writing a more extensive "work biography," consciously including descriptions of what you have done. Then, when you have that before you, cull from it the values that are really yours, the principles that are yours wherever you may be, the wisdom you have gained that now can serve as a window on your inner self.

"What are you trying to prove, and to whom?" is the question transitioning executives hear from Donald Perkins, former chairman of Jewel Food and now a senior adviser in the Chicago office of Jannotta, Bray. He does this to encourage a client to cut through the brush and move on to the "who am I?" and "what do I want to do?" questions.

Words applied by John Naisbitt and Patricia Abdurene to organizations are even more applicable to individuals: Only a person "with a real mission or sense of purpose that comes out of an intuitive or spiritual dimension will capture people's hearts. And you must have people's hearts to inspire the hard work required to realize a vision" (*Re-Inventing the Corporation*, Warner, 1985, p. 22).

So probe your deeper dimensions, here in Step 1, to mine from within yourself the elements of your Step 2 mission statement. If it emerges from within, it can shore up your own heart for the hard work of realizing your vision, and capture the interest, and possibly the heart, of someone who could hire you according to your plan. This important point is given a very practical extension by the observation of an ousted division manager who obtained a vice presidency in the chemical industry: "People fail to find work because they try to sell their experiences and accomplishments without translating these personal assets into the 'value added' the prospective employer would gain by hiring them." The work of identifying your assets and translating them into value added language is part of your Step 1 activity.

The second step is also time-consuming. It amounts to the composition of a personal mission or goals statement: "Here is what I want to do." It is wise to take time at this juncture to come to terms with the question of whether you really prefer to work for yourself or for someone else and, if you are not going to be your own boss, whether you prefer a large or small organization. This kind of reflection led one of my participants to conclude that he wanted "to build smaller fires and have more balance in my life."

Ends, Means, and Résumés

There is nothing wrong with keeping a mission statement general, broad enough to cover many possibilities within the area defined by your general goal. Specification can be supplied by a supplemental statement of particulars that is not necessarily shared immediately with readers of your résumé.

This is an ends-and-means situation. The particulars can be so tightly linked to your goal that they are not just means (stepping stones) to an end (the goal), but ends in themselves. Or the particulars—e.g., your desire to live in the Middle Atlantic states, work in sales management, and be employed in the telecommunications industry—can be immediate objectives to be achieved on your way to the ultimate goal—e.g., top management in a Fortune-500 company. After careful assessment of your values, interests, training, experience, temperament, vulnerabilities, needs, and preferences, you state your goal. For example, your goal (or, as those who use the terms interchangeably would say, your objective) might be a senior-level management position. Your mission in the world of work may be to hold a senior financial management position in a not-for-profit organization, or to be a chief operating officer in a financial services corporation. You may want to put your strong suit—e.g., human resource management—to work in transportation, perhaps, or in higher education; and you may want to say so explicitly. You can sharpen the description of your general goal—senior-level management—and specify it on your résumé. You can, if you wish, specify skill, sector, industry, and geography as part of your goal. Or, you can have just a general goal statement on your résumé, and modify it, as needed (word processors make this easy!) by adding information that will address the specific expectations of a potential employer. It comes down to a question of when (and, since letters and résumés must necessarily appear in print, where) you want to highlight your comparative advantage, that which sets you apart—apart, in the present example, from those who are also seeking senior-level management positions.

One of the authors I mentioned earlier in this chapter, Martin Yates, offers readers of *Knock 'Em Dead* an excellent suggestion for an add-on sheet to the normal résumé. He calls it the Executive Briefing. On a single sheet of paper, you list on the left side the company's stated requirements for the job to be filled. On the right side, you list your experience, matching your skills point by point with the potential employer's specific needs. Yates recommends that you attach an Executive Briefing whenever you send out your résumé. That, by the way, will force you to research the firm and the vacancy carefully before you apply.

Perhaps the Executive Briefing device could have prevented the following mistake. Here is an example of one man's objective as stated in a "Personal Marketing Plan" reduced to a single sheet for review by potential employers—"Objective: An advertising agency account management position in which I can apply my OTC [over-the-counter] drug advertising and marketing expertise." He then lists his "skills and experience" in advertising ("copy strategy development; TV, print, radio production; media planning, buying; copy and consumer research; people management/motivation") and in marketing ("marketing plan development; new product development; trade and consumer promotion; advertising copy evaluation; presentation to senior management").

Next, he lists in "bullet" style four "Key Accomplishments" in both advertising and marketing, and names the advertising agencies he has worked for and the accounts he handled. Reaction from his support group to all this was negative. "Don't you realize that no ad agency anywhere is hiring anyone your age these days to do what you propose to do here?" was the candid question raised by a good friend (thus fulfilling the old adage that "the best mirror is an old friend.") This close friend happened to have had years of senior-level ad agency experience in human resource management.

This is not to say that a Personal Marketing Plan succinctly stated is not a good idea; this particular plan was simply not right for this job seeker. The example also illustrates the understandable tendency we all have to define our potential in terms of our past achievements. This can be a strategic error, even for one who wants to remain in the familiar territory of past employment success. This tendency can blind a person to other possibilities where skills and experience from the past can fit nicely into new opportunities in previously unexplored fields.

Job seekers typically labor over the preparation of their résumés, and many are never comfortable with the result. Should it be chronological, date specific, narrative format, more than one page, achievement-focused, or what? I favor the idea of an "overlay" sheet—a crisp, descriptive summary of who you are and what you've done—that could easily serve to introduce you if you were giving a speech. Attach it as a cover page to your formal résumé, which can be formatted in whatever style and length you select as best for introducing yourself to a potential employer. The how-to-do-it books will give you many examples of model résumés, from one-page career highlights to a full *curriculum vitae*.

Here is an example of a succinct cover-page statement that worked well for one of the participants in my study:

NAME
ADDRESS
PHONE

I am looking for a company, or division of a company, that is not happy with its current revenue or profit growth, or is simply in trouble. I seek a CEO, COO, or Senior V.P. position. Areas in which I have demonstrated special strength are: profit improvement, sales, marketing, product development, brand identification, manufacturing improvement, and cost reduction. I have a consistent record of improving operating results and bringing companies to a position of national market leadership. *I am a strong leader and motivator of people. My experience includes acquisitions, new ventures (both high and low tech), divestitures and closures. International assignments are welcomed. I headed the international company at Ameritech.*

My most recent position was as COO at Maxwell Macmillan, where in a period of fifteen months we were able to bring an unprofitable, troubled business to a point where it was an attractive acquisition. The business was sold at a profit.

If you need additional information, please call—[outplacement office and home numbers].

This brief summary accompanied a full four-page résumé. The writer eventually moved into the presidency of a small company.

It will not surprise you to learn that an accountant was one of the more effective strategic thinkers and planners among the executives I interviewed. After a top-level, commendation-studded, twenty-five-year executive career with the Internal Revenue Service, this man left government to become a banker in the private sector. His timing for his exit from the IRS was fine, but not his timing for his subsequent entry into the presidency of a savings and loan operation. He soon found himself unemployed, without pension or benefits, as the Resolution Trust Corporation shut down his banking operation.

His first step after the separation: time off to think. He stimulated his thinking process by reading *What Color Is Your Parachute?*

> *All of my thirty-two years in the workforce had been in the area of accounting, finance, taxes, and management. I had done quite a bit of volunteer work for charitable and not-for-profit organizations and found the experience most rewarding. So, after giving it a lot of thought, I set out to find a job from my heart and not my head. I decided to focus on the not-for-profit sector.*

It took him three months to find one—executive director of a church-related publishing operation with 125 employees and an annual budget of over $8 million.

Fitness of Mind and Body

From the outset, looking for work was a full-time job for this man. Since, by his estimate, 15 percent of the jobs were filled by respondents to advertisements (experts would drop that figure by two-thirds for senior managers), he spent 15 percent of his eight-hour search day responding to the ads. He belonged to five networking groups and made it a point "to be on someone's calendar each day of the week—to get in front of somebody and to walk away with four or five names." He became friendly with a research librarian, "a walking encyclopedia," who helped him get background information on prospective employers. Every Friday afternoon took him to a place in his suburban Chicago community where updated job listings from the schools were posted. The remainder of each Friday afternoon was spent filling out his calendar to make up a full schedule for his next forty-hour week.

A two-mile run was on his schedule three days a week; both Mass and calisthenics were part of the daily regimen. And for him, it worked. "I've never had a more satisfying job and have never been happier," he told me. As others have remarked, the bright side of being pushed from the nest is finding that you still have wings!

A vice president for communications at a large food conglomerate lost his job at age forty-two and had one full year's severance pay. He spent "much time," he told me, "analyzing likes, dislikes, past history, goals, dreams." And then he began "to explore again, at middle age, with the enthusiasm of a twenty-year-old. I read heavily in many fields, saw every old film I ever wanted to see, learned to play golf and Rollerblade, indulged in long talks with family and friends—the kind we always mean to have but never get around to." But all of this, he noted, "came on top of a forty-hour-a-week search for the right job," which took him three years to find. Another respondent, out of work at age fifty-six, "treated each day as if I were gainfully employed. I appeared at the outplacement office before 9:00 each morning and did not leave until 5:00. I made sure that each hour in between contributed in a defined way to the job-search process." Within six months he had a new job with more responsibility and higher pay.

An ex-IBMer, an accountant by training but a systems manager for the corporation, did none of the above and lost time and money as a result. Not only did he not do any serious self-assessment, he neglected to check carefully before committing himself to a franchising opportunity that took him to a distant state and cost him $35,000 before he cut his losses after about a year. He moved his family back to where they had lived before, then figured out what he wanted to do. His advice to any displaced executive sitting down to map a job-seeking strategy: "Focus on your education and past experience; they will always be part of you. You may want to separate yourself from them altogether, but don't do that without first being convinced that they aren't going to work for you in opening up new opportunities." He had never bothered to sit for his CPA, having stepped right out of college into the corporation to begin a successful career that lasted twenty-two years. He could have stayed with IBM, as he had planned, to age fifty-five ("I always knew I wouldn't stay a second longer"), but at age forty-six he "had grown tired of the culture" and decided to take an attractive severance while that window was still open. (At IBM they now call this the ITO, the "individual transition option.") After the franchising misfire and the return to his roots, it dawned on him that he really liked accounting and could succeed in private practice.

He took a CPA exam-preparation course, passed the test on his first try, framed his certificate, and went into business for himself. "Happiness is being your own boss," he says contentedly.

Two weeks after having lunch in New York with Kevin Dolan, an experienced human resources executive who is singularly generous and effective in helping others find work, and who himself, at that time, had been unemployed for eight months, I received a letter from him saying that reflection on our conversation prompted him to put on paper the key lessons he has learned while in transition. These come from his personal job-search experience and also from running support groups for other job seekers over the past four years. He prefaced his list with the general observation that "anyone who is unemployed must avoid the debilitative feeling of hopelessness, powerlessness, loneliness, and little control of one's life"—the common experience of job seekers. He therefore "laid out a program to minimize these negative feelings as much as possible." Here are his suggestions for "a solid job campaign that will allow one to maintain one's dignity and a positive, upbeat attitude during the difficult transition of unemployment." What follows in Categories I, II, and III is all Kevin Dolan.

Category I. Personal Actions

Attitude—*This is the most important aspect of a job search. It is a time to grow, try new things, meet stimulating and exciting people, and smell the roses. Recognizing that it is a transition (it will end) and that it is a unique opportunity to do things that one cannot normally do while working can energize one to be excited about the job search and challenge. A positive mental attitude is the key to a successful job search.*

Spiritual—*This is the province of prayer, church, ministers, soulmates, and inspirational meetings. All are needed to maintain the positive attitude. The extra time one has during a job search allows for some deep reflection on life and its mysteries. I started most days with twenty minutes of spiritual reading and ended with fifteen minutes of reflection at night.*

Physical fitness—*While working, most of us don't have time to exercise properly. Now there are no excuses. It is important to set some goals here. Mine were to lose between fifteen and twenty pounds and to walk forty-five minutes a day at least six days a week. I have done this, and it gives me a feeling of control and success (weight loss). It also keeps the mind in shape; nature is wonderful in uplifting one's spirit.*

Mental fitness—*This is a great opportunity to read all those books you could never get to. My goal was to read a new book every two weeks, or two books a month on average. I chose books that were inspirational, motivational, businesslike, and religious. Some books that I have read include:* Covey's The Seven Habits of Highly Effective People; *Tichy's* Control Your Own Destiny (Or Someone Else Will); Transitions *by Bridges;* Seven Story Mountain *by Merton; Lester Thurow's* Head to Head; *some of the works of William James, Ralph Waldo Emerson, and Thoreau; Sheehan's* Personal Best, *and numerous religious pocket books. I have personally found that when I was feeling low or depressed, a nature walk and an inspirational book lifted my spirits tremendously.*

[The "nature walk" prescription recommended by Kevin Dolan and many others I met during the course of this study reminds me of lines from one of Countee Cullen's poems:

And I am somewhere worlds away
In God's rich autumn tinted lanes,
Where heart at ease from life's dismay,
My soul's high song beats back the rains.]

Financial management—*To assure peace of mind and avoid panic, I took out an extended home equity line to provide sufficient income to ensure survival over a twelve-month period of unemployment. Additionally, a zero-based budget (critical items only) allows me to see exactly what a given month's shortfall is and how much*

I should be borrowing from home equity. This is my fiscal conscience.

Family—*Your relationship to both spouse and children is key to maintaining your positive attitude. Regular family meetings are important. You must always be honest and frank with your family, but you have to try to remain positive, optimistic, and in control, offering reassurances about finances and job leads. Without communicating false expectations about a job, you have to feel and act as if one is just around the corner. You keep their spirits up by telling them about the people you are meeting and the network you are building.*

Category II. Outside activities

Support group—*To keep your spirits up, you must have a support group or two. More than three groups is counterproductive. Avoid becoming a support group "junkie," moving from group to group instead of developing your own wider network of personal contacts. It is also personally uplifting to do some pro bono charitable work.*

Friends and acquaintances—This is a time to lean on your friends for moral support over lunch, coffee, golf, and meetings to develop network contacts. Friends keep you sane and help you realize that you haven't changed. Genuine friends will shine in this period.

Networking—*This, of course, is a key element in your job-search strategy, although it is often overused, even abused. It is important to learn how to network and not be intrusive or overbearing in the process. Divide your network contacts into two groups: (a) job source leads, persons who can connect you with decision makers or are themselves decision makers, and (b) stimulating people, real friends, soulmates, clergy, psychologists, anyone who can make you feel good and lift your spirits. I set goals of ten to fifteen new network calls a week, usually resulting in a half dozen future meetings; the rest (those with whom meetings were not arranged) received a letter and my résumé. One or two of my weekly appointments are with friends or "inspirational" contacts as a means of keeping the spirits up. I know that out-placement firms often recommend that fifteen to twenty networking calls be made each day, but I would be wary of overload and burnout. Be sure, after each appoint-ment, to send a follow-up letter of thanks.*

Category III. Overall tips

Active lifestyle—*This is essential to a stimulating job search. Sitting at home waiting for the phone to ring is debilitating; you should get out of the house every day, preferably to an office or to a desk with a phone. Friends can be very helpful here—providing space, keeping you active, goal-oriented, and motivated. This is the way to avoid feelings of loneliness and helplessness. All you need is access (for just a half day, two or three days a week) to a desk, phone, and fax.*

Pacing and balance—*Like any new job or endeavor, your transition activity requires that you learn to pace yourself and balance your time evenly across the spectrum. This is not easy; it is also a matter of your unique, individual choice. I found that I would normally go to my office in New York [space provided by former employer] three or four days a week and spend a day or two at home in New Jersey making appointments for the other days. Having an answering machine at home, of course, helps a lot.*

Balance is so important! You can burn out during a job search faster than you can under conditions of full-time employment. That is why the spiritual motivation and personal reflection are needed to maintain your sense of wonder and appreciation of life, even in this difficult time of transition.

Kevin Dolan and others will suggest that if you are a golfer, you should make time for the game during your job campaign. This is not just to weave new networking contacts, but to maintain a proper balance in your life. I was amused by a comment about golf that novelist David Noonan puts on the lips of his character Jim Mooney in *Memoirs of a Caddy* (Simon & Schuster), and I'm grateful to *New York Times* book critic Christopher Lehmann-Haupt for highlighting it in his review: "One of the appeals of golf is that you can do all the things you would normally do in a bar while engaging in an actual sport—you can eat, drink, talk and smoke cigarettes." While in transition, you should use the game, if you enjoy it, for needed recreation, but also as a context for reflection on yourself. Consider the game of golf as a metaphor for the course of your own career; it can be a lens for the examination of your life. Golfers are by definition achievement-oriented; it is instructive to observe how they deal with success and failure on the course. As a regular caddy at a country club about an hour's drive from New York City, Jim Mooney, the novel's seventeen-year-old narrator, has become something of a judge of character as revealed by a player's conduct on the course. Here is how he sizes up one Sean Butterworth:

> *Sean was a good golfer with a bad temper that kept him from being a great golfer. Great golfers expect to make bad shots now and then and when they do they learn from them and then let them go. Not Sean. He hated bad shots and when he made one he got mad at himself and the world and cursed and threw clubs and talked to himself and got all worked up and then, very often, followed the first bad shot with another just as bad or even worse. The energized calm that golf required, the relaxed tension of it, eluded him. He wanted to kill the ball.*

You can learn a lot about yourself from your approach to the game of golf. Some job seekers learn that it is better to leave the clubs in the bag and just go for a long walk!

Personal Finances

Dolan and others warn that you must be careful about personal finances. In addition to looking for work, you have to talk to creditors, reduce expenses, and be realistic. Know with precision what your fixed and variable expenses have been over the past year or so. Be realistic as you look at the year ahead. For instance, if the winter months are approaching, you know that higher fuel bills are coming. Don't use last October's gas bill to estimate your monthly outlay; use December's. This is some of the practical advice for the jobless that Mary A. Malgoire, a financial planner, gave in an interview with *The Washington Post* (Oct. 21, 1990). "And if you use oil, take the number of gallons from last year, but use this year's prices." The next step is to total up your liquid or near-liquid assets, including severance pay, and divide that total by your monthly expenses. There you have the number of months you can manage without new income. If it is not too late, negotiate with your employer for generous severance, outplacement services, help with the health insurance premiums that you will otherwise have to pay yourself, and technical assistance on how to handle the tax implications of what you do with your pension plan.

Be sure to talk to creditors, and prepare yourself for pleasant surprises. The wife of an out-of-work manager told me she will shop at Sears as long as she lives "because they were so human and helpful in carrying us, without penalty, over a very difficult year." Your creditors are interested in you and your money; they will only alienate you and lose the money if you and they are unable to work something out.

Professionalize the Search

You will have noticed already that conflicting, although not necessarily contradictory, advice will come your way. What works for some might not work for others. What some recommend as an essential early step might be recommended as a later move by others. You have to decide what's best for you after considering what has worked for those who have traveled this road before you. However you choose to sequence the process, be sure to professionalize it. That's the advice of a veteran executive search consultant who spoke to me about the advice he gives to the typical displaced male manager: "When you lather up tomorrow morning, look at yourself. You can't let yourself say, 'I'm not important anymore.' So professionalize the search process for yourself. Take it as a challenge. Get your employer to provide you with space, secretary, and fax. Whatever you do, don't do it at home!" One of the participants in my study, a very senior partner in a national accounting firm, reported that he "maintained professionalism" after forced retirement, and this was key to his successful transition.

The sad fact of the matter is that the interval between jobs is lengthening for many managers. Patience as well as professionalism must be maintained, and longer-term job seekers must adjust the search strategy. An article in the business section of the *New York Times* (July 18, 1993) speaks of "the after-18-months strategy." Craig E. Schneier, a management consultant, is quoted: "A year is almost some sort of grace period; a prospective employer is willing to attribute that to a tough economy. But 18 months is when it starts to get dicey. You need some strategies to crawl out of the hole that time puts you in." One of the recommended strategies is to do something other than looking for work. This is not to suggest that you give up the search, but that you continue it in combination with other productive, although uncompensated, work—volunteering your services to a charitable organization, for example, and using your professional skills in that volunteer activity. "If all you've done is stand in the unemployment line," says Mr. Schneier, "it's going to start to show." If, however, you've professionalized your search to the extent of making time for unpaid community service that uses the same skills you are trying to market, you can, after eighteen or more months of unemployment, have something positive to show when you present yourself for an interview. Otherwise, both you and your search show all the signs of failure.

From the ashes of your own discontent, confusion, anger, and injured pride, you now have to build your reconnection strategy. You know that Step 1 is self-assessment and Step 2 is drawing up your mission statement. The steps that follow need not be taken in an ordered sequence; circumstances will suggest different steps at different times for different persons pursuing their individual job campaigns.

Dick Wedemeyer, coauthor of *In Transition*, the book I recommended above, thinks it is a good idea not only to view yourself as a "corporation," but to appoint for yourself a "board of directors." I would recommend this step as a good strategic move. I heard Wedemeyer discuss this idea in a presentation he made to about fifty white-collar job seekers assembled in a midtown Manhattan corporate auditorium, where they meet once a month to listen to an expert and share ideas. Your board of five or six "directors" does not have to meet. They are there for you individually, however, at the end of a phone line at any time; or, if you really perfect this art, you can convene them by conference call to get their reaction to whatever you propose about yourself and your job plan. Boards do not manage; they oversee management and set policy. You can benefit from the reaction of firm but friendly overseers to you and any or all elements of your strategy.

Inviting others to react to you is a humbling, but necessary strategic step. One person who did this learned that "I had a frown in my voice" when speaking on the phone. The suggested remedy: "Install a mirror near your phone and check often to make sure you are smiling when you talk to anyone who doesn't know you well, but who might help you find employment." Solitary self-assessment cannot detect that sort of thing; frank reaction to you and to the way you come across from a trusted friend can. This is what George Herbert must have had in mind when he remarked, "The best mirror is an old friend."

Your board of directors will be particularly helpful if you are at all inclined toward opening a franchise or going into business for yourself, particularly in a recession. Hesitancy about laying out such plans, with all the numbers, is a sure sign that you haven't given the matter sufficient thought. And that's what boards are for: to make sure that your plans are well thought out, that you are not undercapitalized, and that you have not underestimated the length of your sales cycle before you go into business for yourself.

Similarly, having one of your board members as an editor (and spellchecker!) of anything you commit to paper is a good idea. This is more common-sense, standard operating procedure than basic strategy, but it is insurance against the embarrassment (that's two r's and two s's) of misspelled words, grammatical mistakes, and poor style. You will not eliminate the "uhm's," "ah's," "you know's," "like's," "I mean's," and "stuff" from your oral presentations unless a friendly critic rings some kind of a bell for you upon hearing them. Grammatical errors, such as "just between you and I," are the spoken equivalent of bad breath in a job interview.

Within the comfort and confines of a support group, you can role-play the job interview. This is always beneficial, especially when it is recorded on videotape so that you can function as your most severe critic. But the criticism you need should go beyond style into substance. For example, one job seeker I tried to assist was good with words, but not so good at keeping his partisan political prejudices, really ideological biases, to himself. If you are an ideologue, you should avoid, during a job interview, discussion of government policies and their impact on the economy (even though you are convinced that those policies cost you your job). The man I have in mind could not resist bad-mouthing current political leadership and praising the defeated persons and party of the previous administration. It had not occurred to him that he ran the risk of alienating an interviewer whose political points of view, not to mention biases, were not congruent with his own. I encouraged him to read the business press and current business authors, like Emshoff and Handy, so that he could build a mental file of topical points for intelligent conversation about business and its environment. The objective is to impress, not alienate, the interviewer. Sometimes you need a friendly critic to keep you from forgetting that.

It is also good strategy for the job seeker (and good sense for anyone intent upon broadening his or her ensemble of skills) to practice writing. Let your written sentences fall like pebbles to the ground, someone once advised me. This means direct, concise, crisp, clear writing. If you possess that skill, it will serve you well on a daily basis in any managerial position. Letters, memos, speeches, discussion papers, occasional articles, and even books—these are arrows in the executive's quiver, implements in the managerial tool kit. An executive with whom I discussed this study told me that he looks for writing skills in persons he hires and uses the following procedure to evaluate their potential for writing well. At the conclusion of the interview, he invites the candidate to sit down at a desk in an outer office to "write a summary paragraph or two of the highlights of our conversation; I'd like to be sure we have a clear mutual understanding of what we discussed, and I'll keep what you write as part of the record of our meeting." He does this for two good reasons. First, to find out whether or not the job applicant can, unassisted, write well, and second, to see if the person thinks clearly and really grasped the essentials of the conversation.

Readers of the novel *The Man in the Gray Flannel Suit* will recall the interview the job-seeking protagonist Tom Rath had at the United Broadcasting Corporation. He met with "a fat pale man sitting in a high-backed upholstered chair behind a kidney-shaped desk with nothing on it but a blotter and pen." The interview concluded with the question, "Can you write?" The startled applicant was given a typewriter, a cubicle, and one hour to write his "autobiography." "Write anything you want, but at the end of your last page, I'd like you to finish this sentence: 'The most significant fact about me is ...'"

So, although the idea may not be altogether original with the executive who described for me his way of screening candidates, I mention his unusual but not unfair practice by way of encouraging job seekers to hone their writing skills. You never know! Among those you select for service on your board or membership in your support group should be persons capable of critiquing your writing.

Practicing your communications skills fits right in with advice conveyed to job seekers by a short note in *The Wall Street Journal's* "Labor Letter" (May 11, 1993) under the heading: "*Stay Active, personnel professionals advise the unemployed.*" The newspaper surveyed outplacement consultants, executive recruiters, and personnel managers, who suggest that "people out of work should do volunteer work, take classes, learn a new language" and give some thought to "making speeches, lecturing at schools and contributing to industry publications." If you include writing for publication in your job-search strategy (understanding "publication" to include op-ed essays or just letters to the editor), you may find yourself with an impressive piece of published writing to append to your résumé or job application. That can work to your comparative advantage by clearly setting you apart from other applicants.

Keeping your board of directors in place, at least for a while, after you return to work is a good idea. Many reconnected managers live in fear that separation is going to happen again. Dick Hanscom, Director of Operations of the Career Initiatives Center in Cleveland, told me that one CIC client found a job but waited six weeks before telling Dick of his good fortune. His reason? Fear that he would lose the job or prove not up to it. Dick's advice for dealing with this fear is to find a "mentor" in your new employment setting and also keep in touch with a support group—the board of directors idea.

You may not need a board of directors or consultants to advise you on the financial aspects of your search, but the availability of that kind of advice has been helpful to many. Refinancing your mortgage can be facilitated by seeing knowledgeable friends before you talk to the bankers. An important piece of the financial question is your estimate of what you need and want in salary and benefits from your next employer. Although no one linked his or her thinking in this regard to the reported Japanese practice of often reducing compensation for older workers, some of the job seekers I spoke to, whose most recent employment had been very highly paid, acknowledged a willingness to work for considerably less. They reasoned that top jobs for them were more likely to open up in smaller firms, and the pay levels would not be what they had received in the recent past. But their homes were clear, their children were out of college, and only their pride, not their reasonable need, urged them to seek top dollar. Once free psychologically to work for less, they became enthusiastic about taking jobs with fewer perks and lower salaries. A constant in the compensation calculus, however, is the need for adequate, lifetime health insurance if the person is returning to a payroll, or a sufficiently high income stream to afford full health coverage for those planning to freelance or otherwise go it alone.

One of my respondents, age fifty-two, who lost his position as vice president and treasurer of a college, advises those willing to listen not to cut themselves off from others in their field, "no matter how secure your position seems to be." Keep debt down and, when you lose your job, "be prepared to accept less in dollars so that you can establish a platform for a serious job search." He thinks that "too many outplacement advisers are telling people to wait for the six-figure opportunity." You won't get that advice from Bill Morin, who says a good working principle for the job seeker is "take a job to get a job."

The "how to do it" books go into much detail about salary negotiations for your next job. I found considerable unease in the minds and hearts of job seekers as they anticipated having conversations on this point with prospective employers. They typically wanted the job more than they wanted the best possible salary for doing that job, and they feared losing the job opportunity by asking for an excessive salary. They also were familiar with the conventional wisdom that the one who specifies a number first, loses the salary negotiation. And, of course, no one wants to be "taken" in salary negotiations.

My suggestion to an anxious job seeker in these circumstances would be simply to say to a prospective employer at the opportune time, "Look, you know what the market is these days and what this position would typically command; perhaps you feel you are unable to meet that number right now. I know what that number is too, and maybe I'd be willing to work for you for less. My house is clear; my kids are out of college. My needs are not what they were five years ago. So let's try to settle on a number right now and agree to look at it again in six months, when you'll have a better measure of my value-added, as well as a better handle on your ability to pay."

Another factor to be considered when you size up the organization you might decide to join for the next stage of your career is the likelihood of change in the composition of the board of directors or those in top management to whom you will be reporting. The probability of involuntary separation rises dramatically when a senior-level manager finds him- or herself reporting to a new CEO or working with a reorganized board. You should be wary of walking into a situation where personnel changes at the higher levels could mean derivative turnover that could affect you. Although most of your strategic thinking and decisions are centered primarily on you, your needs, and what you bring to a new employment situation, you cannot afford not to survey your prospective employer for present fit and future stability.

Many transitioning executives speak of the need to watch personal expenses, trim vacation plans, reduce entertainment outlays, and defer maintenance on automobiles and other property. One, however, turned this belt-tightening tendency into a do-it-yourself, confidence-building strategy. "I continued my regular work schedule and fitness routine," he told me. "My average workday was ten hours. I curtailed entertainment and did cost-saving things like cooking and car repairs in order to build my confidence and extend my ability to live well without income." Resourcefulness along these lines should be part of any job-search strategy. You have to stay social; you can't drop out.

"Fishing with my sons" was an element factored into his transition strategy by one man. "I'm glad I decided to do that," he told me, "because we had never fished together before, and we continue to do it now that I'm back at work."

Read Your Way Back to Work

Books should be factored into your job-search strategy. Some books will provide how-to-do-it help focused on the specifics of preparing your résumé, presenting yourself in interviews, negotiating salary, and avoiding pitfalls along the way. Other books will broaden your outlook, deepen your self-understanding, and sharpen your awareness of what is happening in the world of work. Let a good librarian, not just a job counselor, be your guide, and use the library to keep up with newspapers and periodical literature, particularly the business and technical journals. If, by the way, you want the job seeker's equivalent of one-stop shopping for practical information, ask your reference librarian for the 1131-page *Job Hunter's Sourcebook: Where to Find Employment Leads and Other Job Search Resources*, edited by Michelle LeCompte (Detroit: Gale Research, Inc., 1993). Bob Adams, Inc. publishes a "job bank" series—*The Carolina Job Bank*, *The Los Angeles Job Bank*, and about twenty others that provide current and comprehensive information for job seekers in specific geographic areas.

As promised, I will now pass along to you information about some of the reading my interviewees have found helpful. I will cluster book titles, with brief comments on their contents, under headings that correspond to the main themes of this book—the self you serve, spousal support, dealing with discouragement, the relevance of religion, and the new corporate culture.

The self you serve will be helped enormously by one or all of the three books mentioned earlier in this chapter. *What Color Is Your Parachute? A Practical Manual for Job Hunters & Career Changers*, by Richard Nelson Bolles (Ten Speed Press), drills home a point that you must come to grasp and fully appreciate:

> *Know your skills. Know what you want to do. Talk to people who have done it. Find out how they did it. Do the homework, on yourself and the companies, thoroughly. Seek out the person who actually has the power to hire; use contacts to get in to see him or her. Show them how you can help them with their problems. Cut no corners, take no shortcuts.*

This book was mentioned more than any other by those I interviewed, and was given high marks for its practical utility.

Richard A. Wedemeyer and Mary Lindley Burton drew on their experience with the Harvard Business School Club of New York's Career Development Seminar to coauthor *In Transition* (Harper Business). Believe them when they say, "The biggest factor in the success or failure of your job search is your state of mind." And read what they have to offer by way of practical advice so that you can connect your steady-state, positively oriented mind with an effective, pretested search strategy.

Parting Company: How to Survive the Loss of a Job and Find Another Successfully (Harcourt Brace Jovanovich), written by William J. Morin and James C. Cabrera, the two top executives of the outplacement firm of Drake Beam Morin, draws valuable information from, as the authors say, DBM's "knowledge base," and puts it all in one place, between the covers of this helpful book. The authors are "career continuation consultants" who have found that despite the changing corporate climate, "one thing has remained the same: the reaction of a person who loses a job." You may see yourself in the person they describe. "Almost everyone encounters shock, anger, and surprise, plus a psychological inability to deal with these unpleasant emotions and a host of practical problems connected to finding a new job or choosing a new direction." Their book addresses these practical problems.

If you are not ready to go immediately to the practical, try John W. Gardner's *Self-Renewal: The Individual and the Innovative Society* (Harper), a short, wisdom-packed paperback. This book first appeared thirty years ago, so the author was clearly ahead of his time in saying, before the word *downsizing* was coined, that "top management can put its finger on almost any function within the organization and decree that henceforth that function will be performed by an outside organization on contract." This book will help you understand an important point: "In the ever-renewing society what matures is a system or framework within which continuous innovation, renewal and rebirth can occur." It will also help you figure out how to become part of that system, and how to function within that framework.

Many of my respondents praised Stephen R. Covey's *The Seven Habits of Highly Effective People: Powerful Lessons in Personal Change* (Simon & Schuster). This is a book to be read with felt-tip pen in hand (as, for that matter, are all books that belong to you and not to a library or one of your friends!) so that you can underline the basic argument. It is not by any means abstruse, just a bit involved as it traces out for you a "character ethic," buttressed with seven basic principles, around which you can organize your life.

Spousal support will be more readily forthcoming and sustained during the job search if Deborah Tannen's *You Just Don't Understand: Women and Men in Conversation* (Ballantine) is read and appreciated. The author is a professor of linguistics whose work rests on solid psychological grounds. I would recommend that "his" and "hers" copies (the book is inexpensive) be read separately by each partner, with each taking care to underline for the other what he or she thinks the other needs to know. In effect, by exchanging the underlined copies, each can say to the other, "Here, this is what 'you just don't understand' about me and the way I converse with you."

One couple I worked with during the course of this project highly recommend John Gray's *Men Are from Mars, Women Are from Venus: A Practical Guide for Improving Communication and Getting What You Want in Your Relationships* (HarperCollins). Forget about the subtitle and just consider what you might learn from the text appearing under these several headings: "How Men Unknowingly Start Arguments," "How Women Unknowingly Start Arguments," "When He Needs Her Approval the Most," "How to Express Your Differences without Arguing," "Giving Support at Difficult Times." And there are many more. The woman in the couple that brought this book to my attention "had no idea" that all men, including her husband, needed occasionally to "go to their caves," to withdraw. Nor did he realize that she, like other women, is like a wave. "When she feels loved," says Gray,

> *her self-esteem rises and falls in a wave motion. When she is feeling really good, she will reach a peak, but then suddenly her mood may change and her wave crashes down. This crash is temporary. After she reaches bottom suddenly her mood will shift and she will again feel good about herself. Automatically her wave begins to rise back up.*

Dealing with discouragement may require that you put yourself on *The Road Less Traveled*, M. Scott Peck's book, which is subtitled *A New Psychology of Love, Traditional Values and Spiritual Growth* (Simon & Schuster). Peck is a psychiatrist who acknowledges that at an earlier stage in his life,

> *during the process of giving up my desire to always win [at games] I was depressed. This is because the feeling associated with giving up something loved—or at least something that is a part of ourselves and familiar—is depression. Since mentally healthy human beings must grow, and since giving up or loss of the old self is an integral part of the process of mental and spiritual growth, depression is a normal and basically healthy phenomenon. It becomes abnormal or unhealthy only when something interferes with the giving-up process, with the result that the depression is prolonged and cannot be resolved by the completion of the process.*

A number of my respondents found this book to be quite helpful.

Also helpful is Gilbert Brim's *Ambition: How We Manage Success and Failure throughout Our Lives* (Basic Books). A theme that runs throughout this book is the need we have to live in a way that keeps us at a level of "just manageable difficulties," a phrase Brim borrows from the psychologist Nicholas Hobbs. Failure to do that can generate a lot of discouragement. A technique for keeping difficulties manageable is what Brim calls "scaling down the dream." I have often thought of this in terms of facing up to the tyranny that can come upon us from the promises we make to ourselves. Brim concludes a chapter on changing levels of aspiration with these words:

> *Some aspirations are of little importance to us, and we can reduce them with ease. Others mean more to us, and we may never get over our failure to fulfill them. Psychiatrists may say that giving up part of our lives should cause mourning over the loss. This may indeed happen during the transition, and may last longer than that in some cases. But the more likely emotion is joy at finally ridding ourselves of hopes that have turned heavy with disappointment. In the end it is relief, not grief, we feel as we relax into a state of lowered ambition.*

The relevance of religion came through in a variety of ways during this study, as the contents of Chapter 6 can attest. Religious books, notably the Bible, were mentioned often, and within the Bible, the Psalms and the Book of Job were mentioned most frequently. The Bible is a source, as I noted in Chapter 8, of principles that, once internalized, can guide a life as well as a job search. With the spiritual needs of job seekers in mind, I edited 125 of the 150 psalms for a book that borrows its title from the 27th Psalm: *Take Courage; Be Stouthearted: Psalms of Support and Encouragement* (Sheed & Ward).

This is an area where near-religious and explicitly religious "little books" are both treasured and traded within support groups. The respondent whose religious commitment I described as "Main Street traditional" in Chapter 6 lives by Russell H. Conwell's tiny tract *Acres of Diamonds* (Jove Books/Berkley Publishing Group).

This executive freely distributes copies to job-seeking friends so that they can get Conwell's motivational message to, in effect, "bloom where you are planted." The story is based on an Arab tale about a man who sold his home and property to search for a diamond mine, only to die a pauper never knowing that the property he sold rested atop an "acre of diamonds."

Jean-Pierre de Caussade's *Abandonment to Divine Providence* (Doubleday Image Books) is a Christian classic that speaks to the soul of the troubled believer, who is invited by this booklet to accept its basic proposition: "All will be well if we abandon ourselves to God." This and another short book, *Daily Readings from the Cloud of Unknowing* (Templegate), are distributed like business cards to job seekers by a senior executive who has himself been through several involuntary separations.

An ex-IBM executive told me that he has personally given away about 200 copies of Fenelon's *Let Go* (Whitaker) and Granger E. Westberg's *Good Grief* (Fortress), books that he found helpful in managing the emotional and spiritual crisis his unemployment produced.

He Leadeth Me (Doubleday Image Books) is a spiritual reflection, a "testament of faith," written by an American Jesuit priest, Walter J. Ciszek, who was "convicted" of espionage in Russia in 1941 and spent twenty-three years in Soviet prisons and the labor camps of Siberia. "Through the long years of isolation and suffering," writes Father Ciszek,

> God had led me to an understanding of life and his love that only those who have experienced it can fathom. He had stripped away from me many of the external consolations, physical and religious, that men rely on and had left me with a core of seemingly simple truths to guide me. And yet what a profound difference they made in my life, what strength they gave me, what courage to go on!

The new corporate contract is a phrase I heard often as displaced managers mumbled about the "contract with corporate America" being broken. I mentioned earlier James R. Emshoff's *The New Rules of the Game: The Four Key Experiences Managers Must Have to*

Thrive in the Non-Hierarchical 90s and Beyond (Harper Business), a book I read after conversations with Emshoff and recommended to others as a source of informed talking points for managers preparing for job interviews. Management "closer to the ground," which also means "closer to the customer," is not just a fad but a genuine new trend that has explanatory value at either end of the hiring-firing decision process. In other words, this trend could explain your release as well as explaining your prospects for reemployment.

A book that influenced Emshoff and many others is Charles Handy's *The Age of Unreason* (Harvard Business School Press). The writer is British, a fact that may provide helpful perspective for his view of corporate America. He writes:

> *The new organization will seek to bind its core executives to itself for as long as it thinks it needs them. The new executives, however, will be less ready to be tied, particularly if they have some sort of qualification as a passport.... Companies ... will be reluctant to guarantee careers for life to everyone, even in the core. More contracts will be for fixed periods of years; more appointments will be tied to particular roles or jobs with no guarantee of further promotion. The help-wanted pages of the papers already reflect this trend: the advertisements offer a job more often than they promise a career.*

A book with an industry-specific starting point but written to broaden the thinking of displaced executives who consider themselves wedded to that one industry is *Career Alternatives for Bankers* (Magellan Press), co-authored by William King, Dean Graber, and Rebecca Newton and sponsored by the American Bankers Association. The first 100 pages of this book convey helpful advice to anyone, not just those with career backgrounds in banking. The applicability of banking skills to opportunities in other fields occupies more than half of this book and ranges from "banking outsourcers" through education, government, real estate, insurance, self-employment, and other possibilities. Included to stimulate the thinking of the more venturesome reader is a "Directory of Outsourcers and Other Companies Selling Products and Services to Banks."

I heard many job seekers refer to *John Lucht's Rites of Passage at $100,000+* (Viceroy); its lengthy subtitle, *The Insider's Lifetime Guide to Executive Job-Changing and Faster Career Progress*, provides a hint that is confirmed in the first chapter. "As an upwardly-mobile executive, there's a good chance that sometime during your career you'll be involved with all the 'professions' that move executives around. Therefore, it's worthwhile to take this once-and-for-all-in-a-hurry opportunity to see how you should deal with each to best serve your *self interest*, which often does not match theirs." Although helpful to the out-of-work executive, this book is more suitable for those who are fully employed but anxious to move onward and upward, often with the assistance of executive search consultants. Readers will get the promised "insider's" look at the different ways recruiters work; they will also be introduced to a variety of search techniques that they can implement on their own. Displaced executives will find much to help them in this book. In my view, most helpful of all for the ousted executive attempting a rebound will be the hard-headed assessment of what works and does not work in "Networking: Pursuing the People You Don't Know" (Chapter 4).

Intended to help you think ahead is *Reengineering the Corporation* by Michael Hammer and James Champy (Harper Business). The central thesis of the book is "that American corporations must undertake nothing less than a radical reinvention of how they do their work." Read it so that you can understand what is happening out there and thus be more likely to reconnect with an organization that is not standing still.

Put Your Thoughts on Paper

No doubt, in this age of nutritional awareness, you have often heard it said that "You are what you eat," and you are familiar with the good advice about diet, cholesterol, and calories associated with that dictum. Consider, as you are laying out your job-search strategy, that it is not too wide of the mark to suggest that "You think what you read." So look around for reading material that can keep you thinking, not just strategically about your job campaign, but deeply about the meaning of life. The point of mentioning this here, of course, is to acknowledge that there should be a place for scheduled reading time in the structured day your search strategy imposes on you (and in all the days that follow, once you are back at work but still in need of intellectual broadening and mental nourishment).

Your strategic Step 1 statement of who you are, composed after reflection and self-assessment, might well take the form of a "Letter to Myself"—for your eyes only, if you want to keep it that way, or share it with others as you wish. You should read it once a month during a job search, for two reasons: to see if your activities are consistent with who you say you are, and to consider whether more recent reading and reflection may now prompt you to make revisions in this personal baseline document.

Step 2 of your job-search strategy also requires that you reduce your thoughts to writing, in this instance stating clearly what you want to do. This is the statement of your mission. It is a more "public" document, even though it is personal and brief. For you personally and privately, it can function as a foreword in your search-strategy playbook, the longer list of strategic steps you intend to take. Your desk calendar should now become for you a planning tool, as quantifiable goals—contacts made, people interviewed, books read, miles walked, journal entries made, days off—are specified and written down.

A job search does not mean that you are starting all over again. You are simply changing. To live is to change. You do, however, have a blank page in front of you that requires immediate attention. For every question running through your mind, look for an answer from within. Consider yourself an author. The strategic plan is your story outline; get it down on paper. Don't succumb to writer's block. Start working on that story now, with the unshakable conviction that there is someone, somewhere, not just interested in what you have to say, but ready and willing to "buy your book."

The
Questionnaire

Executives in Transition

This questionnaire is designed to gather information on what may have been a stressful experience in your life—the separation, whether voluntary or involuntary, from a position of executive responsibility. At any point in this questionnaire, you are welcome to make the marginal note "Confidential" if you wish. If you want all of your responses to be held in confidence, just enter a check mark here: _____.

Please bear in mind that these questions focus on your severance from a specific position of executive responsibility. If that happened to you more than once, and if you care to comment on more than one instance, just duplicate the questionnaire and use a separate copy for each case.

1. The company or organization you left—
Name: _____
Address: _____

2. Your position there: _____

3. How long had you held that position? _____

4. How long had you been with that company? _____

5. The year of separation: _____

6. Your age at that time: _____

7. Shortly before you left, say within a year or so, did you find yourself relating or reporting to a new boss or a realigned board?
Yes _____; No _____.

8. Sometimes restructuring and the offer of attractive severance benefits complicate an answer to this question, so let me put it this way: If you resigned, but in your heart of hearts did not really want to, your separation would, for purposes of this study, be considered "involuntary severance." With that in mind, was your separation (a) voluntary _____, or (b) involuntary _____?

9. If your release was involuntary, was it directed at you individually? Yes _____; No _____. Or, was it part of a wider-spread layoff? Yes _____; No _____.

10. If you left involuntarily, did the release come as a surprise? Yes _____; No _____. Did you have any "inklings"? Yes _____; No _____.

11. How much advance notice did you give/receive?

_____

12. Did the company provide you with severance compensation? Yes _____; No _____.

13. Over how long a period did the severance payments extend?

14. Did you view the severance compensation at that time to be:
(a) adequate _____; inadequate _____; more than adequate _____?
(b) If you care to, please give the dollar value of your severance package: $ _____
(c) It would also be helpful to know the estimated dollar value of the benefits you lost: $_____
(d) What were the major benefits lost?

_____

_____

_____

15. What was your annual compensation in the job you left or lost? (a) cash (salary, bonus, etc., exclusive of stock options and any severance package): $_____
(b) value of additional benefits that year: $ _____

If you were married at the time of severance and subsequent transition, please reflect now on the extent to which you drew support from your spouse at that time.

16. Your marital status at that time: (a) married _____, (b) divorced _____, (c) separated _____, (d) single _____.

17. If you were divorced, separated, or single, did you have a close friend or companion in whom you could confide and from whom you drew emotional support? Yes _____; No _____.

18. Did you discuss the problem immediately with your spouse _____ or close friend _____? Yes _____; No _____.

19. Was the response one of ...
    (a) personal support? Yes _____; No _____.
    (b) criticism? Yes _____; No _____.
    (c) anxiety? Yes _____; No _____.
    (d) understanding? Yes _____; No _____.
    (e) If other words would better describe the response, please list them here:

    _____

    _____

    _____

20. Had your spouse "sensed" earlier on that a severance might be in the works, and said so to you? Yes _____; No _____.

21. Before your severance, did your spouse have paid employment? Yes _____; No _____. After the severance? Yes _____; No _____.

22. Would you characterize your spouse as being, at that time, on a parallel growth path to your own, through either a career or other interests? Yes _____; No _____.

23. After the severance, (a) did you separate from your spouse? Yes _____; No _____; (b) did you consider getting a divorce? Yes _____; No _____; (c) did you actually get a divorce? Yes _____; No _____.

24. Did the transition require sacrifices on the part of your dependent child or children? Yes _____; No _____. If yes, would you please describe those sacrifices?

25. How did he/she/they react?

_____

_____

_____

26. Please give their age(s) at that time:

_____

_____

_____

27. If the transition period required downward adjustments in your living style, which were the hardest to accept?

_____

_____

_____

28. It would be helpful to know the difference in age between you and your spouse (_____ years) and how long you had been married at the time of the severance (_____ years).

29. What "bits of wisdom" have served you well in preparing for or working your way through this transition?

_____

_____

_____

30. What advice would you give to another couple in anticipation of either one of them experiencing involuntary severance from a mid-career executive position?

_____

_____

_____

(Feel free to write more if you wish on additional sheets.)

If you are identified in any way with organized religion, it would be of interest to know whether, at the time of your severance, you found any support in religious faith or religious practice.

31. If you identified with a religious denomination at that time, please name it here: _____; if you did not identify with organized religion but had your own brand of "spirituality" in your life, please so indicate by making a check mark here: _____.

32. Before the severance, did you attend religious services? Yes _____; No _____. If Yes, more often than once a week? Yes _____; No _____.

33. At the time of the severance, did you seek pastoral counseling? Yes _____; No _____.

34. Did you make a religious retreat? Yes _____; No _____.

35. Did you pray privately? Yes _____; No _____.

36. Did you pray with your spouse? Yes _____; No _____.

37. Would you say your spouse was, prior to the severance, a religious person? Yes _____; No _____. Were you? Yes _____; No _____.

38. Did you pray with a friend or friends? Yes _____; No _____.

39. Did you read parts of the Bible? Yes _____; No _____. If Yes, please list any parts or passages that may have proved particularly helpful to you at that time:

_____

_____

_____

40. Did you read other religious books? Yes _____; No _____.

41. Please list any books—religious or not—that you found to be helpful at that time:

_____

_____

_____

42. Did you receive any help at all through church-related support or self-help groups? Yes _____; No _____. If Yes, you may want to mention the church and the group:

_____

_____

_____

43. Please outline here, in as many words as you choose to use, the relevance of religion to you when you experienced the severance and started looking for another job.

_____

_____

_____

(Feel free to write more and use additional sheets.)

This section of the questionnaire deals with the length of time it took to reposition yourself and some of the factors that helped you.

44. Have you now found what you consider to be suitable employment? Yes _____; No _____. (If you are working, but consider the position to be unsuitable, please check here: _____.)

45. How long did it take you to find suitable reemployment?_____; (just check _____ if you are still looking).

46. Are you now in a new industry? Yes _____; No _____.

47. Would you say that the severance opened up an entirely new career for you? Yes _____; No _____.

48. Is your present position as fulfilling _____, more fulfilling _____, or less fulfilling _____ than the one you left?

49. Did any outside activities or interests you maintained during your prior employment help you in making the transition? Yes _____; No _____. If Yes, could you describe the interest or activity?

_____

_____

_____

50. What factors, persons, networks, or events proved most helpful to you in making your transition?

_____

_____

_____

51. Would you care to write a paragraph or two here on how you spent the time between jobs and what you learned from this experience? (You may not think of it this way, but you do have a lot of wisdom to share!)

_____

_____

_____

(Feel free to write more and use additional sheets.)

It would be helpful to have some current information on you at the conclusion of this inquiry. Just check here _____, if you want all of it to be considered confidential. You may, of course, write "Confidential" in the margin next to any item below that you want to be held in confidence.

52. Name: _____

53. Present Position: _____

54. Company: _____

55. Address:

_____

_____

56. Phone: (work) _____; (home) _____

57. If you are now retired, give the year in which you retired: _____

58. Your present age: _____

59. Your religion: _____

60. Your marital status: (a) married _____, (b) divorced _____, (c) separated _____, (d) single _____. If married, are you married to the same person who was your spouse at the time of the severance? Yes _____; No _____.

61. Would you be willing to participate in a phone or face-to-face interview by way of follow-up to any of the information or opinions you have given here? Yes _____; No _____. If Yes, would you prefer a phone call during the day _____, or evening _____, at work _____, or at home _____?

62. Perhaps your spouse would like to add a page of personal reflections stimulated by this questionnaire; if so, they would be most welcome. Just attach those comments to these pages. The experience touched you both, of course; each of you has a lot of wisdom to share with others. Communication of that wisdom is the purpose of the book I want to write!

Many, many thanks for your cooperation! Any additional comments you may want to add will be most welcome. Again, thank you!

PERMISSIONS

Acknowledgment is gratefully given to the copyright holders who granted permission for use of material excerpted from:

Updike, John. *Rabbit Redux, Rabbit Is Rich, Rabbit at Rest.* Copyright © 1971, 1981, and 1990, respectively, by John Updike; reprinted by permission of Alfred A. Knopf, Inc.

Motherwit by Onnie Lee Logan, as told to Katherine Clark. Copyright © 1989 by Katherine Clark and Onnie Lee Logan. Used by permission of Dutton Signet, a division of Penguin Books USA Inc.

When Smart People Fail by Carole Hyatt and Linda Gottlieb. Copyright © 1987 by Carol Hyatt and Linda Gottlieb; reprinted by permission of Simon & Schuster, Inc.

Pack Your Own Parachute by Paul Hirsch. Copyright © 1987 by Paul Hirsch. Reprinted by permission of Addison-Wesley Publishing Company, Inc.

Re-Inventing the Corporation by John Naisbitt and Patricia Abdurene. Copyright © 1985 by Megatrends Ltd.; used by permission of Warner Books, Inc.

The New Individualists by Paul Leinberger and Bruce Tucker. Copyright © 1991 by Paul Leinberger and Bruce Tucker; used by permission of HarperCollins Publishers.

"The Hawaiian Room" (*Manager's Journal*) by John Rocchi. Reprinted with permission of The Wall Street Journal © 1980, Dow Jones & Company, Inc. All rights reserved.

Men Astutely Trained by Peter McDonough. Copyright © 1992 by Peter McDonough; reprinted with permission of The Free Press, Macmillan Publishing Company.

"When Women Lose Their Jobs," by Stanlee Phelps and Marguerite Mason, copyright August 1991. Reprinted with the permission of *Personnel Journal*, ACC Communications, Inc., Costa Mesa, California; all rights reserved.

Protocols of Reading by Robert Scholes. Copyright © 1989 by Yale University; reprinted with permission of Yale University Press.

INDEX